The Editor

D. M. R. Bentley is Professor of English at the University of Western Ontario. He is the author of *The Gay]Grey Moose: Essays on the Ecologies and Mythologies of Canadian Poetry, 1690–1990*; *Mimic Fires: Accounts of Early Long Poems on Canada*; *Mnemographia Canadensis: Essays on Memory, Community, and Environment in Canada*; and *The Confederation Group of Canadian Poets, 1880–1897*. The founding and continuing editor of *Canadian Poetry: Studies, Documents, Reviews* (1977–) and the Canadian Poetry Press series of Scholarly Editions of Early Canadian Long Poems (1986–), he is also the author of numerous articles on Canadian fiction, Canadian culture, and Victorian literature and art. His previous scholarly and critical editions include *Malcolm's Katie* by Isabella Valancy Crawford, *Essays and Reviews* by Archibald Lampman, *Letters to Margaret Lawrence* by Bliss Carman, and *Arcadian Adventures with the Idle Rich* by Stephen Leacock.

A NORTON CRITICAL EDITION

Stephen Leacock

SUNSHINE SKETCHES OF
A LITTLE TOWN

AUTHORITATIVE TEXT
BACKGROUNDS AND CONTEXTS
CRITICISM

Edited by

D. M. R. BENTLEY

UNIVERSITY OF WESTERN ONTARIO

W. W. NORTON & COMPANY • *New York* • *London*

W. W. Norton & Company has been independent since its founding in 1923, when William Warder Norton and Mary D. Herter Norton first published lectures delivered at the People's Institute, the adult education division of New York City's Cooper Union. The Nortons soon expanded their program beyond the Institute, publishing books by celebrated academics from America and abroad. By mid-century, the two major pillars of Norton's publishing program—trade books and college texts—were firmly established. In the 1950s, the Norton family transferred control of the company to its employees, and today—with a staff of four hundred and a comparable number of trade, college, and professional titles published each year—W. W. Norton & Company stands as the largest and oldest publishing house owned wholly by its employees.

The text of this book is composed in Fairfield Medium
with the display set in Bernhard Modern.
Composition by PennSet, Inc.
Manufacturing by the Maple-Vail Book Group, Binghamton, NY.
Production manager: Benjamin Reynolds.

Library of Congress Cataloging-in-Publication Data
Leacock, Stephen, 1869–1944.
Sunshine sketches of a little town: an authoritative text,
backgrounds and contexts, criticism / Stephen Leacock; edited
by D.M.R. Bentley.
p. cm. — (A Norton critical edition)
Includes bibliographical references (p.).

ISBN 0–393–92634–6

1. Canada—Social life and customs—Fiction. 2. Leacock, Stephen,
1869–1944. Sunshine sketches of a little town. 3. City and town life
in literature. 4. City and town life—Fiction. 5. Canada—In literature.
I. Bentley, D. M. R. II. Title. III. Series.

PR9199.3.L367S86 2005
813'.52—dc22

2005052328

W. W. Norton & Company, Inc., 500 Fifth Avenue, New York, N.Y. 10110-0017
www.wwnorton.com

W. W. Norton & Company Ltd., Castle House,
75/76 Wells Street, London W1T 3QT

1 2 3 4 5 6 7 8 9 0

Contents

Acknowledgements

In the course of producing this Norton Critical Edition I have incurred numerous debts to many people. First and foremost, I would like to have been able to thank Stephen Leacock himself for the hours of pleasure that he has given me. Editing *Sunshine Sketches of a Little Town* has been a joy from start to finish and has greatly increased my admiration both for the book and for its author. I also owe great debts of thanks to Gerald Lynch and to Carl Spadoni, two scholars who have done superb work in recent years to further our appreciation and understanding of Leacock and who have given me the benefit of their hugely valuable findings and insights. To Carol Bemis for asking me to tackle a Norton Critical Edition and to Brian B. Baker for guiding me through the production process, I am deeply grateful, as I am to Amanda J. Stamos for her careful work in entering the text of *Sunshine Sketches of a Little Town* and to Marybeth Curtin for her invaluable assistance in proofreading it and in collecting critical materials. Steven Artelle, Chris Brown, Angela Esterhammer, Ronald N. Harpelle, Shelley Hulan, Ian MacLaren, Andre Narbonne, Brian Trehearne, and Fred and Tina Belinsky have my thanks for helping in various ways. So, too, do the authors and copyright holders who have granted me permission to reprint critical materials. Finally (and also foremost in so many ways), my heartfelt thanks go to my wife, Susan, for her help in proofreading the edition and to our children, Michael, Simon, and Diana, companions each and all in hope and sunshine.

Introduction

Apparently begun by Stephen Leacock (1869–1944) in January 1912, *Sunshine Sketches of a Little Town* was first published as a series of twelve instalments in the *Montreal Daily Star* between February 17 and June 22, 1912.[1] With the ink scarcely dry on the second of these instalments (February 24), Leacock wrote to his publisher, John Lane of The Bodley Head, in the hopes of arranging for publication of the sketches in serial and then book form in England and the United States. No further serialization occurred, but in August and September 1912 *Sunshine Sketches of a Little Town* was published in London and New York under the imprint of John Lane, The Bodley Head and in Toronto under the imprint of Bell and Cockburn. It was enthusiastically reviewed in Britain and the United States as well as Canada, and it has seldom, if ever, been out of print since. A play centred on one of its characters quickly followed its initial appearances and in due course there were excerptings, recordings, and translations into Finnish (1951), Chinese (1982), and French (1986).[2] Together with the collection of sketches that many scholars regard as its somewhat more acerbic companion, *Arcadian Adventures with the Idle Rich* (1914), *Sunshine Sketches of a Little Town* represents Canada's greatest comic writer at his most accomplished and complex. For popular appeal and scholarly interest, it has few rivals in Canadian literature.

When he published *Sunshine Sketches of a Little Town*, Leacock's reputation as a writer was based primarily on three components of

1. Leacock's preliminary "Plan and Ideas for a series of sketches about a little country town & the people in it" is dated "Jan 7. 1912." It is held by the Stephen Leacock Memorial Home and Museum in Orillia, Ontario, and printed in facsimile in Stanley Cohen, " 'Sunshine Sketches' Outline: More Original Leacock Found," *Montreal Star* 31 (August 1966) and in transcript in Appendix A of Carl Spadoni's edition of *Sunshine Sketches of a Little Town* (Peterborough, ON: Broadview, 2002), 166–67. Spadoni's edition also includes variant tables of contents for the book (168–69) and the pertinent correspondence between Leacock and his publishers (170–77). All Leacock scholars are in Spadoni's debt for his magisterial *Bibliography of Stephen Leacock* (Toronto: ECW, 1998).

2. The play, entitled *Jeff*, by Michael Morton ran for a week in Montreal in 1916, but did not meet with the approval of Leacock, who attempted to do better in *Sunshine Sketches: A Play in Four Acts* based on "The Mariposa Bank Mystery Sketch" and published in *Maclean's Magazine* (Toronto) in May, June, and July 1917. Leacock's play is reprinted as Appendix E of Spadoni's edition of *Sunshine Sketches of a Little Town*, 201–72.

his work: a textbook in the discipline that he taught at Montreal's McGill University (*Elements of Political Science* [1906]), two books on Canadian history (*Greater Canada* [1907] and *Baldwin, Lafontaine, Hicks* [1907]), and two collections of what the London *Spectator* called "fantasies and burlesques" (*Literary Lapses* [1910] and *Nonsense Novels* [1911]).[3] Each of these elements of Leacock's prior work is intensely pertinent to his first sustained venture into fiction, for it was with a pen dipped in political science and Canadian history that he recorded the progress of the sketches' principal character, Josh Smith, from small-town hotelier (and, at the outset of his illustrious career, cook in a lumber camp) to federal politician, and it was with a pencil sharpened by "burlesque" and parody that he sketched the characters and antics of Dean Drone, Peter Pupkin, and their fellow Mariposans and delineated his own experiences and accomplishments in the "Preface" that is scarcely less integral to the work than "L'Envoi" with which it elegiacally concludes.

In addition to being the offspring of Leacock's previous work and the antecedent of *Arcadian Adventures with the Idle Rich, Sunshine Sketches of a Little Town* has roots in the fertile soils of the English comic novel and American local colour writing, each of which provided Leacock with a principal inspiration and model for his own humourous fiction and persona—the former in Charles Dickens and the latter in Mark Twain. Leacock's Canada is the land "full of hope and promise" that Dickens describes in *American Notes* (1842),[4] his Missinaba County is a Canadian twin of the locale of Twain's *The Celebrated Jumping Frog of Calaveras County and Other Sketches* (1867). Indeed, the very genre that he chose to people with such caricatures as the barber Jefferson Thorpe, and the undertaker Golgotha Gingham is the genre of both Twain's collection and Dickens's *Sketches by Boz* (1836–37). (Not surprisingly, Leacock's *Essays and Literary Studies* [1916] contain admiring discussions of both Dickens and Twain, and both writers are towering presences in his later *Humor: Its Theory and Technique* [1935] and *Humour and Humanity* [1937].) It is a testament to Leacock that even as it draws on Dickens, Twain, and, of course, several other writers, *Sunshine Sketches of a Little Town* is so deeply imbued with the distinctive imprint of its author and locale that it belongs beside the most astute and evocative depictions of small-town life in Canada and continues to elicit the smiles and laughter of anyone capable of responding to Leacock's signature brand of kindly humour.[5]

---

3. See this Norton Critical Edition, p. 154.
4. *American Notes for General Circulation* (London: Chapman and Hall, 1842), 207.
5. The most extended and perceptive discussions of Leacock's theory of humour and its relation to his work are in Gerald Lynch, *Stephen Leacock: Humour and Humanity* (Montreal and Kingston: McGill-Queen's UP, 1988).

For all these and numerous other reasons, *Sunshine Sketches of a Little Town* is a refulgent addition to the Norton Critical Editions. At the heart of the volume in hand is an authoritative text of the work accompanied by explanatory notes and followed by a list of editorial emendations. Also included in the volume is a selection of contemporary reviews and critical materials that will enable readers to study responses to *Sunshine Sketches of a Little Town* from the time of its first appearance to the early years of the present century.

The Present Text

Sunshine Sketches of a Little Town was first published by John Lane, The Bodley Head, in London, England, on August 9, 1912. An American issue and a Canadian issue followed on September 20, and by the end of 1912 four additional impressions (printings) of the book were in existence. The text in the present Norton Critical Edition is based on the second and subsequent impressions of the first edition, the reason being that they contain numerous changes that almost without exception are obvious corrections of errors in the first impression.

The presence of those errors probably stems from the haste and circumstances in which the final manuscript of the book was submitted to the publisher and proofread (or not) by Leacock. The correspondence between Leacock and Lane concerning *Sunshine Sketches of a Little Town*[6] reveals that Leacock left Montreal for a holiday in France on May 12, 1912, having told Lane some five weeks earlier (on April 3) that he was not satisfied with the sketches that he had submitted up to that time and that in due course he would send "a revised and corrected form" of the entire manuscript "so as to minimize proof reading." When he arrived in Paris sometime after the middle of May, he informed Lane that the manuscript "had been delayed in coming" (presumably it was being typed in Montreal) and that he would mail it to him as soon as he had "looked [it] over." A few days later, on June 4, he wrote to B. W. Willet of John Lane, The Bodley Head, to say that he was "very anxious to get the proofs . . . at the earliest possible moment" so that he could "correct them" before leaving France from Le Havre on June 15, adding that he would "only need galley proofs" and would "leave the rest" to the press. Lane, he observed, had assured him that "the whole thing could be set up"—that is, typeset—"in a week." Finally, on June 10, he wrote to Lane himself, asking that the proofs be sent directly to his Paris hotel (rather than care of his

---

6. All quotations from the correspondence are taken from Spadoni's edition, 174–76.

travel agent) in order to save time and expressing his regret that he will be unable to come to London because "time is all too short." In the absence of further correspondence concerning *Sunshine Sketches of a Little Town* until December 1912, it is only possible to speculate about what happened next, but the shortness of time between Leacock's letter of June 10 (Monday) and his departure from Paris or Le Havre on June 15 (Saturday), coupled with the fact that the first impression of the book contains over sixty errors that are corrected in the second and subsequent impressions, suggests four scenarios: (1) that the galleys arrived in Paris before Leacock's departure[7] and that he corrected them hurriedly; (2) that the galleys did not arrive in time and the first impression went to press without authorial correction; (3) that the galleys were sent to Canada and that they were returned too late for corrections to be made in the first impression; and (4) that the corrections that appear in the second impression were made by the publisher rather than by Leacock, a possibility that seems less likely because some of the changes appear to be authorial.

Whatever the case, it is apparent from the presence of the corrections made to the second impression in all subsequent impressions that they were approved if not actually made by Leacock. From this and from the absence of any evidence of Leacock's involvement in any later edition of *Sunshine Sketches of a Little Town*, an editor faces a clear but hardly crucial decision with respect to copy-text and procedures: either select the first impression and emend it so as to include the corrections present in the second impression as well as any other changes deemed necessary, or select the second impression and emend it only as deemed necessary. For this Norton Critical Edition the latter option was chosen; however, the list of editorial emendations that follows the text identifies all the changes between the first and second impressions.

None of this means that the first impression of *Sunshine Sketches of a Little Town* is without interest or significance. Like the versions of the sketches in the incomplete manuscript in the Stephen Leacock Memorial Home and Museum in Orillia, Ontario, and like those that were published in instalments in the *Montreal Daily Star*, the first impression of the book is part of its textual history and, as such, furnishes interesting insights into its evolution as a creative and social document. The three extant versions of some or all of the sketches that precede the version used as the basis for this Norton Critical Edition can be studied in the texts and lists of

---

7. As argued by Spadoni, *Bibliography*, 115. Albert Moritz and Theresa Moritz are less certain, however, stating only that "Leacock . . . may have read proofs before embarking for Canada from Le Havre on 15 June" (*Stephen Leacock: His Remarkable Life* [Toronto: Fitzhenry and Whiteside, 2002], 151).

variants provided by Carl Spadoni in the edition of *Sunshine Sketches of a Little Town* published by Broadview Press in 2002.

The emendations to the second impression of the John Lane, The Bodley Head text of *Sunshine Sketches of a Little Town* that follow the text in this Norton Critical Edition have been made in order to correct typographical errors, to correct spelling mistakes that are clearly not present for effect, and to achieve consistency of spelling within the text.

The Text of
SUNSHINE SKETCHES
OF A LITTLE TOWN

Sunshine Sketches
of a Little Town

Preface

I know no way in which a writer may more fittingly introduce his work to the public than by giving a brief account of who and what he is. By this means some of the blame for what he has done is very properly shifted to the extenuating circumstances of his life.

I was born at Swanmoor, Hants,[1] England, on December 30, 1869. I am not aware that there was any particular conjunction of the planets at the time, but should think it extremely likely. My parents migrated to Canada in 1876, and I decided to go with them.[2] My father took up a farm near Lake Simcoe, in Ontario. This was during the hard times of Canadian farming, and my father was just able by great diligence to pay the hired men and, in years of plenty, to raise enough grain to have seed for the next year's crop without buying any. By this process my brothers and I were inevitably driven off the land, and have become professors, business men, and engineers, instead of being able to grow up as farm labourers. Yet I saw enough of farming to speak exuberantly in political addresses of the joy of early rising and the deep sleep, both of body and intellect, that is induced by honest manual toil.

I was educated at Upper Canada College, Toronto, of which I was head boy in 1887.[3] From there I went to the University of Toronto, where I graduated in 1891.[4] At the University I spent my entire time in the acquisition of languages, living, dead, and half-dead, and knew nothing of the outside world. In this diligent pursuit of words I spent about sixteen hours of each day. Very soon after graduation I had forgotten the languages, and found myself intellectually bankrupt. In other words I was what is called a

---

1. Hampshire, a county in southern England.
2. Stephen Leacock was one of eleven children, and the third son, of Peter and Agnes Leacock, both of whom came from well-to-do families. After trying unsuccessfully to farm in South Africa and the United States, they moved to Canada in 1876 and took up land near Sutton in Georgina Township, Ontario, south of Lake Simcoe. Peter Leacock was no more successful at farming in Canada than elsewhere, however, and in 1887 he abandoned his farm and family altogether.
3. Upper Canada College was and is Canada's most prestigious private boys' school.
4. Leacock's degree was an honours B.A. with an emphasis on classical and modern languages.

distinguished graduate, and, as such, I took to school teaching as the only trade I could find that needed neither experience nor intellect. I spent my time from 1891 to 1899 on the staff of Upper Canada College,[5] an experience which has left me with a profound sympathy for the many gifted and brilliant men who are compelled to spend their lives in the most dreary, the most thankless, and the worst paid profession in the world. I have noted that of my pupils, those who seemed the laziest and the least enamoured of books are now rising to eminence at the bar, in business, and in public life; the really promising boys who took all the prizes are now able with difficulty to earn the wages of a clerk in a summer hotel or a deck hand on a canal boat.

In 1899 I gave up school teaching in disgust, borrowed enough money to live upon for a few months, and went to the University of Chicago to study economics and political science.[6] I was soon appointed to a Fellowship in political economy, and by means of this and some temporary employment by McGill University,[7] I survived until I took the degree of Doctor of Philosophy in 1903. The meaning of this degree is that the recipient of instruction is examined for the last time in his life, and is pronounced completely full. After this, no new ideas can be imparted to him.

From this time, and since my marriage, which had occurred at this period,[8] I have belonged to the staff of McGill University, first as lecturer in Political Science, and later as head of the department of Economics and Political Science. As this position is one of the prizes of my profession, I am able to regard myself as singularly fortunate. The emolument[9] is so high as to place me distinctly above the policemen, postmen, street-car conductors, and other salaried officials of the neighbourhood, while I am able to mix with the poorer of the business men of the city on terms of something like equality. In point of leisure, I enjoy more in the four corners of a single year than a business man knows in his whole life. I thus have what the business man can never enjoy, an ability to think, and, what is still better, to stop thinking altogether for months at a time.

I have written a number of things in connection with my college life—a book on Political Science,[1] and many essays, magazine arti-

5. In fact, Leacock began teaching at Upper Canada College in 1889 in order to help finance his university education.
6. The topic of Leacock's doctoral dissertation is "The Doctrine of *Laissez Faire*." It has been published in conjunction with his reminiscences of the University of Chicago in *My Recollection of Chicago and the Doctrine of Laissez Faire*, edited by Carl Spadoni (1998).
7. Leacock began to work as a sessional lecturer at McGill University, Montreal, in the summer of 1900 and was appointed to a full-time position in 1903 and made head of the political science department in 1908.
8. Leacock was married to Beatrix Hamilton, the daughter of a wealthy Toronto businessman, in the summer of 1900. They had one child, Stephen, who was born in 1915.
9. Salary.
1. *Extension Lectures on the Elements of Political Economy* (1910).

cles, and so on.[2] I belong to the Political Science Association of America,[3] to the Royal Colonial Institute,[4] and to the Church of England.[5] These things, surely, are a proof of respectability. I have had some small connection with politics and public life. A few years ago I went all round the British Empire delivering addresses on Imperial organization.[6] When I state that these lectures were followed almost immediately by the Union of South Africa,[7] the Banana Riots in Trinidad,[8] and the Turco-Italian war,[9] I think the reader can form some idea of their importance. In Canada I belong to the Conservative party, but as yet I have failed entirely in Canadian politics, never having received a contract to build a bridge, or make a wharf, nor to construct even the smallest section of the Transcontinental Railway.[1] This, however, is a form of national ingratitude to which one becomes accustomed in this Dominion.

Apart from my college work, I have written two books, one called "Literary Lapses" and the other "Nonsense Novels."[2] Each of these is published by John Lane (London and New York), and either of them can be obtained, absurd though it sounds, for the mere sum of three shillings and sixpence. Any reader of this preface, for example, ridiculous though it appears, could walk into a bookstore and buy both of these books for seven shillings. Yet these works are of so humorous a character that for many years it was found impossible to print them. The compositors fell back from their task suffocated with laughter and gasping for air. Nothing but the invention of the linotype machine[3]—

2. See Carl Spadoni, *A Bibliography of Stephen Leacock* (1998), for Leacock's publications prior to 1912.
3. The professional organization of teachers of political science.
4. Founded in 1868 as the Colonial Society, the Royal Colonial Society existed under that name until 1928, when it became the Royal Empire Society, which, in 1958, became the Royal Commonwealth Society. Its purpose was to promote knowledge in and about the British Empire.
5. The Anglican branch of the Western (or Latin) church. Since the Reformation, the Church of England has rejected the authority of the Pope and taken the British monarch as its titular head. Its tenets are set out in the Thirty-nine Articles and its services, as Leacock would have known them, in the Book of Common Prayer. Its equivalent in the United States is the Episcopalian Church.
6. Leacock's lecture tour of the British Empire took him to New Zealand and Australia in 1907 and South Africa and England in 1908.
7. The act creating the Union of South Africa came into force on October 31, 1910.
8. There were no Banana Riots in Trinidad in the period following Leacock's lecture tour or at any other time. Perhaps he had in mind the Water Riots of March 23, 1903, in Port-of-Spain, Trinidad, and confused these with the Belmanna Riots of 1876 in Roxborough, Tobago. Precipitated by the colonial government's attempt to make the people of Port-of-Spain pay for water by installing water meters, the Water Riots resulted in sixteen deaths and the destruction of principal government buildings in the town.
9. The Turco-Italian or Italo-Turkish War began on September 29, 1911, and ended with the Treaty of Ouchy on October 15, 1912.
1. The Canadian Pacific Railway (C.P.R.).
2. *Literary Lapses: A Book of Sketches* was published in 1910 and *Nonsense Novels* in 1911.
3. Invented in 1884 by Ottmar Mergenthaler, the linotype machine was operated from a keyboard like that of a typewriter. Because it produced metal slugs corresponding to single lines of type as set by hand by traditional printers, it greatly improved the speed and reduced the cost of printing.

or rather, of the kind of men who operate it—made it possible to print these books. Even now people have to be very careful in circulating them, and the books should never be put into the hands of persons not in robust health.

Many of my friends are under the impression that I write these humorous nothings in idle moments when the wearied brain is unable to perform the serious labours of the economist. My own experience is exactly the other way. The writing of solid, instructive stuff fortified by facts and figures is easy enough. There is no trouble in writing a scientific treatise on the folk-lore of Central China, or a statistical enquiry into the declining population of Prince Edward Island. But to write something out of one's own mind, worth reading for its own sake, is an arduous contrivance only to be achieved in fortunate moments, few and far between. Personally, I would sooner have written "Alice in Wonderland"[4] than the whole Encyclopædia Britannica.[5]

In regard to the present work I must disclaim at once all intention of trying to do anything so ridiculously easy as writing about a real place and real people. Mariposa[6] is not a real town. On the contrary, it is about seventy or eighty of them. You may find them all the way from Lake Superior to the sea, with the same square streets and the same maple trees and the same churches and hotels, and everywhere the sunshine of the land of hope.

Similarly, the Reverend Mr. Drone is not one person, but about eight or ten. To make him I clapped the gaiters of one ecclesiastic round the legs of another, added the sermons of a third and the character of a fourth, and so let him start on his way in the book to pick up such individual attributes as he might find for himself. Mullins and Bagshaw and Judge Pepperleigh and the rest are, it is true, personal friends of mine. But I have known them in such a variety of forms, with such alternations of tall and short, dark and fair, that, individually, I should have much ado to know them. Mr. Pupkin is found whenever a Canadian bank opens a branch in a county town and needs a teller. As for Mr. Smith, with his two hundred and eighty pounds, his hoarse voice, his loud check suit, his diamonds, the roughness of his address and the goodness of his heart,—all of this is known by everybody to be a necessary and universal adjunct of the hotel business.

4. *Alice's Adventures in Wonderland* by Lewis Carroll (Charles Dodgson) (1835–1910) was first published in 1865.
5. The eleventh edition of the *Encyclopaedia Britannica* was published in 1910–11.
6. Despite Leacock's protestations in this and the ensuing paragraph, the settings and many of the characters in the book derive to some extent from actual places and people in and around the town of Orillia, Ontario, near which Leacock had grown up and, in 1908–1909, built the cottage where he spent most of his summers. In Appendix C in his edition of *Sunshine Sketches of a Little Town* (178–81), Carl Spadoni assembles information and speculations from various sources, including Leacock himself, on the Orillian counterparts of people and places in the book.

The inspiration of the book,—a land of hope and sunshine where little towns spread their square streets and their trim maple trees beside placid lakes almost within echo of the primeval forest,[7]—is large enough. If it fails in its portrayal of the scenes and the country that it depicts the fault lies rather with an art that is deficient than in an affection that is wanting.

STEPHEN LEACOCK

McGill University,
June, 1912.

Chapter I

The Hostelry of Mr. Smith

I don't know whether you know Mariposa. If not, it is of no consequence, for if you know Canada at all, you are probably well acquainted with a dozen towns just like it.

There it lies in the sunlight, sloping up from the little lake that spreads out at the foot of the hillside on which the town is built. There is a wharf beside the lake, and lying alongside of it a steamer that is tied to the wharf with two ropes of about the same size as they use on the Lusitania.[1] The steamer goes nowhere in particular, for the lake is landlocked and there is no navigation for the Mariposa Belle except to "run trips" on the first of July and the Queen's Birthday,[2] and to take excursions of the Knights of Pythias[3] and the Sons of Temperance[4] to and from the Local Option Townships.[5]

In point of geography the lake is called Lake Wissanotti and the river running out of it the Ossawippi, just as the main street of Mariposa is called Missinaba Street and the county Missinaba County. But these names do not really matter. Nobody uses them.

---

7. A possible allusion to the opening words of Henry Wadsworth Longfellow's *Evangeline* (1847): "This is the forest primeval."
1. British passenger ship that would be sunk by a German submarine off the coast of Ireland on May 7, 1915, with great loss of life. See also p. 42, n. 6.
2. July 1 was Dominion (now Canada) Day and May 24 is the birthday of Queen Victoria (1819–1901), who ascended to the throne of Great Britain, Ireland, and Britain's overseas dominions in 1837.
3. Named for Damon and Pythias, two youths in ancient Greek mythology whose loyalty to each other came to epitomize true friendship, the Knights of Pythias is a social organization for men that was founded in 1864 and had lodges in both Canada and the United States.
4. The Order of the Sons of Temperance was founded in New York in 1842 and quickly established "divisions" in other parts of the United States and then in Canada and elsewhere. Its members took a vow to abstain from alcoholic drinks and to combat the effects and spread of intemperance.
5. Townships that had exercised the option of deciding by popular vote whether or not to allow the sale of alcoholic drinks within their borders. The Dunkin Act of 1864 gave the local option to all counties and municipalities in Canada East (Quebec) and Canada West (Ontario) and in 1878 the right was extended throughout the Dominion by the Canadian Temperance Act.

People simply speak of the "lake" and the "river" and the "main street," much in the same way as they always call the Continental Hotel, "Pete Robinson's" and the Pharmaceutical Hall, "Eliot's Drug Store." But I suppose this is just the same in every one else's town as in mine, so I need lay no stress on it.

The town, I say, has one broad street that runs up from the lake, commonly called the Main Street. There is no doubt about its width. When Mariposa was laid out there was none of that short-sightedness which is seen in the cramped dimensions of Wall Street and Piccadilly.[6] Missinaba Street is so wide that if you were to roll Jeff Thorpe's barber shop over on its face it wouldn't reach half way across. Up and down the Main Street are telegraph poles of cedar of colossal thickness, standing at a variety of angles and carrying rather more wires than are commonly seen at a trans-atlantic cable station.

On the Main Street itself are a number of buildings of extraordinary importance,—Smith's Hotel and the Continental and the Mariposa House, and the two banks (the Commercial and the Exchange), to say nothing of McCarthy's Block (erected in 1878), and Glover's Hardware Store with the Oddfellows' Hall[7] above it. Then on the "cross" street that intersects Missinaba Street at the main corner there is the Post Office and the Fire Hall and the Young Men's Christian Association and the office of the Mariposa Newspacket,—in fact, to the eye of discernment a perfect jostle of public institutions comparable only to Threadneedle Street or Lower Broadway.[8] On all the side streets there are maple trees and broad sidewalks, trim gardens with upright calla lilies, houses with verandahs, which are here and there being replaced by residences with piazzas.[9]

To the careless eye the scene on the Main Street of a summer afternoon is one of deep and unbroken peace. The empty street sleeps in the sunshine. There is a horse and buggy tied to the hitching post in front of Glover's hardware store. There is, usually and commonly, the burly figure of Mr. Smith, proprietor of Smith's Hotel, standing in his chequered waistcoat on the steps of his hostelry, and perhaps, further up the street, Lawyer Macartney going for his

6. Major thoroughfares in New York City and London, England.
7. With origins in eighteenth-century fraternal organizations that had secret rites supposedly resembling those of the Freemasons, the Independent Order of Oddfellows was formed in Manchester, England, about 1813 and thereafter grew into a vast organization with lodges in the United States as well as Britain, Canada, and other countries. In 1842 the American lodges broke away to become a large organization in its own right.
8. Threadneedle Street in London, England, is the site of the Bank of England, which is known as "The Old Lady of Threadneedle Street." Lower Broadway in New York City is the site of many large commercial buildings.
9. From meaning a covered walk or arcade along the front of a building, "piazza" came in North America to mean a "verandah." In Leacock's usage here and later, it appears to refer to the spacious verandah of a large house.

afternoon mail, or the Rev. Mr. Drone, the Rural Dean of the Church of England Church,[1] going home to get his fishing rod after a mothers' auxiliary meeting.

But this quiet is mere appearance. In reality, and to those who know it, the place is a perfect hive of activity. Why, at Netley's butcher shop (established in 1882) there are no less than four men working on the sausage machines in the basement; at the News-packet office there are as many more job-printing; there is a long distance telephone with four distracting girls on high stools wearing steel caps and talking incessantly; in the offices in McCarthy's block are dentists and lawyers, with their coats off, ready to work at any moment; and from the big planing factory down beside the lake where the railroad siding is, you may hear all through the hours of the summer afternoon the long-drawn music of the running saw.

Busy—well, I should think so! Ask any of its inhabitants if Mariposa isn't a busy, hustling, thriving town. Ask Mullins, the manager of the Exchange Bank, who comes hustling over to his office from the Mariposa House every day at 10.30 and has scarcely time all morning to go out and take a drink with the manager of the Commercial; or ask—well, for the matter of that, ask any of them if they ever knew a more rushing go-a-head town than Mariposa.

Of course if you come to the place fresh from New York, you are deceived. Your standard of vision is all astray. You do think the place is quiet. You do imagine that Mr. Smith is asleep merely because he closes his eyes as he stands. But live in Mariposa for six months or a year and then you will begin to understand it better; the buildings get higher and higher; the Mariposa House grows more and more luxurious; McCarthy's block towers to the sky; the 'buses[2] roar and hum to the station; the trains shriek; the traffic multiplies; the people move faster and faster; a dense crowd swirls to and fro in the post-office and the five and ten cent store—and amusements! well, now! lacrosse, baseball, excursions, dances, the Firemen's Ball every winter and the Catholic picnic every summer; and music— the town band in the park every Wednesday evening, and the Odd-fellows' brass band on the street every other Friday; the Mariposa Quartette, the Salvation Army—why, after a few months' residence you begin to realize that the place is a mere mad round of gaiety.

In point of population, if one must come down to figures, the Canadian census puts the numbers every time at something round five thousand. But it is very generally understood in Mariposa that the census is largely the outcome of malicious jealousy. It is usual

1. A relatively senior clergyman who, under a bishop, has the responsibility of supervising the clergy in certain parishes. "Church of England Church": Anglican church.
2. Omnibuses: large vehicles for transporting passengers between hotels and railway stations.

that after the census the editor of the Mariposa Newspacket makes a careful re-estimate (based on the data of relative non-payment of subscriptions), and brings the population up to 6,000. After that the Mariposa Times-Herald makes an estimate that runs the figures up to 6,500. Then Mr. Gingham, the undertaker, who collects the vital statistics for the provincial government, makes an estimate from the number of what he calls the "demised" as compared with the less interesting persons who are still alive, and brings the population to 7,000. After that somebody else works it out that it's 7,500; then the man behind the bar of the Mariposa House offers to bet the whole room that there are 9,000 people in Mariposa. That settles it, and the population is well on the way to 10,000, when down swoops the federal census taker on his next round and the town has to begin all over again.

Still, it is a thriving town and there is no doubt of it. Even the transcontinental railways,[3] as any townsman will tell you, run through Mariposa. It is true that the trains mostly go through at night and don't stop. But in the wakeful silence of the summer night you may hear the long whistle of the through train for the west as it tears through Mariposa, rattling over the switches and past the semaphores[4] and ending in a long, sullen roar as it takes the trestle bridge over the Ossawippi. Or, better still, on a winter evening about eight o'clock you will see the long row of the Pullmans and diners[5] of the night express going north to the mining country, the windows flashing with brilliant light, and within them a vista of cut glass and snow-white table linen, smiling negroes and millionaires with napkins at their chins whirling past in the driving snowstorm.

I can tell you the people of Mariposa are proud of the trains, even if they don't stop! The joy of being on the main line lifts the Mariposa people above the level of their neighbours in such places as Tecumseh[6] and Nichols Corners into the cosmopolitan atmosphere of through traffic and the larger life. Of course, they have their own train, too—the Mariposa Local, made up right there in the station yard, and running south to the city a hundred miles away. That, of course, is a real train, with a box stove on end in the passenger car, fed with cordwood[7] upside down, and with seven-

---

3. The tracks of the Canadian Pacific Railway.
4. Railway signals consisting of an upright with arms that can be turned up or down.
5. Sleeping cars (or cars with seats) and dining cars.
6. Village or town named for the Shawnee war chief who participated in a futile attempt in the early 1790s to preserve his native Ohio Valley from American settlement and allied his followers with the British and Canadian forces in the War of 1812. Tecumseh was revered as a hero for his capture and merciful treatment of prisoners at Fort Meigs (May 1813) and for his steadfastness and death at the Battle of Moraviantown (October 5, 1813) on the Thames River in what is now southwestern Ontario.
7. Firewood sold by the cord.

teen flat cars of pine lumber set between the passenger car and the locomotive so as to give the train its full impact when shunting.

Outside of Mariposa there are farms that begin well but get thinner and meaner as you go on, and end sooner or later in bush and swamp and the rock of the north country. And beyond that again, as the background of it all, though it's far away, you are somehow aware of the great pine woods of the lumber country reaching endlessly into the north.

Not that the little town is always gay or always bright in the sunshine. There never was such a place for changing its character with the season. Dark enough and dull it seems of a winter night, the wooden sidewalks creaking with the frost, and the lights burning dim behind the shop windows. In olden times the lights were coal oil lamps; now, of course, they are, or are supposed to be, electricity,—brought from the power house on the lower Ossawippi nineteen miles away. But, somehow, though it starts off as electricity from the Ossawippi rapids, by the time it gets to Mariposa and filters into the little bulbs behind the frosty windows of the shops, it has turned into coal oil again, as yellow and bleared as ever.

After the winter, the snow melts and the ice goes out of the lake, the sun shines high and the shanty-men[8] come down from the lumber woods and lie round drunk on the sidewalk outside of Smith's Hotel—and that's spring time. Mariposa is then a fierce, dangerous lumber town, calculated to terrorize the soul of a newcomer who does not understand that this also is only an appearance and that presently[9] the rough-looking shanty-men will change their clothes and turn back again into farmers.

Then the sun shines warmer and the maple trees come out and Lawyer Macartney puts on his tennis trousers, and that's summer time. The little town changes to a sort of summer resort. There are visitors up from the city. Every one of the seven cottages along the lake is full. The Mariposa Belle churns the waters of the Wissanotti into foam as she sails out from the wharf, in a cloud of flags, the band playing and the daughters and sisters of the Knights of Pythias dancing gaily on the deck.

That changes too. The days shorten. The visitors disappear. The golden rod[1] beside the meadow droops and withers on its stem. The maples blaze in glory and die. The evening closes dark and chill, and in the gloom of the main corner of Mariposa the Salvation Army around a naphtha lamp[2] lift up the confession of their sins—

---

8. Men who work for all or, as here, part of the year as lumbermen, living in crude huts (shanties) in the bush.
9. Soon; in due course.
1. Plants with rod-like stems and yellow flowers that bloom late in summer.
2. Lamp that burns a liquid obtained from distilling petroleum.

and that is autumn. Thus the year runs its round, moving and changing in Mariposa, much as it does in other places.

If, then, you feel that you know the town well enough to be admitted into the inner life and movement of it, walk this June afternoon half way down the Main Street—or, if you like, half way up from the wharf—to where Mr. Smith is standing at the door of his hostelry. You will feel as you draw near that it is no ordinary man that you approach. It is not alone the huge bulk of Mr. Smith (two hundred and eighty pounds as tested on Netley's scales). It is not merely his costume, though the chequered waistcoat of dark blue with a flowered pattern forms, with his shepherd's plaid[3] trousers, his grey spats and patent-leather boots, a colour scheme of no mean order. Nor is it merely Mr. Smith's finely mottled face. The face, no doubt, is a notable one,—solemn, inexpressible, unreadable, the face of the heaven-born hotel keeper. It is more than that. It is the strange dominating personality of the man that somehow holds you captive. I know nothing in history to compare with the position of Mr. Smith among those who drink over his bar, except, though in a lesser degree, the relation of the Emperor Napoleon to the Imperial Guard.[4]

When you meet Mr. Smith first you think he looks like an overdressed pirate. Then you begin to think him a character. You wonder at his enormous bulk. Then the utter hopelessness of knowing what Smith is thinking by merely looking at his features gets on your mind and makes the Mona Lisa[5] seem an open book and the ordinary human countenance as superficial as a puddle in the sunlight. After you have had a drink in Mr. Smith's bar, and he has called you by your Christian name, you realize that you are dealing with one of the greatest minds in the hotel business.

Take, for instance, the big sign that sticks out into the street above Mr. Smith's head as he stands. What is on it? Simply: "JOS. SMITH, PROP."[6] Nothing more, and yet the thing was a flash of

3. A pattern of small black and white checks.
4. The relationship between Napoleon Bonaparte (1769–1821), Napoleon I of the French, and the élite troops of the Imperial Guard that protected him is legendary. Napoleon's defeat at Waterloo is sometimes ascribed to his reluctance to send the Imperial Guard into the battle.
5. The enigmatic smile of the *Mona Lisa* (*La Giaconda*) painted by Leonardo da Vinci has given rise to much speculation, including an extensive description in Walter Pater's *The Renaissance: Studies in Art and History* (1873), where the "subtle expression . . . on the face" of the woman in the portrait is described as "expressive of what in the ways of a thousand years men had come to desire . . . All the thoughts and experience of the world are etched and moulded there, in that which they have of power to refine and make expressive the outward form, the animalism of Greece, the lust of Rome, the mysticism of the middle ages with its spiritual ambition and imaginative loves, the return of the Pagan world, the sins of the Borgias" (Oxford World's Classic edition, ed. Adam Phillips, [Oxford: Oxford UP 1986], 79, 80).
6. "Jos." is probably an abbreviation of Joshua, and "Josh" (as Smith is later called) is North American slang for a good-natured joke and for making good-natured fun of someone. "Prop" is an abbreviation of proprietor (owner).

genius. Other men who had had the hotel before Mr. Smith had called it by such feeble names as the Royal Hotel and the Queen's and the Alexandria. Every one of them failed. When Mr. Smith took over the hotel he simply put up the sign with "JOS. SMITH, PROP.," and then stood underneath in the sunshine as a living proof that a man who weighs nearly three hundred pounds is the natural king of the hotel business.

But on this particular afternoon, in spite of the sunshine and deep peace, there was something as near to profound concern and anxiety as the features of Mr. Smith were ever known to express.

The moment was indeed an anxious one. Mr. Smith was awaiting a telegram from his legal adviser who had that day journeyed to the county town to represent the proprietor's interest before the assembled License Commissioners.[7] If you know anything of the hotel business at all, you will understand that as beside the decisions of the License Commissioners of Missinaba County, the opinions of the Lords of the Privy Council[8] are mere trifles.

The matter in question was very grave. The Mariposa court had just fined Mr. Smith for the second time for selling liquors after hours. The Commissioners, therefore, were entitled to cancel the license.

Mr. Smith knew his fault and acknowledged it. He had broken the law. How he had come to do so, it passed his imagination to recall. Crime always seems impossible in retrospect. By what sheer madness of the moment could he have shut up the bar on the night in question, and shut Judge Pepperleigh, the district judge of Missinaba County, outside of it? The more so inasmuch as the closing up of the bar under the rigid license law of the province was a matter that the proprietor never trusted to any hands but his own. Punctually every night at 11 o'clock Mr. Smith strolled from the desk of the "rotunda"[9] to the door of the bar. If it seemed properly full of people and all was bright and cheerful, then he closed it. If not, he kept it open a few minutes longer till he had enough people inside to warrant closing. But never, never unless he was assured that Pepperleigh, the judge of the court, and Macartney, the prosecuting attorney, were both safely in the bar, or the bar parlour, did the proprietor venture to close up. Yet on this fatal night Pepperleigh and Macartney had been shut out—actually left on the street without a drink, and compelled to hammer and beat at the street door of the bar to gain admittance.

7. Officials responsible for licensing the sale of alcoholic drinks.
8. The British monarch's advisory council, a body whose importance had long since been greatly diminished by the transference of the duties of government to the cabinet.
9. Pretentious term for the hotel's lobby: a rotunda is a round hall or building, especially one with a dome.

This was the kind of thing not to be tolerated. Either a hotel must be run decently or quit. An information was laid next day and Mr. Smith convicted in four minutes, his lawyers practically refusing to plead. The Mariposa court, when the presiding judge was cold sober, and it had the force of public opinion behind it, was a terrible engine of retributive justice.

So no wonder that Mr. Smith awaited with anxiety the message of his legal adviser.

He looked alternately up the street and down it again, hauled out his watch from the depths of his embroidered pocket, and examined the hour hand and the minute hand and the second hand with frowning scrutiny.

Then wearily, and as one mindful that a hotel man is ever the servant of the public, he turned back into the hotel.

"Billy," he said to the desk clerk, "if a wire[1] comes bring it into the bar parlour."

The voice of Mr. Smith is of a deep guttural such as Plancon or Edouard de Reske[2] might have obtained had they had the advantages of the hotel business. And with that, Mr. Smith, as was his custom in off moments, joined his guests in the back room. His appearance, to the untrained eye, was merely that of an extremely stout hotel-keeper walking from the rotunda to the back bar. In reality, Mr. Smith was on the eve of one of the most brilliant and daring strokes ever effected in the history of licensed liquor. When I saw that it was out of the agitation of this situation that Smith's Ladies' and Gent's Café originated, anybody who knows Mariposa will understand the magnitude of the moment.

Mr. Smith, then, moved slowly from the doorway of the hotel through the "rotunda," or more simply the front room with the desk and the cigar case in it, and so to the bar and thence to the little room or back bar behind it. In this room, as I have said, the brightest minds of Mariposa might commonly be found in the quieter part of a summer afternoon.

To-day there was a group of four who looked up as Mr. Smith entered, somewhat sympathetically, and evidently aware of the perplexities of the moment.

Henry Mullins and George Duff, the two bank managers, were both present. Mullins is a rather short, rather round, smooth-shaven man of less than forty, wearing one of those round banking suits of pepper and salt, with a round banking hat of hard straw, and with the kind of gold tie-pin and heavy watch-chain and seals necessary to inspire confidence in matters of foreign exchange. Duff is just as round

1. Telegram.
2. Pol-Henri Plancon (1854–1914) was a famous French operatic bass singer and Édouard de Reske (Reszke) (1853–1917) a famous Polish one.

and just as short, and equally smoothly shaven, while his seals and straw hat are calculated to prove that the Commercial is just as sound a bank as the Exchange. From the technical point of view of the banking business, neither of them had any objection to being in Smith's Hotel or to taking a drink as long as the other was present. This, of course, was one of the cardinal principles of Mariposa banking.

Then there was Mr. Diston, the high school teacher, commonly known as the "one who drank." None of the other teachers ever entered a hotel unless accompanied by a lady or protected by a child. But as Mr. Diston was known to drink beer on occasions and to go in and out of the Mariposa House and Smith's Hotel, he was looked upon as a man whose life was a mere wreck. Whenever the School Board raised the salaries of the other teachers, fifty or sixty dollars per annum at one lift, it was well understood that public morality wouldn't permit of an increase for Mr. Diston.

Still more noticeable, perhaps, was the quiet, sallow looking man dressed in black, with black gloves and with black silk hat heavily craped and placed hollow-side-up on a chair. This was Mr. Golgotha Gingham,[3] the undertaker of Mariposa, and his dress was due to the fact that he had just come from what he called an "interment." Mr. Gingham had the true spirit of his profession, and such words as "funeral" or "coffin" or "hearse" never passed his lips. He spoke always of "interments," of "caskets," and "coaches," using terms that were calculated rather to bring out the majesty and sublimity of death than to parade its horrors.

To be present at the hotel was in accord with Mr. Gingham's general conception of his business. No man had ever grasped the true principles of undertaking more thoroughly than Mr. Gingham. I have often heard him explain that to associate with the living, uninteresting though they appear, is the only way to secure the custom of the dead.

"Get to know people really well while they are alive," said Mr. Gingham; "be friends with them, close friends, and then when they die you don't need to worry. You'll get the order every time."

So, naturally, as the moment was one of sympathy, it was Mr. Gingham who spoke first.

"What'll you do, Josh," he said, "if the Commissioners go against you?"

"Boys," said Mr. Smith, "I don't rightly know. If I have to quit, the next move is to the city. But I don't reckon that I will have to quit. I've got an idee that I think's good every time."

3. A kind of cotton cloth woven from coloured yarns into stripes or checks. "Golgotha": the hill (also called Calvary) where Jesus Christ was crucified, so named in Mark 15.22: "And they bring him unto the place named Golgotha, which is, being interpreted, the place of a skull."

"Could you run a hotel in the city?" asked Mullins.

"I could," said Mr. Smith. "I'll tell you. There's big things doin' in the hotel business right now, big chances if you go into it right. Hotels in the city is branching out. Why, you take the dining-room side of it," continued Mr. Smith, looking round at the group, "there's thousands in it. The old plan's all gone. Folks won't eat now in an ordinary dining-room with a high ceiling and windows. You have to get 'em down underground in a room with no windows and lots of sawdust round and waiters that can't speak English. I seen them places last time I was in the city. They call 'em Rats' Coolers.[4] And for light meals they want a Caff,[5] a real French Caff, and for folks that come in late another place that they call a Girl Room[6] that don't shut up at all. If I go to the city that's the kind of place I mean to run. What's yours, Gol? It's on the house?"

And it was just at the moment when Mr. Smith said this that Billy, the desk clerk, entered the room with the telegram in his hand.

But stop—it is impossible for you to understand the anxiety with which Mr. Smith and his associates awaited the news from the Commissioners, without first realizing the astounding progress of Mr. Smith in the three past years, and the pinnacle of public eminence to which he had attained.

Mr. Smith had come down from the lumber country of the Spanish River, where the divide is toward the Hudson Bay,—"back north" as they called it in Mariposa.

He had been, it was said, a cook in the lumber shanties. To this day Mr. Smith can fry an egg on both sides with a lightness of touch that is the despair of his own "help."

After that, he had run a river driver's boarding-house.[7]

After that, he had taken a food contract for a gang of railroad navvies[8] on the transcontinental.

After that, of course, the whole world was open to him.

He came down to Mariposa and bought out the "inside" of what had been the Royal Hotel.

Those who are educated understand that by the "inside" of a hotel is meant everything except the four outer walls of it—the fittings, the furniture, the bar, Billy the desk-clerk, the three dining-room girls, and above all the license granted by King Edward VII, and ratified further by King George,[9] for the sale of intoxicating liquors.

4. Rathskellers: beer halls or restaurants modelled on the German type in the cellar (*keller*) of a town hall (*rat*).
5. Café.
6. Grill Room.
7. A house where lumbermen engaged in the process of floating or driving logs down river can obtain meals and lodging.
8. Labourers.
9. Edward VII (1841–1910) was sovereign of Great Britain and its overseas dominions from 1901 to 1910. He was succeeded in 1910 by George V (1865–1936).

Till then the Royal had been a mere nothing. As "Smith's Hotel" it broke into a blaze of effulgence.

From the first, Mr. Smith, as a proprietor, was a wild, rapturous success.

He had all the qualifications.

He weighed two hundred and eighty pounds.

He could haul two drunken men out of the bar each by the scruff of the neck without the faintest anger or excitement.

He carried money enough in his trousers pockets to start a bank, and spent it on anything, bet it on anything, and gave it away in handfuls.

He was never drunk, and, as a point of chivalry to his customers, never quite sober. Anybody was free of the hotel who cared to come in. Anybody who didn't like it could go out. Drinks of all kinds cost five cents, or six for a quarter. Meals and beds were practically free. Any persons foolish enough to go to the desk and pay for them, Mr. Smith charged according to the expression of their faces.

At first the loafers and the shanty men settled down on the place in a shower. But that was not the "trade" that Mr. Smith wanted. He knew how to get rid of them. An army of charwomen,[1] turned into the hotel, scrubbed it from top to bottom. A vacuum cleaner, the first seen in Mariposa, hissed and screamed in the corridors. Forty brass beds were imported from the city, not, of course, for the guests to sleep in, but to keep them out. A bar-tender with a starched coat and wicker sleeves[2] was put behind the bar.

The loafers were put out of business. The place had become too "high toned" for them.

To get the high class trade, Mr. Smith set himself to dress the part. He wore wide cut coats of filmy serge,[3] light as gossamer; chequered waistcoats with a pattern for every day in the week; fedora hats[4] light as autumn leaves; four-in-hand ties[5] of saffron and myrtle green with a diamond pin the size of a hazel nut. On his fingers there were as many gems as would grace a native prince of India; across his waistcoat lay a gold watch-chain in huge square links and in his pocket a gold watch that weighed a pound and a half and marked minutes, seconds and quarter seconds. Just to look at Josh Smith's watch brought at least ten men to the bar every evening.

Every morning Mr. Smith was shaved by Jefferson Thorpe, across the way. All that art could do, all that Florida water[6] could effect, was lavished on his person.

1. Domestic cleaners.
2. Woven cuff protectors designed to guard men's shirt sleeves against stains.
3. Strong fabric woven so as to show diagonal lines.
4. Felt hats dented lengthwise, usually with curled brim.
5. Neckties tied with a flat slip-knot.
6. A commercially prepared toilet water or cologne consisting of a blend of floral oils in a water and alcohol base.

Mr. Smith became a local character. Mariposa was at his feet. All the reputable business-men drank at Mr. Smith's bar, and in the little parlour behind it you might find at any time a group of the brightest intellects in the town.

Not but what there was opposition at first. The clergy, for example, who accepted the Mariposa House and the Continental as a necessary and useful evil, looked askance at the blazing lights and the surging crowd of Mr. Smith's saloon. They preached against him. When the Rev. Dean Drone led off with a sermon on the text "Lord be merciful even unto this publican Matthew Six,"[7] it was generally understood as an invitation to strike Mr. Smith dead. In the same way the sermon at the Presbyterian church the week after was on the text "Lo what now doeth Abiram in the land of Melchisideck Kings Eight and Nine?"[8] and it was perfectly plain that what was meant was, "Lo, what is Josh Smith doing in Mariposa?"

But this opposition had been countered by a wide and sagacious philanthropy. I think Mr. Smith first got the idea of that on the night when the steam merry-go-round came to Mariposa. Just below the hostelry, on an empty lot, it whirled and whistled, steaming forth its tunes on the summer evening while the children crowded round it in hundreds. Down the street strolled Mr. Smith, wearing a soft fedora to indicate that it was evening.

"What d'you charge for a ride, boss?" said Mr. Smith.

"Two for a nickel," said the man.

"Take that," said Mr. Smith, handing out a ten-dollar bill from a roll of money, "and ride the little folks free all evening."

That night the merry-go-round whirled madly till after midnight, freighted to capacity with Mariposa children, while up in Smith's Hotel, parents, friends and admirers, as the news spread, were standing four deep along the bar. They sold forty dollars' worth of lager alone that night, and Mr. Smith learned, if he had not already suspected it, the blessedness of giving.

The uses of philanthropy went further. Mr. Smith subscribed to

---

7. Publicans (that is, tax collectors) are mentioned in Matthew 5.46, 11.19, and 18.16, but not in Matthew 6, which is the central chapter of Jesus' Sermon on the Mount and contains the words of the Lord's Prayer (or "Our Father") as well as some of Christianity's central exhortations and ethical principles, including Christ's injunctions again the public display of charitable acts, the accumulation of wealth, and personal adornment. Erroneous though it is, Dean Drone's citation of Matthew 6 directs the reader to values by which Josh Smith and other Mariposans may be judged.

8. Abiram is one of the men who rebel against Moses in Numbers 16. In punishment they are "swallowed . . . up together" by the earth (Numbers 26.10). Melchizedek was a priest and king of Salem (Jerusalem) who blessed Abraham in the name of the Most High and received tithes from him. References to him appear in Genesis 14.18, Psalm 110.4, and Hebrews 5.6–10 and 6.20 and 27, but not in either book of Kings. The misspelling of his name may be an error on Leacock's part or a further indication of the faulty knowledge of the preacher in the Presbyterian church.

everything, joined everything, gave to everything. He became an Oddfellow, a Forester,[9] a Knight of Pythias and a Workman.[1] He gave a hundred dollars to the Mariposa Hospital and a hundred dollars to the Young Men's Christian Association.

He subscribed to the Ball Club, the Lacrosse Club, the Curling Club, to anything, in fact, and especially to all those things which needed premises to meet in and grew thirsty in their discussions.

As a consequence the Oddfellows held their annual banquet at Smith's Hotel and the Oyster Supper of the Knights of Pythias was celebrated in Mr. Smith's dining-room.

Even more effective, perhaps, were Mr. Smith's secret benefactions, the kind of giving done by stealth of which not a soul in town knew anything, often, for a week after it was done. It was in this way that Mr. Smith put the new font in Dean Drone's church, and handed over a hundred dollars to Judge Pepperleigh for the unrestrained use of the Conservative party.

So it came about that, little by little, the antagonism had died down. Smith's Hotel became an accepted institution in Mariposa. Even the temperance people were proud of Mr. Smith as a sort of character who added distinction to the town. There were moments, in the earlier quiet of the morning, when Dean Drone would go so far as to step in to the "rotunda" and collect a subscription. As for the Salvation Army, they ran in and out all the time unreproved.

On only one point difficulty still remained. That was the closing of the bar. Mr. Smith could never bring his mind to it,—not as a matter of profit, but as a point of honour. It was too much for him to feel that Judge Pepperleigh might be out on the sidewalk thirsty at midnight, that the night hands of the Times-Herald on Wednesday might be compelled to go home dry. On this point Mr. Smith's moral code was simplicity itself,—do what is right and take the consequences. So the bar stayed open.

Every town, I suppose, has its meaner spirits. In every genial bosom some snake is warmed,—or, as Mr. Smith put it to Golgotha Gingham—"there are some fellers even in this town skunks enough to inform."

At first the Mariposa court quashed all indictments. The presiding judge, with his spectacles on and a pile of books in front of him, threatened the informer with the penitentiary. The whole bar of

9. A member of the Ancient Order of Foresters, a friendly or benevolent society founded in England in 1834, but having its origins in the eighteenth-century Royal Foresters. By the late nineteenth century, the Foresters had courts or lodges in the United States, Canada, and elsewhere as well as Britain. Women were admitted in 1892.

1. A member of the Ancient Order of United Workmen, a friendly or benevolent society founded in the United States in 1868 by John Jordan Upchurch, a Mason. By the late nineteenth century the Workmen had branches in Canada and elsewhere as well as the United States.

Mariposa was with Mr. Smith. But by sheer iteration the informations had proved successful. Judge Pepperleigh learned that Mr. Smith had subscribed a hundred dollars for the Liberal party and at once fined him for keeping open after hours. That made one conviction. On the top of this had come the untoward incident just mentioned and that made two. Beyond that was the deluge. This then was the exact situation when Billy, the desk clerk, entered the back bar with the telegram in his hand.

"Here's your wire, sir," he said.

"What does it say?" said Mr. Smith.

He always dealt with written documents with a fine air of detachment. I don't suppose there were ten people in Mariposa who knew that Mr. Smith couldn't read.

Billy opened the message and read, "Commissioners give you three months to close down."

"Let me read it," said Mr. Smith, "that's right, three months to close down."

There was dead silence when the message was read. Everybody waited for Mr. Smith to speak. Mr. Gingham instinctively assumed the professional air of hopeless melancholy.

As it was afterwards recorded, Mr. Smith stood and "studied" with the tray in his hand for at least four minutes. Then he spoke.

"Boys," he said, "I'll be darned if I close down till I'm ready to close down. I've got an idee. You wait and I'll show you."

And beyond that, not another word did Mr. Smith say on the subject.

But within forty-eight hours the whole town knew that something was doing. The hotel swarmed with carpenters, bricklayers and painters. There was an architect up from the city with a bundle of blue prints in his hand. There was an engineer taking the street level with a theodolite, and a gang of navvies with shovels digging like fury as if to dig out the back foundations of the hotel.

"That'll fool 'em," said Mr. Smith.

Half the town was gathered round the hotel crazy with excitement. But not a word would the proprietor say.

Great dray² loads of square timber, and two-by-eight pine joists kept arriving from the planing mill. There was a pile of matched spruce sixteen feet high lying by the sidewalk.

Then the excavation deepened and the dirt flew, and the beams went up and the joists across, and all the day from dawn till dusk the hammers of the carpenters clattered away, working overtime at time and a half.

"It don't matter what it costs," said Mr. Smith; "get it done."

2. Large vehicle suitable for transporting heavy loads.

Rapidly the structure took form. It extended down the side street, joining the hotel at a right angle. Spacious and graceful it looked as it reared its uprights into the air.

Already you could see the place where the row of windows was to come, a veritable palace of glass, it must be, so wide and commodious were they. Below it, you could see the basement shaping itself, with a low ceiling like a vault and big beams running across, dressed, smoothed, and ready for staining. Already in the street there were seven crates of red and white awning.

And even then nobody knew what it was, and it was not till the seventeenth day that Mr. Smith, in the privacy of the back bar, broke the silence and explained.

"I tell you, boys," he says, "it's a caff—like what they have in the city—a ladies' and gent's caff, and that underneath (what's yours, Mr. Mullins?) is a Rats' Cooler. And when I get her started, I'll hire a French Chief[3] to do the cooking, and for the winter I will put in a 'girl room,' like what they have in the city hotels. And I'd like to see who's going to close her up then."

Within two more weeks the plan was in operation. Not only was the caff built but the very hotel was transformed. Awnings had broken out in a red and white cloud upon its face, its every window carried a box of hanging plants, and above in glory floated the Union Jack. The very stationery was changed. The place was now Smith's Summer Pavillion. It was advertised in the city as Smith's Tourists' Emporium, and Smith's Northern Health Resort. Mr. Smith got the editor of the Times-Herald to write up a circular all about ozone[4] and the Mariposa pine woods, with illustrations of the maskinonge (piscis mariposis)[5] of Lake Wissanotti.

The Saturday after that circular hit the city in July, there were men with fishing rods and landing nets pouring in on every train, almost too fast to register. And if, in the face of that, a few little drops of whiskey were sold over the bar, who thought of it?

But the caff! that, of course, was the crowning glory of the thing, that and the Rats' Cooler below.

Light and cool, with swinging windows open to the air, tables with marble tops, palms, waiters in white coats—it was the standing marvel of Mariposa. Not a soul in the town except Mr. Smith, who knew it by instinct, ever guessed that waiters and palms and marble tables can be rented over the long distance telephone.

Mr. Smith was as good as his word. He got a French Chief with an aristocratic saturnine countenance, and a moustache and imperial[6]

3. Chef.
4. An imagined constituent of the air that was supposed to have health-giving properties.
5. A large species of pike (Esox masquinongy).
6. A tuft of hair below the lower lip.

that recalled the late Napoleon III.[7] No one knew where Mr. Smith got him. Some people in the town said he was a French marquis. Others said he was a count and explained the difference.

No one in Mariposa had ever seen anything like the caff. All down the side of it were the grill fires, with great pewter dish covers that went up and down on a chain, and you could walk along the row and actually pick out your own cutlet and then see the French marquis throw it on to the broiling iron; you could watch a buckwheat pancake whirled into existence under your eyes and see fowls' legs devilled, peppered, grilled, and tormented till they lost all semblance of the original Mariposa chicken.

Mr. Smith, of course, was in his glory.

"What have you got to-day, Alf?" he would say, as he strolled over to the marquis. The name of the Chief was, I believe, Alphonse, but "Alf" was near enough for Mr. Smith.

The marquis would extend to the proprietor the menu, "Voilà, m'sieu, la carte du jour."

Mr. Smith, by the way, encouraged the use of the French language in the caff. He viewed it, of course, solely in its relation to the hotel business, and, I think, regarded it as a recent invention.

"It's comin' in all the time in the city," he said, "and y'aint expected to understand it."

Mr. Smith would take the carte between his finger and thumb and stare at it. It was all covered with such devices as Potage à la Mariposa—Filet Mignon à la proprietaire—Côtelette à la Smith, and so on.

But the greatest thing about the caff were the prices. Therein lay, as everybody saw at once, the hopeless simplicity of Mr. Smith.

The prices stood fast at 25 cents a meal. You could come in and eat all they had in the caff for a quarter.

"No, sir," Mr. Smith said stoutly, "I ain't going to try to raise no prices on the public. The hotel's always been a quarter and the caff's a quarter."

Full? Full of people?

Well, I should think so! From the time the caff opened at 11 till it closed at 8.30, you could hardly find a table. Tourists, visitors, travellers, and half the people of Mariposa crowded at the little tables; crockery rattling, glasses tinkling on trays, corks popping, the waiters in their white coats flying to and fro, Alphonse whirling the cutlets and pancakes into the air, and in and through it all, Mr. Smith, in a white flannel suit and a broad crimson sash about his waist. Crowded and gay from morning to night, and even noisy in its hilarity.

7. Louis Napoleon Bonaparte (1808–1873), French emperor (1852–70).

Noisy, yes; but if you wanted deep quiet and cool, if you wanted to step from the glare of a Canadian August to the deep shadow of an enchanted glade,—walk down below into the Rats' Cooler. There you had it; dark old beams (who could believe they were put there a month ago?), great casks set on end with legends[8] such as Amontillado Fino done in gilt on a black ground, tall steins filled with German beer soft as moss, and a German waiter noiseless as moving foam. He who entered the Rats' Cooler at three of a summer afternoon was buried there for the day. Mr. Golgotha Gingham spent anything from four to seven hours there of every day. In his mind the place had all the quiet charm of an interment, with none of its sorrows.

But at night, when Mr. Smith and Billy, the desk clerk, opened up the cash register and figured out the combined losses of the caff and the Rats' Cooler, Mr. Smith would say:

"Billy, just wait till I get the license renood, and I'll close up this damn caff so tight they'll never know what hit her. What did that lamb cost? Fifty cents a pound, was it? I figure it, Billy, that every one of them hogs eats about a dollar's worth a grub for every twenty-five cents they pay on it. As for Alf—by gosh, I'm through with him."

But that, of course, was only a confidential matter as between Mr. Smith and Billy.

I don't know at what precise period it was that the idea of a petition to the License Commissioners first got about the town. No one seemed to know just who suggested it. But certain it was that public opinion began to swing strongly towards the support of Mr. Smith. I think it was perhaps on the day after the big fish dinner that Alphonse cooked for the Mariposa Canoe Club (at twenty cents a head) that the feeling began to find open expression. People said it was a shame that a man like Josh Smith should be run out of Mariposa by three license commissioners. Who were the license commissioners, anyway? Why, look at the license system they had in Sweden; yes, and in Finland and in South America. Or, for the matter of that, look at the French and Italians, who drink all day and all night. Aren't they all right? Aren't they a musical people? Take Napoleon, and Victor Hugo;[9] drunk half the time, and yet look what they did.

I quote these arguments not for their own sake, but merely to indicate the changing temper of public opinion in Mariposa. Men

8. Inscriptions.
9. Among other things, Napoleon Bonaparte distinguished himself as a great military leader and tactician. The achievements of the French writer Victor Hugo (1802–1885), who was a central figure in the Romantic movement, include *Nôtre Dame de Paris* (1831) and *Les Misérables* (1862).

would sit in the caff at lunch perhaps for an hour and a half and talk about the license question in general, and then go down into the Rats' Cooler and talk about it for two hours more.

It was amazing the way the light broke in in the case of particular individuals, often the most unlikely, and quelled their opposition.

Take, for example, the editor of the Newspacket. I suppose there wasn't a greater temperance advocate in town. Yet Alphonse queered him with an Omelette à la License in one meal.

Or take Pepperleigh himself, the judge of the Mariposa court. He was put to the bad[1] with a game pie,—pâté normand aux fine herbes—the real thing, as good as a trip to Paris in itself. After eating it, Pepperleigh had the common sense to realize that it was sheer madness to destroy a hotel that could cook a thing like that.

In the same way, the secretary of the School Board was silenced with a stuffed duck à la Ossawippi.

Three members of the town council were converted with a Dindon farci à la Josh Smith.

And then, finally, Mr. Diston persuaded Dean Drone to come, and as soon as Mr. Smith and Alphonse saw him they landed him with a fried flounder that even the apostles would have appreciated.[2]

After that, every one knew that the license question was practically settled. The petition was all over the town. It was printed in duplicate at the Newspacket and you could see it lying on the counter of every shop in Mariposa. Some of the people signed it twenty or thirty times.

It was the right kind of document too. It began—"Whereas in the bounty of providence the earth putteth forth her luscious fruits and her vineyards for the delight and enjoyment of mankind—" It made you thirsty just to read it. Any man who read that petition over was wild to get to the Rats' Cooler.

When it was all signed up they had nearly three thousand names on it.

Then Nivens, the lawyer, and Mr. Gingham (as a provincial official) took it down to the county town, and by three o'clock that afternoon the news had gone out from the long distance telephone office that Smith's license was renewed for three years.

Rejoicings! Well, I should think so! Everybody was down wanting to shake hands with Mr. Smith. They told him that he had done more to boom[3] Mariposa than any ten men in town. Some of them said he ought to run for the town council, and others wanted to

---

1. Brought to moral ruin.
2. In Matthew 4.19, Christ tells Andrew and Peter, who are fishermen, that if they become his disciples he will make them "fishers of men."
3. Advertize.

make him the Conservative candidate for the next Dominion election. The caff was a mere babel of voices,[4] and even the Rats' Cooler was almost floated away from its moorings.

And in the middle of it all, Mr. Smith found time to say to Billy, the desk clerk: "Take the cash registers out of the caff and the Rats' Cooler and start counting up the books."

And Billy said: "Will I write the letters for the palms and the tables and the stuff to go back?"

And Mr. Smith said: "Get 'em written right away."

So all evening the laughter and the chatter and the congratulations went on, and it wasn't till long after midnight that Mr. Smith was able to join Billy in the private room behind the "rotunda." Even when he did, there was a quiet and a dignity about his manner that had never been there before. I think it must have been the new halo of the Conservative candidacy that already radiated from his brow. It was, I imagine, at this very moment that Mr. Smith first realised that the hotel business formed the natural and proper threshold of the national legislature.[5]

"Here's the account of the cash registers," said Billy.

"Let me see it," said Mr. Smith. And he studied the figures without a word.

"And here's the letters about the palms, and here's Alphonse up to yesterday—"

And then an amazing thing happened.

"Billy," said Mr. Smith, "tear 'em up. I ain't going to do it. It ain't right and I won't do it. They got me the license for to keep the caff and I'm going to keep the caff. I don't need to close her. The bar's good for anything from forty to a hundred a day now, with the Rats' Cooler going good, and that caff will stay right here."

And stay it did.

There it stands, mind you, to this day. You've only to step round the corner of Smith's Hotel on the side street and read the sign: LADIES' AND GENTS CAFÉ, just as large and as imposing as ever.

Mr. Smith said that he'd keep the caff, and when he said a thing he meant it!

Of course there were changes, small changes.

I don't say, mind you, that the fillet de beef that you get there now is perhaps quite up to the level of the filet de bœufs aux champignons of the days of glory.

No doubt the lamb chops in Smith's Caff are often very much the same, nowadays, as the lamb chops of the Mariposa House or the Continental.

4. Confusion of noise, especially voices; scene of confusion (on the basis of the story of the tower of Babel in Genesis 11.1–9).
5. House of Commons.

Of course, things like Omelette aux Trufles practically died out when Alphonse went. And, naturally, the leaving of Alphonse was inevitable. No one knew just when he went, or why. But one morning he was gone. Mr. Smith said that "Alf had to go back to his folks in the old country."

So, too, when Alf left, the use of the French language, as such, fell off tremendously in the caff. Even now they use it to some extent. You can still get fillet de beef, and saucisson au juice, but Billy the desk clerk has considerable trouble with the spelling.

The Rats' Cooler, of course, closed down, or rather Mr. Smith closed it for repairs, and there is every likelihood that it will hardly open for three years. But the caff is there. They don't use the grills, because there's no need to, with the hotel kitchen so handy.

The "girl room," I may say, was never opened. Mr. Smith promised it, it is true, for the winter, and still talks of it. But somehow there's been a sort of feeling against it. Every one in town admits that every big hotel in the city has a "girl room" and that it must be all right. Still, there's a certain—well, you know how sensitive opinion is in a place like Mariposa.

Chapter II

The Speculations of Jefferson Thorpe

It was not until the mining boom, at the time when everybody went simply crazy over the Cobalt and Porcupine mines of the new silver country near the Hudson Bay, that Jefferson Thorpe reached what you might call public importance in Mariposa.

Of course everybody knew Jeff and his little barber shop that stood just across the street from Smith's Hotel. Everybody knew him and everybody got shaved there. From early morning, when the commercial travellers off the 6.30 express got shaved into the resemblance of human beings, there were always people going in and out of the barber shop.

Mullins, the manager of the Exchange Bank, took his morning shave from Jeff as a form of resuscitation, with enough wet towels laid on his face to stew him and with Jeff moving about in the steam, razor in hand, as grave as an operating surgeon.

Then, as I think I said, Mr. Smith came in every morning and there was a tremendous outpouring of Florida water and rums,[1] essences and revivers and renovators, regardless of expense. What with Jeff's white coat and Mr. Smith's flowered waistcoat and the

---

1. Commercially prepared toilet waters or colognes consisting of bay leaves and bayberry in a water and alcohol base.

red geranium in the window and the Florida water and the double extract of hyacinth, the little shop seemed multi-coloured and luxurious enough for the annex of a Sultan's harem.

But what I mean is that, till the mining boom, Jefferson Thorpe never occupied a position of real prominence in Mariposa. You couldn't, for example, have compared him with a man like Golgotha Gingham, who, as undertaker, stood in a direct relation to life and death, or to Trelawney, the postmaster, who drew money from the Federal Government of Canada, and was regarded as virtually a member of the Dominion Cabinet.

Everybody knew Jeff and liked him, but the odd thing was that till he made money nobody took any stock in his ideas at all. It was only after he made the "clean up" that they came to see what a splendid fellow he was. "Level-headed" I think was the term; indeed in the speech of Mariposa, the highest form of endowment was to have the head set on horizontally as with a theodolite.[2]

As I say, it was when Jeff made money that they saw how gifted he was, and when he lost it,—but still, there's no need to go into that. I believe it's something the same in other places, too.

The barber shop, you will remember, stands across the street from Smith's Hotel, and stares at it face to face.

It is one of those wooden structures—I don't know whether you know them—with a false front that sticks up above its real height and gives it an air at once rectangular and imposing. It is a form of architecture much used in Mariposa and understood to be in keeping with the pretentious and artificial character of modern business. There is a red, white and blue post in front of the shop and the shop itself has a large square window out of proportion to its little flat face.

Painted on the panes of the window is the remains of a legend that once spelt BARBER SHOP, executed with flourishes that prevailed in the golden age of sign painting in Mariposa. Through the window you can see the geraniums in the window shelf and behind them Jeff Thorpe with his little black skull cap[3] on and his spectacles drooped upon his nose as he bends forward in the absorption of shaving.

As you open the door, it sets in violent agitation a coiled spring up above and a bell that almost rings. Inside, there are two shaving chairs of the heavier, or electrocution pattern, with mirrors in front of them and pigeon holes with individual shaving mugs. There must be ever so many of them, fifteen or sixteen. It is the current supposition of each of Jeff's customers that everyone else but him-

2. A surveying instrument for measuring horizontal and vertical angles.
3. Close-fitting cap worn on the back of the head: a beanie or possibly a yarmulke (and, if so, a sign that Jefferson Thorpe is Jewish).

self uses a separate mug. One corner of the shop is partitioned off
and bears the sign: HOT AND COLD BATHS, 50 cents. There has
been no bath inside the partition for twenty years—only old newspapers and a mop. Still, it lends distinction somehow, just as do the
faded cardboard signs that hang against the mirror with the legends: TURKISH SHAMPOO, 75 cents, and ROMAN MASSAGE,
$1.00.

They said commonly in Mariposa that Jeff made money out of
the barber shop. He may have, and it may have been that that
turned his mind to investment. But it's hard to see how he could. A
shave cost five cents, and a hair-cut fifteen (or the two, if you liked,
for a quarter), and at that it is hard to see how he could make
money, even when he had both chairs going and shaved first in one
and then in the other.

You see, in Mariposa, shaving isn't the hurried, perfunctory thing
that it is in the city. A shave is looked upon as a form of physical
pleasure and lasts anywhere from twenty-five minutes to three-
quarters of an hour.

In the morning hours, perhaps, there was a semblance of haste
about it, but in the long quiet of the afternoon, as Jeff leaned forward towards the customer and talked to him in a soft confidential
monotone, like a portrait painter, the razor would go slower and
slower, and pause and stop, move and pause again, till the shave
died away into the mere drowse of conversation.

At such hours, the Mariposa barber shop would become a very
Palace of Slumber, and as you waited your turn in one of the
wooden arm-chairs beside the wall, what with the quiet of the hour,
and the low drone of Jeff's conversation, the buzzing of the flies
against the window pane and the measured tick of the clock above
the mirror, your head sank dreaming on your breast, and the Mariposa Newspacket rustled unheeded on the floor. It makes one
drowsy just to think of it!

The conversation, of course, was the real charm of the place. You
see, Jefferson's forte, or specialty, was information. He could tell
you more things within the compass of a half-hour's shave than you
get in days of laborious research in an encyclopædia. Where he got
it all, I don't know, but I am inclined to think it came more or less
out of the newspapers.

In the city, people never read the newspapers, not really, only little bits and scraps of them. But in Mariposa it's different. There
they read the whole thing from cover to cover, and they build up on
it, in the course of years, a range of acquirement that would put a
college president to the blush. Anybody who has ever heard Henry
Mullins and Peter Glover talk about the future of China will know
just what I mean.

And, of course, the peculiarity of Jeff's conversation was that he could suit it to his man every time. He had a kind of divination about it. There was a certain kind of man that Jeff would size up sideways as he stropped the razor, and in whose ear he would whisper: "I see where Saint Louis has took four straight games off Chicago,"—and so hold him fascinated to the end.

In the same way he would say to Mr. Smith: "I see where it says that this 'Flying Squirl' run a dead heat for the King's Plate."[4]

To a humble intellect like mine he would explain in full the relations of the Keesar[5] to the German Rich Dog.[6]

But first and foremost, Jeff's specialty in the way of conversation was finance and the money market, the huge fortunes that a man with the right kind of head could make.

I've known Jefferson to pause in his shaving with the razor suspended in the air as long as five minutes while he described, with his eye half closed, exactly the kind of a head a man needed in order to make a "haul" or a "clean up." It was evidently simply a matter of the head, and as far as one could judge, Jeff's own was the very type required.

I don't know just at what time or how Jefferson first began his speculative enterprises. It was probably in him from the start. There is no doubt that the very idea of such things as Traction Stock and Amalgamated Asbestos went to his head: and whenever he spoke of Mr. Carnegie and Mr. Rockefeller,[7] the yearning tone of his voice made it as soft as lathered soap.

I suppose the most rudimentary form of his speculation was the hens. That was years ago. He kept them out at the back of his house,—which itself stood up a grass plot behind and beyond the barber shop,—and in the old days Jeff would say, with a certain note of pride in his voice, that The Woman had sold as many as two dozen eggs in a day to the summer visitors.

But what with reading about Amalgamated Asbestos and Consolidated Copper and all that, the hens began to seem pretty small business, and, in any case, the idea of two dozen eggs at a cent apiece almost makes one blush. I suppose a good many of us have felt just as Jeff did about our poor little earnings. Anyway, I remember Jeff telling me one day that he could take the whole lot of the hens and sell them off and crack the money into Chicago wheat on margin and turn it over in twenty-four hours. He did it too. Only

---

4. The most important Canadian horse race.
5. Kaiser: the title of German emperors from 1871 to 1918.
6. Reichstag: the German legislative assembly.
7. The founder of a dynasty of American capitalists and philanthropists, John Davison Rockefeller (1839–1937) was the president of the Standard Oil Company from 1870 to 1911. Andrew Carnegie (1831–1919) was an immigrant to the United States from Scotland who built up an immense fortune that he used for philanthropic purposes.

somehow when it was turned over it came upside down on top of the hens.

After that the hen house stood empty and The Woman had to throw away chicken feed every day, at a dead loss of perhaps a shave and a half. But it made no difference to Jeff, for his mind had floated away already on the possibilities of what he called "displacement" mining[8] on the Yukon.

So you can understand that when the mining boom struck Mariposa, Jefferson Thorpe was in it right from the very start. Why, no wonder; it seemed like the finger of Providence. Here was this great silver country spread out to north of us, where people had thought there was only a wilderness. And right at our very doors! You could see, as I saw, the night express going north every evening; for all one knew Rockefeller or Carnegie or anyone might be on it! Here was the wealth of Calcutta, as the Mariposa Newspacket put it, poured out at our very feet.

So no wonder the town went wild! All day in the street you could hear men talking of veins, and smelters and dips[9] and deposits and faults,—the town hummed with it like a geology class on examination day. And there were men about the hotels with mining outfits and theodolites and dunnage bags,[1] and at Smith's bar they would hand chunks of rock up and down, some of which would run as high as ten drinks to the pound.

The fever just caught the town and ran through it! Within a fortnight they put a partition down Robertson's Coal and Wood Office and opened the Mariposa Mining Exchange, and just about every man on the Main Street started buying scrip. Then presently[2] young Fizzlechip, who had been teller in Mullins's Bank and that everybody had thought a worthless jackass before, came back from the Cobalt country with a fortune, and loafed round in the Mariposa House in English khaki and a horizontal hat,[3] drunk all the time, and everybody holding him up as an example of what it was possible to do if you tried.

They all went in. Jim Eliot mortgaged the inside of the drug store and jammed it into Twin Tamagami. Pete Glover at the hardware store bought Nippewa stock at thirteen cents and sold it to his brother at seventeen and bought it back in less than a week at nineteen. They didn't care! They took a chance. Judge Pepperleigh put

8. Place mining: the separation of particles of gold and other minerals from deposits through the process of washing.
9. Receptacles or the liquids that they contain for cooling or coating metals.
1. Bags of camp equipment.
2. Soon.
3. Probably a pinch-crowned, straight-brimmed hat of the sort worn by miners of the time (and nowadays by the Royal Canadian Mounted Police and American state troopers) or, less likely, a flat-crowned, straight-brimmed hat made of straw and sporting a colourful ribbon hatband: a boater or skimmer.

the rest of his wife's money into Temiskaming Common, and
Lawyer Macartney got the fever, too, and put every cent that his
sister possessed into Tulip Preferred.

And even when young Fizzlechip shot himself in the back room
of the Mariposa House, Mr. Gingham buried him in a casket with
silver handles and it was felt that there was a Monte Carlo[4] touch
about the whole thing.

They all went in—or all except Mr. Smith. You see, Mr. Smith
had come down from there, and he knew all about rocks and mining and canoes and the north country. He knew what it was to eat
flour-baked dampers[5] under the lee side of a canoe propped among
the underbrush, and to drink the last drop of whiskey within fifty
miles. Mr. Smith had mighty little use for the north. But what he
did do, was to buy up enough early potatoes to send fifteen carload
lots into Cobalt at a profit of five dollars a bag.

Mr. Smith, I say, hung back. But Jeff Thorpe was in the mining
boom right from the start. He bought in on the Nippewa mine even
before the interim prospectus was out. He took a "block" of 100
shares of Abbitibbi Development at fourteen cents, and he and
Johnson, the livery stable-keeper next door, formed a syndicate and
got a thousand shares of Metagami Lake at $3\frac{1}{4}$ cents and then "un-
loaded" them on one of the sausage men at Netley's butcher shop
at a clear cent per cent advance.

Jeff would open the little drawer below the mirror in the barber
shop and show you all kinds and sorts of Cobalt country mining
certificates,—blue ones, pink ones, green ones, with outlandish and
fascinating names on them that ran clear from the Mattawa to the
Hudson Bay.

And right from the start he was confident of winning.

"There ain't no difficulty to it," he said, "there's lots of silver up
there in that country and if you buy some here and some there you
can't fail to come out somewhere. I don't say," he used to continue,
with the scissors open and ready to cut, "that some of the green-
horns[6] won't get bit. But if a feller knows the country and keeps his
head level, he can't lose."

Jefferson had looked at so many prospectuses and so many pictures of mines and pine trees and smelters, that I think he'd forgotten that he'd never been in the country. Anyway, what's two
hundred miles!

To an onlooker it certainly didn't seem so simple. I never knew
the meanness, the trickery, of the mining business, the sheer obsti-
nate determination of the bigger capitalists not to make money

4. Resort town in Monaco renowned for its gambling casinos.
5. Confections made of unfermented bread.
6. Inexperienced people.

when they might, till I heard the accounts of Jeff's different mines. Take the case of the Corona Jewel. There was a good mine, simply going to ruin for lack of common sense.

"She ain't been developed," Jeff would say. "There's silver enough in her so you could dig it out with a shovel. She's full of it. But they won't get at her and work her."

Then he'd take a look at the pink and blue certificates of the Corona Jewel and slam the drawer on them in disgust.

Worse than that was the Silent Pine,—a clear case of stupid incompetence! Utter lack of engineering skill was all that was keeping the Silent Pine from making a fortune for its holders.

"The only trouble with that mine," said Jeff, "is they won't go deep enough. They followed the vein down to where it kind o' thinned out and then they quit. If they'd just go right into her good, they'd get it again. She's down there all right."

But perhaps the meanest case of all was the Northern Star. That always seemed to me, every time I heard of it, a straight case for the criminal law. The thing was so evidently a conspiracy.

"I bought her," said Jeff, "at thirty-two, and she stayed right there tight, like she was stuck. Then a bunch of these fellers in the city started to drive her down and they got her pushed down to twenty-four, and I held on to her and they shoved her down to twenty-one. This morning they've got her down to sixteen, but I don't mean to let go. No, sir."

In another fortnight[7] they shoved her, the same unscrupulous crowd, down to nine cents, and Jefferson still held on.

"They're working her down," he admitted, "but I'm holding her."

No conflict between vice and virtue was ever grimmer.

"She's at six," said Jeff, "but I've got her. They can't squeeze me."

A few days after that, the same criminal gang had her down further than ever.

"They've got her down to three cents," said Jeff, "but I'm with her. Yes, sir, they think they can shove her clean off the market, but they can't do it. I've boughten in Johnson's shares, and the whole of Netley's, and I'll stay with her till she breaks."

So they shoved and pushed and clawed her down—that unseen nefarious crowd in the city—and Jeff held on to her and they writhed and twisted at his grip, and then—

And then—well, that's just the queer thing about the mining business. Why, sudden as a flash of lightning, it seemed, the news came over the wire to the Mariposa Newspacket, that they had struck a vein of silver in the Northern Star as thick as a sidewalk, and that the stock had jumped to seventeen dollars a share, and

7. Two weeks.

even at that you couldn't get it! And Jeff stood there flushed and half-staggered against the mirror of the little shop, with a bunch of mining scrip[8] in his hand that was worth forty thousand dollars!

Excitement! It was all over the town in a minute. They ran off a news extra at the Mariposa Newspacket, and in less than no time there wasn't standing room in the barber shop, and over in Smith's Hotel they had three extra bar-keepers working on the lager beer pumps.

They were selling mining shares on the Main Street in Mariposa that afternoon and people were just clutching for them. Then at night there was a big oyster supper in Smith's caff, with speeches, and the Mariposa band outside.

And the queer thing was that the very next afternoon was the funeral of young Fizzlechip, and Dean Drone had to change the whole text of his Sunday sermon at two days' notice for fear of offending public sentiment.

But I think what Jeff liked best of it all was the sort of public recognition that it meant. He'd stand there in the shop, hardly bothering to shave, and explain to the men in the arm-chairs how he held her, and they shoved her, and he clung to her, and what he'd said to himself—a perfect Iliad[9]—while he was clinging to her.

The whole thing was in the city papers a few days after with a photograph of Jeff, taken specially at Ed Moore's studio (upstairs over Netley's). It showed Jeff sitting among palm trees, as all mining men do, with one hand on his knee, and a dog, one of those regular mining dogs, at his feet, and a look of piercing intelligence in his face that would easily account for forty thousand dollars.

I say that the recognition meant a lot to Jeff for its own sake. But no doubt the fortune meant quite a bit to him too on account of Myra.

Did I mention Myra, Jeff's daughter? Perhaps not. That's the trouble with the people in Mariposa; they're all so separate and so different—not a bit like the people in the cities—that unless you hear about them separately and one by one you can't for a moment understand what they're like.

Myra had golden hair and a Greek face and would come bursting through the barber shop in a hat at least six inches wider than what they wear in Paris. As you saw her swinging up the street to the Telephone Exchange in a suit that was straight out of the Delineator[1] and brown American boots, there was style written all over her,—the kind of thing that Mariposa recognised and did homage

---

8. Stock or share certificates.
9. Tale of many trials and sorrows, after the ancient Greek epic of the same name.
1. A monthly magazine of fashion, culture, and fine arts for women, published in New York from 1873 to 1937.

to. And to see her in the Exchange,—she was one of the four girls
that I spoke of,—on her high stool with a steel cap on,—jabbing
the connecting plugs in and out as if electricity cost nothing—well,
all I mean is that you could understand why it was that the commercial travellers would stand round in the Exchange calling up all
sorts of impossible villages, and waiting about so pleasant and genial!—it made one realize how naturally good-tempered men are.
And then when Myra would go off duty and Miss Cleghorn, who
was sallow, would come on, the commercial men would be off
again like autumn leaves.

It just shows the difference between people. There was Myra
who treated lovers like dogs and would slap them across the face
with a banana skin to show her utter independence. And there was
Miss Cleghorn, who was sallow, and who bought a forty cent
Ancient History to improve herself: and yet if she'd hit any man
in Mariposa with a banana skin, he'd have had her arrested for
assault.

Mind you, I don't mean that Myra was merely flippant and
worthless. Not at all. She was a girl with any amount of talent. You
should have heard her recite "The Raven,"[2] at the Methodist Social! Simply genius! And when she acted Portia in the Trial Scene of
the Merchant of Venice[3] at the High School concert, everybody in
Mariposa admitted that you couldn't have told it from the original.

So, of course, as soon as Jeff made the fortune, Myra had her
resignation in next morning and everybody knew that she was to go
to a dramatic school for three months in the fall and become a
leading actress.

But, as I said, the public recognition counted a lot for Jeff. The
moment you begin to get that sort of thing it comes in quickly
enough. Brains, you know, are recognized right away. That was why,
of course, within a week from this Jeff received the first big packet
of stuff from the Cuban Land Development Company, with
coloured pictures of Cuba, and fields of bananas, and haciendas
and insurrectos[4] with machetes and Heaven knows what. They
heard of him, somehow,—it wasn't for a modest man like Jefferson
to say how. After all, the capitalists of the world are just one and
the same crowd. If you're in it, you're in it, that's all! Jeff realized
why it is that of course men like Carnegie or Rockefeller and Morgan[5] all know one another. They have to.

For all I know, this Cuban stuff may have been sent from Morgan

2. Poem by the American writer Edgar Allan Poe (1809–1845), first published in 1845.
3. Act IV, scene i of William Shakespeare's play.
4. Country houses and insurrectionists.
5. John Pierpont Morgan (1837–1913), American banker, financier, art collector, and phi-
lanthropist.

himself. Some of the people in Mariposa said yes, others said no. There was no certainty.

Anyway, they were fair and straight, this Cuban crowd that wrote to Jeff. They offered him to come right in and be one of themselves. If a man's got the brains, you may as well recognize it straight away. Just as well write him to be a director now as wait and hesitate till he forces his way into it.

Anyhow, they didn't hesitate, these Cuban people that wrote to Jeff from Cuba—or from a post-office box in New York—it's all the same thing, because Cuba being so near to New York the mail is all distributed from there. I suppose in some financial circles they might have been slower, wanted guarantees of some sort, and so on, but these Cubans, you know, have got a sort of Spanish warmth of heart that you don't see in business men in America, and that touches you. No, they asked no guarantee. Just send the money—whether by express order or by bank draft or cheque, they left that entirely to oneself, as a matter between Cuban gentlemen.

And they were quite frank about their enterprise—bananas and tobacco in the plantation district reclaimed from the insurrectos. You could see it all there in the pictures—the tobacco plants and the insurrectos—everything. They made no rash promises, just admitted straight out that the enterprise might realise 400 per cent. or might conceivably make less. There was no hint of more.

So within a month, everybody in Mariposa knew that Jeff Thorpe was "in Cuban lands" and would probably clean up half a million by New Year's. You couldn't have failed to know it. All round the little shop there were pictures of banana groves and the harbour of Habana,[6] and Cubans in white suits and scarlet sashes, smoking cigarettes in the sun and too ignorant to know that you can make four hundred per cent. by planting a banana tree.

I liked it about Jeff that he didn't stop shaving. He went on just the same. Even when Johnson, the livery stable man, came in with five hundred dollars and asked him to see if the Cuban Board of Directors would let him put it in, Jeff laid it in the drawer and then shaved him for five cents, in the same old way. Of course, he must have felt proud when, a few days later, he got a letter from the Cuban people, from New York, accepting the money straight off without a single question, and without knowing anything more of Johnson except that he was a friend of Jeff's. They wrote most handsomely. Any friends of Jeff's were friends of Cuba. All money they might send would be treated just as Jeff's would be treated.

One reason, perhaps, why Jeff didn't give up shaving was because it allowed him to talk about Cuba. You see, everybody knew in

6. Havana.

Mariposa that Jeff Thorpe had sold out of Cobalts and had gone into Cuban Renovated Lands—and that spread round him a kind of halo of wealth and mystery and outlandishness—oh, something Spanish. Perhaps you've felt it about people that you know. Anyhow, they asked him about the climate, and yellow fever and what the negroes were like and all that sort of thing.

"This Cubey, it appears, is an island," Jeff would explain. Of course, everybody knows how easily islands lend themselves to making money,—"and for fruit, they say it comes up so fast you can't stop it." And then he would pass into details about the Hash-enders and the resurrectos and technical things like that till it was thought a wonder how he could know it. Still, it was realized that a man with money has got to know these things. Look at Morgan and Rockefeller and all the men that make a pile. They know just as much as Jeff did about the countries where they make it. It stands to reason.

Did I say that Jeff shaved in the same old way? Not quite. There was something even dreamier about it now, and a sort of new element in the way Jeff fell out of his monotone into lapses of thought that I, for one, misunderstood. I thought that perhaps getting so much money,—well, you know the way it acts on people in the larger cities. It seemed to spoil one's idea of Jeff that copper and asbestos and banana lands should form the goal of his thought when, if he knew it, the little shop and the sunlight of Mariposa was so much better.

In fact, I had perhaps borne him a grudge for what seemed to me his perpetual interest in the great capitalists. He always had some item out of the paper about them.

"I see where this here Carnegie has give fifty thousand dollars for one of them observatories," he would say.

And another day he would pause in the course of shaving, and almost whisper: "Did you ever *see* this Rockefeller?"

It was only by a sort of accident that I came to know that there was another side to Jefferson's speculation that no one in Mariposa ever knew, or will ever know now.

I knew it because I went in to see Jeff in his house one night. The house,—I think I said it,—stood out behind the barber shop. You went out of the back door of the shop, and through a grass plot with petunias beside it, and the house stood at the end. You could see the light of the lamp behind the blind, and through the screen door as you came along. And it was here that Jefferson used to sit in the evenings when the shop got empty.

There was a round table that The Woman used to lay for supper, and after supper there used to be a chequered cloth on it and a lamp with a shade. And beside it Jeff would sit, with his spectacles on and the paper spread out, reading about Carnegie and Rockefeller. Near him, but away from the table, was The Woman doing needlework, and Myra, when she wasn't working in the Telephone Exchange, was there too with her elbows on the table reading Marie Corelli[7]—only now, of course, after the fortune, she was reading the prospectuses of Dramatic Schools.

So this night,—I don't know just what it was in the paper that caused it,—Jeff laid down what he was reading and started to talk about Carnegie.

"This Carnegie, I bet you, would be worth," said Jeff, closing up his eyes in calculation, "as much as perhaps two million dollars, if you was to sell him up. And this Rockefeller and this Morgan, either of them, to sell them up clean, would be worth another couple of million—"

I may say in parentheses that it was a favourite method in Mariposa if you wanted to get at the real worth of a man, to imagine him clean sold up, put up for auction, as it were. It was the only way to test him.

"And now look at 'em," Jeff went on. "They make their money and what do they do with it? They give it away. And who do they give it to? Why, to those as don't want it, every time. They give it to these professors and to this research and that, and do the poor get any of it? Not a cent and never will.

"I tell you, boys," continued Jeff (there were no boys present, but in Mariposa all really important speeches are addressed to an imaginary audience of boys)—"I tell you, if I was to make a million out of this Cubey, I'd give it straight to the poor, yes, sir—divide it up into a hundred lots of a thousand dollars each and give it to the people that hadn't nothing."

So always after that I knew just what those bananas were being grown for.

Indeed, after that, though Jefferson never spoke of his intentions directly, he said a number of things that seemed to bear on them. He asked me, for instance, one day, how many blind people it would take to fill one of these blind homes and how a feller could get ahold of them. And at another time he asked whether if a feller advertised for some of these incurables a feller could get enough of them to make a showing. I know for a fact that he got Nivens, the lawyer, to draw up a document that was to give an acre of banana land in Cuba to every idiot[8] in Missinaba County.

But still,—what's the use of talking of what Jeff meant to do? Nobody knows or cares about it now.

---

7. Pseudonym of Mary Mackay (1855–1924), whose frequently melodramatic and far-fetched novels were extremely popular in the decades preceding World War I.
8. Person congenitally afflicted with the severest grade of feeble-mindedness or merely a foolish or unwise person.

The end of it was bound to come. Even in Mariposa some of the people must have thought so. Else how was it that Henry Mullins made such a fuss about selling a draft[9] for forty thousand on New York? And why was it that Mr. Smith wouldn't pay Billy, the desk clerk, his back wages when he wanted to put it into Cuba?

Oh yes; some of them must have seen it. And yet when it came it seemed so quiet,—ever so quiet,—not a bit like the Northern Star mine and the oyster supper and the Mariposa band. It is strange how quiet these things look, the other way round.

You remember the Cuban Land frauds in New York—and Porforio Gomez shooting the detective, and him and Maximo Morez getting clear away with two hundred thousand? No, of course you don't; why, even in the city papers it only filled an inch or two of type, and anyway the names were hard to remember. That was Jeff's money—part of it. Mullins got the telegram, from a broker or someone, and he showed it to Jeff just as he was going up the street with an estate agent to look at a big empty lot on the hill behind the town—the very place for these incurables.

And Jeff went back to the shop so quiet—have you ever seen an animal that is stricken through, how quiet it seems to move?

Well, that's how he walked.

And since that, though it's quite a little while ago, the shop's open till eleven every night now, and Jeff is shaving away to pay back that five hundred that Johnson, the livery man, sent to the Cubans, and—

Pathetic? tut! tut! You don't know Mariposa. Jeff has to work pretty late, but that's nothing—nothing at all, if you've worked hard all your lifetime. And Myra is back at the Telephone Exchange—they were glad enough to get her, and she says now that if there's one thing she hates, it's the stage, and she can't see how the actresses put up with it.

Anyway, things are not so bad. You see it was just at this time that Mr. Smith's caff opened, and Mr. Smith came to Jeff's Woman and said he wanted seven dozen eggs a day, and wanted them handy, and so the hens are back, and more of them, and they exult so every morning over the eggs they lay that if you wanted to talk of Rockefeller in the barber shop you couldn't hear his name for the cackling.

---

9. Order for money drawn by one bank and payable at another to the person designated on it.

Chapter III

The Marine Excursion of the Knights of Pythias

Half-past six on a July morning![1] The Mariposa Belle is at the wharf, decked in flags, with steam up ready to start.

Excursion day!

Half-past six on a July morning, and Lake Wissanotti lying in the sun as calm as glass. The opal colours of the morning light are shot from the surface of the water.

Out on the lake the last thin threads of the mist are clearing away like flecks of cotton wool.

The long call of the loon echoes over the lake. The air is cool and fresh. There is in it all the new life of the land of the silent pine and the moving waters. Lake Wissanotti in the morning sunlight! Don't talk to me of the Italian lakes, or the Tyrol or the Swiss Alps. Take them away. Move them somewhere else. I don't want them.

Excursion Day, at half-past six of a summer morning! With the boat all decked in flags and all the people in Mariposa on the wharf, and the band in peaked caps with big cornets tied to their bodies ready to play at any minute! I say! Don't tell me about the Carnival of Venice and the Delhi Durbar.[2] Don't! I wouldn't look at them. I'd shut my eyes! For light and colour give me every time an excursion out of Mariposa down the lake to the Indian's Island out of sight in the morning mist. Talk of your Papal Zouaves and your Buckingham Palace Guard![3] I want to see the Mariposa band in uniform and the Mariposa Knights of Pythias with their aprons and their insignia and their picnic baskets and their five-cent cigars!

Half-past six in the morning, and all the crowd on the wharf and the boat due to leave in half an hour. Notice it!—in half an hour. Already she's whistled twice (at six, and at six fifteen), and at any minute now, Christie Johnson will step into the pilot house and pull the string for the warning whistle that the boat will leave in half an hour. So keep ready. Don't think of running back to Smith's Hotel for the sandwiches. Don't be fool enough to try to go up to the Greek Store, next to Netley's, and buy fruit. You'll be left behind for sure if you do. Never mind the sandwiches and the fruit! Anyway, here comes Mr. Smith himself with a huge basket of

1. Possibly July 1, Dominion (now Canada) Day.
2. Celebration in Venice before the beginning of the fast of Lent and the reception at Delhi in 1911 to mark the proclamation of the city as capital of India.
3. Until relatively recently, the guard at Buckingham Palace in London was drawn from the British sovereign's household troops. "Papal Zouaves": a corps of soldiers for the protection of the Pope that was founded in 1860 and disbanded in 1871. Its members were predominantly French and wore uniforms based on those of Algerian recruits to the French army, including colourful jackets and voluminous pants.

provender that would feed a factory. There must be sandwiches in
that. I think I can hear them clinking. And behind Mr. Smith is the
German waiter from the caff with another basket—indubitably
lager beer; and behind him, the bar-tender of the hotel, carrying
nothing, as far as one can see. But of course if you know Mariposa
you will understand that why he looks so nonchalant and empty-
handed is because he has two bottles of rye whiskey under his linen
duster. You know, I think, the peculiar walk of a man with two bottles of whiskey in the inside pockets of a linen coat. In Mariposa,
you see, to bring beer to an excursion is quite in keeping with public opinion. But, whiskey,—well, one has to be a little careful.

Do I say that Mr. Smith is here? Why, everybody's here. There's
Hussell the editor of the Newspacket, wearing a blue ribbon on his
coat, for the Mariposa Knights of Pythias are, by their constitution,
dedicated to temperance; and there's Henry Mullins, the manager
of the Exchange Bank, also a Knight of Pythias, with a small flask
of Pogram's Special[4] in his hip pocket as a sort of amendment to
the constitution. And there's Dean Drone, the Chaplain of the Order, with a fishing-rod (you never saw such green bass as lie among
the rocks at Indian's Island), and with a trolling line in case of
maskinonge, and a landing net in case of pickerel, and with his eldest daughter, Lilian Drone, in case of young men. There never was
such a fisherman as the Rev. Rupert Drone.

• • • • •

Perhaps I ought to explain that when I speak of the excursion as
being of the Knights of Pythias, the thing must not be understood
in any narrow sense. In Mariposa practically everybody belongs to
the Knights of Pythias just as they do to everything else. That's the
great thing about the town and that's what makes it so different
from the city. Everybody is in everything.

You should see them on the seventeenth of March,[5] for example,
when everybody wears a green ribbon and they're all laughing and
glad,—you know what the Celtic nature is,—and talking about
Home Rule.[6]

On St. Andrew's Day[7] every man in town wears a thistle and
shakes hands with everybody else, and you see the fine old Scotch
honesty beaming out of their eyes.

---

4. The eponymous hero of Charles Dickens's *Martin Chuzzlewhit* (1843–44), a novel that
   satirizes many aspects of American life, encounters the Honourable Elijah Pogram,
   member of the U.S. Congress and orator extraordinaire, on a steamboat journey through
   the Mississippi Valley.
5. St. Patrick's Day.
6. Self-government for Ireland, which had been a part of Great Britain since in 1801.
   Home Rule was a major issue in British politics from the middle of the nineteenth century onwards.
7. November 30.

And on St. George's Day![8]—well, there's no heartiness like the good old English spirit, after all; why shouldn't a man feel glad that he's an Englishman?

Then on the Fourth of July[9] there are stars and stripes flying over half the stores in town, and suddenly all the men are seen to smoke cigars, and to know all about Roosevelt and Bryan and the Philippine Islands.[1] Then you learn for the first time that Jeff Thorpe's people came from Massachusetts and that his uncle fought at Bunker Hill[2] (it must have been Bunker Hill,—anyway Jefferson will swear it was in Dakota all right enough); and you find that George Duff has a married sister in Rochester and that her husband is all right; in fact, George was down there as recently as eight years ago. Oh, it's the most American town imaginable is Mariposa,—on the fourth of July.

But wait, just wait, if you feel anxious about the solidity of the British connection, till the twelfth of the month,[3] when everybody is wearing an orange streamer in his coat and the Orangemen (every man in town) walk in the big procession. Allegiance! Well, perhaps you remember the address they gave to the Prince of Wales on the platform of the Mariposa station as he went through on his tour to the west.[4] I think that pretty well settled that question.

So you will easily understand that of course everybody belongs to the Knights of Pythias and the Masons[5] and Oddfellows, just as they all belong to the Snow Shoe Club and the Girls' Friendly Society.

And meanwhile the whistle of the steamer has blown again for a quarter to seven:—loud and long this time, for any one not here

8. April 23.
9. Independence Day in the United States.
1. Philippine independence was a burning issue in American politics between the transferral of the islands from Spain to the United States at the end of the Spanish-American War (1898) and the achievement of independence in 1945. Theodore Roosevelt (1858–1919) became president of the United States on the assassination of President McKinley in 1901 and was elected for a second term in 1904. William Jennings Bryan (1860–1925) was a member of the American Congress from 1891 to 1895 and a thrice unsuccessful Democratic nominee for president (1896, 1900, 1908).
2. Hill in Charlestown, Massachusetts, near which the first organized battle of the American War of Independence took place on June 17, 1775.
3. July 12: the day of the parade of the Orange Society, a Protestant and fervently anti-Catholic organization dedicated to the maintenance of the British-Irish Connection and named for William of Orange (William III of England, Scotland, and Ireland), whose victory at the Battle of the Boyne on July 12, 1690, secured England's position in Ireland.
4. George V (1865–1936), who became king in 1910, visited Canada in 1901 as the Duke of Cornwall and York. Between August and November of that year, he and the Duchess of Cornwall and York (later Queen Mary) crossed Canada from east to west, primarily by rail, visiting Orillia on October 10. Leacock was a member of the welcoming party and would later recall the event in My Discovery of England (1922). The duke was crowned Prince of Wales after his return to England in November 1901.
5. The Society of Freemasons, a secret society dating from the Middle Ages with numerous lodges in Europe, North America, and elsewhere.

now is late for certain, unless he should happen to come down in the last fifteen minutes.

What a crowd upon the wharf and how they pile on to the steamer! It's a wonder that the boat can hold them all. But that's just the marvellous thing about the Mariposa Belle.

I don't know,—I have never known,—where the steamers like the Mariposa Belle come from. Whether they are built by Harland and Wolff of Belfast,[6] or whether, on the other hand, they are not built by Harland and Wolff of Belfast, is more than one would like to say offhand.

The Mariposa Belle always seems to me to have some of those strange properties that distinguish Mariposa itself. I mean, her size seems to vary so. If you see her there in the winter, frozen in the ice beside the wharf with a snowdrift against the windows of the pilot house, she looks a pathetic little thing the size of a butternut. But in the summer time, especially after you've been in Mariposa for a month or two, and have paddled alongside of her in a canoe, she gets larger and taller, and with a great sweep of black sides, till you see no difference between the Mariposa Belle and the Lusitania. Each one is a big steamer and that's all you can say.

Nor do her measurements help you much. She draws about eighteen inches forward, and more than that,—at least half an inch more, astern, and when she's loaded down with an excursion crowd she draws a good two inches more. And above the water,—why, look at all the decks on her! There's the deck you walk on to, from the wharf, all shut in, with windows along it, and the after cabin with the long table, and above that the deck with all the chairs piled upon it, and the deck in front where the band stand round in a circle, and the pilot house is higher than that, and above the pilot house is the board with the gold name and the flag pole and the steel ropes and the flags; and fixed in somewhere on the different levels is the lunch counter where they sell the sandwiches, and the engine room, and down below the deck level, beneath the water line, is the place where the crew sleep. What with steps and stairs and passages and piles of cordwood for the engine,—oh no, I guess Harland and Wolff didn't build her. They couldn't have.

Yet even with a huge boat like the Mariposa Belle, it would be impossible for her to carry all of the crowd that you see in the boat

---

6. Shipbuilding company whose yards in Northern Ireland and Scotland built three sister ships that were collectively designated "Olympic Class": *Lusitania*, launched in 1906; *Olympic*, launched in 1910; and *Titanic*, launched in 1912. Each was the largest passenger vessel in existence at the time of its launching and all were victims of disaster: on September 20, 1911, *Olympic* sustained extensive damage in a collision with the British cruiser H.M.S. Hawke; on the night of April 14–15, 1912, *Titanic* struck an iceberg and sank; and on May 7, 1915, *Lusitania* was sunk by a German U-Boat. "The Marine Excursion of the Knights of Pythias" was first published in the *Montreal Star* on March 16, 1912.

and on the wharf. In reality, the crowd is made up of two classes,—all of the people in Mariposa who are going on the excursion and all those who are not. Some come for the one reason and some for the other.

The two tellers of the Exchange Bank are both there standing side by side. But one of them,—the one with the cameo pin and the long face like a horse,—is going, and the other,—with the other cameo pin and the face like another horse,—is not. In the same way, Hussell of the Newspacket is going, but his brother, beside him, isn't. Lilian Drone is going, but her sister can't; and so on all through the crowd.

· · · · ·

And to think that things should look like that on the morning of a steamboat accident.

How strange life is!

To think of all these people so eager and anxious to catch the steamer, and some of them running to catch it, and so fearful that they might miss it,—the morning of a steamboat accident. And the captain blowing his whistle, and warning them so severely that he would leave them behind,—leave them out of the accident! And everybody crowding so eagerly to be in the accident.

Perhaps life is like that all through.

Strangest of all to think, in a case like this, of the people who were left behind, or in some way or other prevented from going, and always afterwards told of how they had escaped being on board the Mariposa Belle that day!

Some of the instances were certainly extraordinary.

Nivens, the lawyer, escaped from being there merely by the fact that he was away in the city.

Towers, the tailor, only escaped owing to the fact that, not intending to go on the excursion he had stayed in bed till eight o'clock and so had not gone. He narrated afterwards that waking up that morning at half-past five, he had thought of the excursion and for some unaccountable reason had felt glad that he was not going.

· · · · ·

The case of Yodel, the auctioneer, was even more inscrutable. He had been to the Oddfellows' excursion on the train the week before and to the Conservative picnic the week before that, and had decided not to go on this trip. In fact, he had not the least intention of going. He narrated afterwards how the night before someone had stopped him on the corner of Nippewa and Tecumseh Streets[7] (he indicated the very spot) and asked: "Are you going to take in the excursion to-morrow?" and he had said, just as simply as he was

---

7. Streets named for a town in Manitoba (Neepawa) and for the Shawnee war chief Tecumseh (see p. 10, n. 6).

talking when narrating it: "No." And ten minutes after that, at the corner of Dalhousie and Brock Streets[8] (he offered to lead a party of verification to the precise place) somebody else had stopped him and asked: "Well, are you going on the steamer trip to-morrow?" Again he had answered: "No," apparently almost in the same tone as before.

He said afterwards that when he heard the rumour of the accident it seemed like the finger of Providence, and he fell on his knees in thankfulness.

There was the similar case of Morison (I mean the one in Glover's hardware store that married one of the Thompsons). He said afterwards that he had read so much in the papers about accidents lately,—mining accidents, and aeroplanes and gasoline,—that he had grown nervous. The night before his wife had asked him at supper: "Are you going on the excursion?" He had answered: "No, I don't think I feel like it," and had added: "Perhaps your mother might like to go." And the next evening just at dusk, when the news ran through the town, he said the first thought that flashed through his head was: "Mrs. Thompson's on that boat."

He told this right as I say it—without the least doubt or confusion. He never for a moment imagined she was on the Lusitania or the Olympic[9] or any other boat. He knew she was on this one. He said you could have knocked him down where he stood. But no one had. Not even when he got half-way down,—on his knees, and it would have been easier still to knock him down or kick him. People do miss a lot of chances.

Still, as I say, neither Yodel nor Morison nor anyone thought about there being an accident until just after sundown when they—

Well, have you ever heard the long booming whistle of a steamboat two miles out on the lake in the dusk, and while you listen and count and wonder, seen the crimson rockets going up against the sky and then heard the fire bell ringing right there beside you in the town, and seen the people running to the town wharf?

That's what the people of Mariposa saw and felt that summer evening as they watched the Mackinaw life-boat[1] go plunging out into the lake with seven sweeps[2] to a side and the foam clear to the gunwale with the lifting stroke of fourteen men!

8. Streets named for George Ramsay, the ninth earl of Dalhousie (1770–1838), the lieutenant governor of Nova Scotia from 1816 to 1819 and governor-in-chief of Canada from 1819 to 1828, and Major-General Sir Isaac Brock (1769–1812), the colonial administrator and military leader who was regarded as the saviour of Upper Canada (Ontario) after he was killed leading British forces to victory over an American invading force at the Battle of Queenston Heights (October 13, 1812) during the War of 1812.
9. See p. 42, n. 6
1. Heavy, flat-bottomed row-boat of the sort used by the Hudson's Bay Company to carry freight.
2. Long oars.

But, dear me, I am afraid that this is no way to tell a story. I suppose the true art would have been to have said nothing about the accident till it happened. But when you write about Mariposa, or hear of it, if you know the place, it's all so vivid and real that a thing like the contrast between the excursion crowd in the morning and the scene at night leaps into your mind and you must think of it.

• • • • •

But never mind about the accident,—let us turn back again to the morning.

The boat was due to leave at seven. There was no doubt about the hour,—not only seven, but seven sharp. The notice in the Newspacket said: "The boat will leave sharp at seven"; and the advertising posters on the telegraph poles on Missinaba Street that began "Ho, for Indian's Island!" ended up with the words: "Boat leaves at seven sharp." There was a big notice on the wharf that said: "Boat leaves sharp on time."

So at seven, right on the hour, the whistle blew loud and long, and then at seven fifteen three short peremptory blasts, and at seven thirty one quick angry call,—just one,—and very soon after that they cast off the last of the ropes and the Mariposa Belle sailed off in her cloud of flags, and the band of the Knights of Pythias, timing it to a nicety, broke into the "Maple Leaf for Ever!"[3]

I suppose that all excursions when they start are much the same. Anyway, on the Mariposa Belle everybody went running up and down all over the boat with deck chairs and camp stools and baskets, and found places, splendid places to sit, and then got scared that there might be better ones and chased off again. People hunted for places out of the sun and when they got them swore that they weren't going to freeze to please anybody; and the people in the sun said that they hadn't paid fifty cents to be roasted. Others said that they hadn't paid fifty cents to get covered with cinders, and there were still others who hadn't paid fifty cents to get shaken to death with the propeller.

Still, it was all right presently. The people seemed to get sorted out into the places on the boat where they belonged. The women, the older ones, all gravitated into the cabin on the lower deck and by getting round the table with needlework, and with all the windows shut, they soon had it, as they said themselves, just like being at home.

All the young boys and the toughs and the men in the band got down on the lower deck forward, where the boat was dirtiest and where the anchor was and the coils of rope.

And upstairs on the after deck there were Lilian Drone and Miss

3. Patriotic song composed in 1867 by Alexander Muir that celebrates Canada as a creation of British imperialism and immigration.

Lawson, the high school teacher, with a book of German poetry,—Gothey[4] I think it was,—and the bank teller and the younger men.

In the centre, standing beside the rail, were Dean Drone and Dr. Gallagher, looking through binocular glasses at the shore.

Up in front on the little deck forward of the pilot house was a group of the older men, Mullins and Duff and Mr. Smith in a deck chair, and beside him Mr. Golgotha Gingham, the undertaker of Mariposa, on a stool. It was part of Mr. Gingham's principles to take in an outing of this sort, a business matter, more or less,—for you never know what may happen at these water parties. At any rate, he was there in a neat suit of black, not, of course, his heavier or professional suit, but a soft clinging effect[5] as of burnt paper that combined gaiety and decorum to a nicety.

• • • • •

"Yes," said Mr. Gingham, waving his black glove in a general way towards the shore, "I know the lake well, very well. I've been pretty much all over it in my time."

"Canoeing?" asked somebody.

"No," said Mr. Gingham, "not in a canoe." There seemed a peculiar and quiet meaning in his tone.

"Sailing, I suppose," said somebody else.

"No," said Mr. Gingham. "I don't understand it."

"I never knowed that you went on to the water at all, Gol," said Mr. Smith, breaking in.

"Ah, not now," explained Mr. Gingham; "it was years ago, the first summer I came to Mariposa. I was on the water practically all day. Nothing like it to give a man an appetite and keep him in shape."

"Was you camping?" asked Mr. Smith.

"We camped at night," assented the undertaker, "but we put in practically the whole day on the water. You see we were after a party that had come up here from the city on his vacation and gone out in a sailing canoe. We were dragging. We were up every morning at sunrise, lit a fire on the beach and cooked breakfast, and then we'd light our pipes and be off with the net for a whole day. It's a great life," concluded Mr. Gingham wistfully.

"Did you get him?" asked two or three together.

There was a pause before Mr. Gingham answered.

"We did," he said,—"down in the reeds past Horseshoe Point. But it was no use. He turned blue on me right away."

After which Mr. Gingham fell into such a deep reverie that the

---

4. Johann Wolfgang von Goethe (1749–1842), the German man of letters whose works include *Hermann and Dorothea* (1797) and *Faust* (1808, 1832).
5. Pleasing or remarkable combination of colour or form, as in a picture.

boat had steamed another half-mile down the lake before anybody broke the silence again.

Talk of this sort,—and after all what more suitable for a day on the water?—beguiled the way.

• • • • •

Down the lake, mile by mile over the calm water, steamed the Mariposa Belle. They passed Poplar Point where the high sand-banks are with all the swallows' nests in them, and Dean Drone and Dr. Gallagher looked at them alternately through the binocular glasses, and it was wonderful how plainly one could see the swallows and the banks and the shrubs,—just as plainly as with the naked eye.

And a little further down they passed the Shingle Beach, and Dr. Gallagher, who knew Canadian history, said to Dean Drone that it was strange to think that Champlain[6] had landed there with his French explorers three hundred years ago; and Dean Drone, who didn't know Canadian history, said it was stranger still to think that the hand of the Almighty had piled up the hills and rocks long before that; and Dr. Gallagher said it was wonderful how the French had found their way through such a pathless wilderness; and Dean Drone said that it was wonderful also to think that the Almighty had placed even the smallest shrub in its appointed place. Dr. Gallagher said it filled him with admiration. Dean Drone said it filled him with awe. Dr. Gallagher said he'd been full of it ever since he was a boy; and Dean Drone said so had he.

Then a little further, as the Mariposa Belle steamed on down the lake, they passed the Old Indian Portage where the great grey rocks are; and Dr. Gallagher drew Dean Drone's attention to the place where the narrow canoe track wound up from the shore to the woods, and Dean Drone said he could see it perfectly well without the glasses.

Dr. Gallagher said that it was just here that a party of five hundred French had made their way with all their baggage and accoutrements across the rocks of the divide and down to the Great Bay. And Dean Drone said that it reminded him of Xenophon leading his ten thousand Greeks over the hill passes of Armenia down to the sea.[7] Dr. Gallagher said that he had often wished he could have seen and spoken to Champlain, and Dean Drone said how much he regretted to have never known Xenophon.

6. Samuel de Champlain (1567–1635), French explorer who in 1615 travelled by canoe with two other French explorers and ten Native Americans to Lake Simcoe (Lake Wissanotti) from Georgian Bay (the "Great Bay").

7. The ancient Greek historian Xenophon (c. 430–c. 355 B.C.E.) was one of the leaders of the retreat of the Greek force (the Ten Thousand) after the Battle of Cunaxa (401 B.C.E.), east of the Euphrates River in Babylonia, to the port of Cotyora on the Black Sea. Xenophon's account of the retreat in his *Anabasis* is one of the most celebrated sections of his most important work.

And then after that they fell to talking of relics and traces of the past, and Dr. Gallagher said that if Dean Drone would come round to his house some night he would show him some Indian arrow heads that he had dug up in his garden. And Dean Drone said that if Dr. Gallagher would come round to the rectory any afternoon he would show him a map of Xerxes' invasion of Greece.[8] Only he must come some time between the Infant Class and the Mothers' Auxiliary.

So presently they both knew that they were blocked out of one another's houses for some time to come, and Dr. Gallagher walked forward and told Mr. Smith, who had never studied Greek, about Champlain crossing the rock divide.

Mr. Smith turned his head and looked at the divide for half a second and then said he had crossed a worse one up north back of the Wahnipitae and that the flies were Hades,[9]—and then went on playing freezeout poker[1] with the two juniors in Duff's bank.

So Dr. Gallagher realized that that's always the way when you try to tell people things, and that as far as gratitude and appreciation goes one might as well never read books or travel anywhere or do anything.

In fact, it was at this very moment that he made up his mind to give the arrows to the Mariposa Mechanics' Institute,[2]—they afterwards became, as you know, the Gallagher Collection. But, for the time being, the doctor was sick of them and wandered off round the boat and watched Henry Mullins showing George Duff how to make a John Collins[3] without lemons, and finally went and sat down among the Mariposa band and wished that he hadn't come.

So the boat steamed on and the sun rose higher and higher, and the freshness of the morning changed into the full glare of noon, and they went on to where the lake began to narrow in at its foot, just where the Indian's Island is,—all grass and trees and with a log wharf running into the water. Below it the Lower Ossawippi runs out of the lake, and quite near are the rapids, and you can see down among the trees the red brick of the power house and hear the roar of the leaping water.

The Indian's Island itself is all covered with trees and tangled

8. Xerxes I (d. 465 B.C.E.), king of ancient Persia (486–465 B.C.E.) and the Ahasuerus of the Bible, invaded Greece in 480 B.C.E. and, despite the heroic defense of Leonides and his Spartans at Thermopylae, occupied Athens. A year later his occupying army was defeated by the Greeks at Plataea, near Thebes (Thivai).
9. In ancient Greek mythology, the abode of the dead ruled over by the god of the underworld; hell.
1. Extremely competitive poker.
2. Institution for the education of skilled workers, usually consisting of a library, a room for classes and lectures, and other amenities. The first Mechanics' Institute was established in London in 1824 and thereafter the concept spread throughout Britain and to North America.
3. Cocktail consisting of either gin or whiskey, soda, and lemon juice and slice.

vines, and the water about it is so still that it's all reflected double and looks the same either way up. Then when the steamer's whistle blows as it comes into the wharf, you hear it echo among the trees of the island, and reverberate back from the shores of the lake.

The scene is all so quiet and still and unbroken, that Miss Cleghorn,—the sallow girl in the telephone exchange, that I spoke of—said she'd like to be buried there. But all the people were so busy getting their baskets and gathering up their things that no one had time to attend to it.

I mustn't even try to describe the landing and the boat crunching against the wooden wharf and all the people running to the same side of the deck and Christie Johnson calling out to the crowd to keep to the starboard and nobody being able to find it. Everyone who has been on a Mariposa excursion knows all about that.

Nor can I describe the day itself and the picnic under the trees. There were speeches afterwards, and Judge Pepperleigh gave such offence by bringing in Conservative politics that a man called Patriotus Canadiensis[4] wrote and asked for some of the invaluable space of the Mariposa Times-Herald and exposed it.

I should say that there were races too, on the grass on the open side of the island, graded mostly according to ages,—races for boys under thirteen and girls over nineteen and all that sort of thing. Sports are generally conducted on that plan in Mariposa. It is realized that a woman of sixty has an unfair advantage over a mere child.

Dean Drone managed the races and decided the ages and gave out the prizes; the Wesleyan minister[5] helped, and he and the young student, who was relieving in the Presbyterian Church, held the string at the winning point.

They had to get mostly clergymen for the races because all the men had wandered off, somehow, to where they were drinking lager beer out of two kegs stuck on pine logs among the trees.

But if you've ever been on a Mariposa excursion you know all about these details anyway.

So the day wore on and presently the sun came through the trees on a slant and the steamer whistle blew with a great puff of white steam and all the people came straggling down to the wharf and pretty soon the Mariposa Belle had floated out on to the lake again and headed for the town, twenty miles away.

• • • • •

4. Canadian Patriot (pseudonym).
5. A minister in the branch of Methodism adhering to the doctrines and church policy of John Wesley (1703–1791). By 1912, the discussions among Methodists, Presbyterians, and Congregationalists that led to the creation in 1925 of the United Church of Canada had already been underway for nearly a decade.

I suppose you have often noticed the contrast there is between an excursion on its way out in the morning and what it looks like on the way home.

In the morning everybody is so restless and animated and moves to and fro all over the boat and asks questions. But coming home, as the afternoon gets later and later and the sun sinks beyond the hills, all the people seem to get so still and quiet and drowsy.

So it was with the people on the Mariposa Belle. They sat there on the benches and the deck chairs in little clusters, and listened to the regular beat of the propeller and almost dozed off asleep as they sat. Then when the sun set and the dusk drew on, it grew almost dark on the deck and so still that you could hardly tell there was anyone on board.

And if you had looked at the steamer from the shore or from one of the islands, you'd have seen the row of lights from the cabin windows shining on the water and the red glare of the burning hemlock from the funnel, and you'd have heard the soft thud of the propeller miles away over the lake.

Now and then, too, you could have heard them singing on the steamer,—the voices of the girls and the men blended into unison by the distance, rising and falling in long-drawn melody: "O—Can-a-da—O—Can-a-da."[6]

You may talk as you will about the intoning choirs of your European cathedrals, but the sound of "O Canada," borne across the waters of a silent lake at evening is good enough for those of us who know Mariposa.

I think that it was just as they were singing like this: "O—Can-a-da," that word went round that the boat was sinking.

If you have ever been in any sudden emergency on the water, you will understand the strange psychology of it,—the way in which what is happening seems to become known all in a moment without a word being said. The news is transmitted from one to the other by some mysterious process.

At any rate, on the Mariposa Belle first one and then the other heard that the steamer was sinking. As far as I could ever learn the first of it was that George Duff, the bank manager, came very quietly to Dr. Gallagher and asked him if he thought that the boat was sinking. The doctor said no, that he had thought so earlier in the day but that he didn't now think that she was.

After that Duff, according to his own account, had said to

---

6. The melody for "O Canada" by Calixa Lavallée and the French words of the song by Adolphe-Basile Routhier were composed in 1880 and the English words by Robert Stanley Weir in 1908. It was Canada's unofficial national anthem for many years prior to its formal adoption as such in 1980.

Macartney, the lawyer, that the boat was sinking, and Macartney said that he doubted it very much.

Then somebody came to Judge Pepperleigh and woke him up and said that there was six inches of water in the steamer and that she was sinking. And Pepperleigh said it was perfect scandal and passed the news on to his wife and she said that they had no business to allow it and that if the steamer sank that was the last excursion she'd go on.

So the news went all round the boat and everywhere the people gathered in groups and talked about it in the angry and excited way that people have when a steamer is sinking on one of the lakes like Lake Wissanotti.

Dean Drone, of course, and some others were quieter about it, and said that one must make allowances and that naturally there were two sides to everything. But most of them wouldn't listen to reason at all. I think, perhaps, that some of them were frightened. You see the last time but one that the steamer had sunk, there had been a man drowned and it made them nervous.

What? Hadn't I explained about the depth of Lake Wissanotti? I had taken it for granted that you knew; and in any case parts of it are deep enough, though I don't suppose in this stretch of it from the big reed beds up to within a mile of the town wharf, you could find six feet of water in it if you tried. Oh, pshaw! I was not talking about a steamer sinking in the ocean and carrying down its screaming crowds of people into the hideous depths of green water. Oh, dear me, no! That kind of thing never happens on Lake Wissanotti.

But what does happen is that the Mariposa Belle sinks every now and then, and sticks there on the bottom till they get things straightened up.

On the lakes round Mariposa, if a person arrives late anywhere and explains that the steamer sank, everybody understands the situation.

You see when Harland and Wolff built the Mariposa Belle, they left some cracks in between the timbers that you fill up with cotton waste[7] every Sunday. If this is not attended to, the boat sinks. In fact, it is part of the law of the province that all the steamers like the Mariposa Belle must be properly corked,[8]—I think that is the word,—every season. There are inspectors who visit all the hotels in the province to see that it is done.

So you can imagine now that I've explained it a little straighter, the indignation of the people when they knew that the boat had

7. Refuse from cotton-mills, used to clean machinery and, here, to press into the seams of the hull to make it watertight.
8. Caulked.

come uncorked and that they might be stuck out there on a shoal or a mud-bank half the night.

I don't say either that there wasn't any danger; anyway, it doesn't feel very safe when you realize that the boat is settling down with every hundred yards that she goes, and you look over the side and see only the black water in the gathering night.

Safe! I'm not sure now that I come to think of it that it isn't worse than sinking in the Atlantic. After all, in the Atlantic there is wireless telegraphy, and a lot of trained sailors and stewards. But out on Lake Wissanotti,—far out, so that you can only just see the lights of the town away off to the south,—when the propeller comes to a stop,—and you can hear the hiss of steam as they start to rake out the engine fires to prevent an explosion,—and when you turn from the red glare that comes from the furnace doors as they open them, to the black dark that is gathering over the lake,—and there's a night wind beginning to run among the rushes,—and you see the men going forward to the roof of the pilot house to send up the rockets to rouse the town,—safe? Safe yourself, if you like; as for me, let me once get back into Mariposa again, under the night shadow of the maple trees, and this shall be the last, last time I'll go on Lake Wissanotti.

Safe! Oh yes! Isn't it strange how safe other people's adventures seem after they happen? But you'd have been scared, too, if you'd been there just before the steamer sank, and seen them bringing up all the women on to the top deck.

I don't see how some of the people took it so calmly; how Mr. Smith, for instance, could have gone on smoking and telling how he'd had a steamer "sink on him" on Lake Nipissing and a still bigger one, a side-wheeler, sink on him in Lake Abbitibbi.

Then, quite suddenly, with a quiver, down she went. You could feel the boat sink, sink,—down, down,—would it never get to the bottom? The water came flush up to the lower deck, and then— thank heaven,—the sinking stopped and there was the Mariposa Belle safe and tight on a reed bank.

Really, it made one positively laugh! It seemed so queer and, anyway, if a man has a sort of natural courage, danger makes him laugh. Danger? pshaw! fiddlesticks! everybody scouted[9] the idea. Why, it is just the little things like this that give zest to a day on the water.

Within half a minute they were all running round looking for sandwiches and cracking jokes and talking of making coffee over the remains of the engine fires.

· · · · ·

9. Mocked; dismissed with disdain.

I don't need to tell at length how it all happened after that.

I suppose the people on the Mariposa Belle would have had to settle down there all night or till help came from the town, but some of the men who had gone forward and were peering out into the dark said that it couldn't be more than a mile across the water to Miller's Point. You could almost see it over there to the left,— some of them, I think, said "off on the port bow," because you know when you get mixed up in these marine disasters, you soon catch the atmosphere of the thing.

So pretty soon they had the davits[1] swung out over the side and were lowering the old lifeboat from the top deck into the water.

There were men leaning out over the rail of the Mariposa Belle with lanterns that threw the light as they let her down, and the glare fell on the water and the reeds. But when they got the boat lowered, it looked such a frail, clumsy thing as one saw it from the rail above, that the cry was raised: "Women and children first!" For what was the sense, if it should turn out that the boat wouldn't even hold women and children, of trying to jam a lot of heavy men into it?

So they put in mostly women and children and the boat pushed out into the darkness so freighted down it would hardly float.

In the bow of it was the Presbyterian student who was relieving the minister, and he called out that they were in the hands of Providence. But he was crouched and ready to spring out of them at the first moment.

So the boat went and was lost in the darkness except for the lantern in the bow that you could see bobbing on the water. Then presently it came back and they sent another load, till pretty soon the decks began to thin out and everybody got impatient to be gone.

It was about the time that the third boat-load put off that Mr. Smith took a bet with Mullins for twenty-five dollars, that he'd be home in Mariposa before the people in the boats had walked round the shore.

No one knew just what he meant, but pretty soon they saw Mr. Smith disappear down below into the lowest part of the steamer with a mallet in one hand and a big bundle of marline[2] in the other.

They might have wondered more about it, but it was just at this time that they heard the shouts from the rescue boat—the big Mackinaw lifeboat—that had put out from the town with fourteen men at the sweeps when they saw the first rockets go up.

I suppose there is always something inspiring about a rescue at sea, or on the water.

After all, the bravery of the lifeboat man is the true bravery,—expended to save life, not to destroy it.

---

1. Pair of small cranes for hoisting lifeboats, stores, and other items.
2. Small rope for winding around a larger one to keep it from wearing.

Certainly they told for months after of how the rescue boat came out to the Mariposa Belle.

I suppose that when they put her in the water the lifeboat touched it for the first time since the old Macdonald Government[3] placed her on Lake Wissanotti.

Anyway, the water poured in at every seam. But not for a moment,—even with two miles of water between them and the steamer,—did the rowers pause for that.

By the time they were half-way there the water was almost up to the thwarts,[4] but they drove her on. Panting and exhausted (for mind you, if you haven't been in a fool boat like that for years, rowing takes it out of you), the rowers stuck to their task. They threw the ballast over and chucked into the water the heavy cork jackets and lifebelts that encumbered their movements. There was no thought of turning back. They were nearer to the steamer than the shore.

"Hang to it, boys," called the crowd from the steamer's deck, and hang they did.

They were almost exhausted when they got them; men leaning from the steamer threw them ropes and one by one every man was hauled aboard just as the lifeboat sank under their feet.

Saved! by Heaven, saved, by one of the smartest pieces of rescue work ever seen on the lake.

There's no use describing it; you need to see rescue work of this kind by lifeboats to understand it.

Nor were the lifeboat crew the only ones that distinguished themselves.

Boat after boat and canoe after canoe had put out from Mariposa to the help of the steamer. They got them all.

Pupkin, the other bank teller, with a face like a horse, who hadn't gone on the excursion,—as soon as he knew that the boat was signalling for help and that Miss Lawson was sending up rockets,—rushed for a row boat, grabbed an oar (two would have hampered him), and paddled madly out into the lake. He struck right out into the dark with the crazy skiff almost sinking beneath his feet. But they got him. They rescued him. They watched him, almost dead with exhaustion, make his way to the steamer, where he was hauled up with ropes. Saved! Saved!!

• • • • •

They might have gone on that way half the night, picking up the rescuers, only, at the very moment when the tenth load of people

3. Canada's first prime minister, Sir John A. Macdonald (1815–1891), had two periods in office, 1867 to 1873 and 1878 to 1891. A Conservative in the tradition of Benjamin Disraeli, Macdonald was a moving force in the creation of Canada and the building of the Canadian Pacific Railway.
4. Rowers' benches.

left for the shore,—just as suddenly and saucily as you please, up came the Mariposa Belle from the mud bottom and floated.

FLOATED?

Why, of course she did. If you take a hundred and fifty people off a steamer that has sunk, and if you get a man as shrewd as Mr. Smith to plug the timber seams with mallet and marline, and if you turn ten bandsmen of the Mariposa band on to your hand pump on the bow of the lower decks—float? why, what else can she do?

Then, if you stuff hemlock into the embers of the fire that you were raking out, till it hums and crackles under the boiler, it won't be long before you hear the propeller thud-thudding at the stern again, and before the long roar of the steam whistle echoes over to the town.

And so the Mariposa Belle, with all steam up again and with the long train of sparks careering from the funnel, is heading for the town.

But no Christie Johnson at the wheel in the pilot house this time.

"Smith! Get Smith!" is the cry.

Can he take her in? Well, now! Ask a man who has had steamers sink on him in half the lakes from Temiscaming to the Bay, if he can take her in? Ask a man who has run a York boat[5] down the rapids of the Moose when the ice is moving, if he can grip the steering wheel of the Mariposa Belle? So there she steams safe and sound to the town wharf!

Look at the lights and the crowd! If only the federal census taker could count us now! Hear them calling and shouting back and forward from the deck to the shore! Listen! There is the rattle of the shore ropes as they get them ready, and there's the Mariposa band,—actually forming in a circle on the upper deck just as she docks, and the leader with his baton,—one—two—ready now,—

"O CAN-A-DA!"

---

5. A wide boat with a shallow draft, the York boat was equipped with a small sail and eight oars. It was named for the Hudson's Bay Company trading post at York Factory on Hudson Bay and was used for carrying large loads.

Chapter IV

The Ministrations of the Rev. Mr. Drone

The Church of England Church in Mariposa is on a side street, where the maple trees are thickest, a little up the hill from the heart of the town. The trees above the church and the grass plot that was once the cemetery, till they made the new one (the Necropolis,[1] over the brow of the hill), fill out the whole corner. Down behind the church, with only the driving shed[2] and a lane between, is the rectory. It is a little brick house with odd angles. There is a hedge and a little gate, and a weeping ash tree with red berries.

At the side of the rectory, churchward, is a little grass lawn with low hedges and at the side of that two wild plum trees, that are practically always in white blossom. Underneath them is a rustic table and chairs, and it is here that you may see Rural Dean Drone, the incumbent[3] of the Church of England Church, sitting, in the chequered light of the plum trees that is neither sun nor shadow. Generally you will find him reading, and when I tell you that at the end of the grass plot where the hedge is highest there is a yellow bee hive with seven bees[4] that belong to Dean Drone, you will realize that it is only fitting that the Dean is reading in the Greek. For what better could a man be reading beneath the blossom of the plum trees, within the very sound of the bees, than the Pastorals of Theocritus?[5] The light trash of modern romance might put a man to sleep in such a spot, but with such food for reflection as Theocritus, a man may safely close his eyes and muse on what he reads without fear of dropping into slumber.

Some men, I suppose, terminate their education when they leave their college. Not so Dean Drone. I have often heard him say that if he couldn't take a book in the Greek out on the lawn in a spare half-hour, he would feel lost. It's a certain activity of the brain that must be stilled somehow. The Dean, too, seemed to have a native feeling for the Greek language. I have often heard people who

1. City of the dead: a cemetery, especially one belonging to an ancient city.
2. Small, low building for the storing of a carriage or automobile.
3. Office holder who performs official duties.
4. A "yellow bee hive with seven bees" appears on various crests and flags and is usually taken to represent industriousness and endeavour. In Masonic lore, a bee-hive surrounded by bees is not only taken as "an emblem of industry . . . [that] recommends the practice of that virtue" and that "teaches us that . . . we should . . . never sit . . . down contented, while our fellow-creatures around us are in want," but also as a sign that "he that will so demean himself as not to be endeavoring to add to the common stock of knowledge and understanding, may be deemed a *drone* in the *hive* of nature, a useless member of society, and unworthy of our protection as Masons" (Charles W. Moore, *The New Masonic Trestle-Board* [1850], 48).
5. Celebrations of the rural life ("pastoral" is from the Latin "pastor": shepherd) by the ancient Greek poet Theocritus (c. 308–240 B.C.E.).

might sit with him on the lawn, ask him to translate some of it. But he always refused. One couldn't translate it, he said. It lost so much in the translation that it was better not to try. It was far wiser not to attempt it. If you undertook to translate it, there was something gone, something missing immediately. I believe that many classical scholars feel this way, and like to read the Greek just as it is, without the hazard of trying to put it into so poor a medium as English. So that when Dean Drone said that he simply couldn't translate it, I believe he was perfectly sincere.

Sometimes, indeed, he would read it aloud. That was another matter. Whenever, for example, Dr. Gallagher—I mean, of course, old Dr. Gallagher, not the young doctor (who was always out in the country in the afternoon)—would come over and bring his latest Indian relics to show to the Dean, the latter always read to him a passage or two. As soon as the doctor laid his tomahawk on the table, the Dean would reach for his Theocritus. I remember that on the day when Dr. Gallagher brought over the Indian skull that they had dug out of the railway embankment, and placed it on the rustic table, the Dean read to him so long from Theocritus that the doctor, I truly believe, dozed off in his chair. The Dean had to wait and fold his hands with the book across his knee, and close his eyes till the doctor should wake up again. And the skull was on the table between them, and from above the plum blossoms fluttered down, till they made flakes on it as white as Dr. Gallagher's hair.

· · · · ·

I don't want you to suppose that the Rev. Mr. Drone spent the whole of his time under the trees. Not at all. In point of fact, the rector's life was one round of activity which he himself might deplore but was powerless to prevent. He had hardly sat down beneath the trees of an afternoon after his mid-day meal when there was the Infant Class at three, and after that, with scarcely an hour between, the Mothers' Auxiliary at five, and the next morning the Book Club, and that evening the Bible Study Class, and the next morning the Early Workers' Guild at eleven-thirty. The whole week was like that, and if one found time to sit down for an hour or so to recuperate it was the most one could do. After all, if a busy man spends the little bit of leisure that he gets in advanced classical study, there is surely no harm in it. I suppose, take it all in all, there wasn't a busier man than the Rural Dean among the Anglican clergy of the diocese.

If the Dean ever did snatch a half-day from his incessant work, he spent it in fishing. But not always that, for as likely as not, instead of taking a real holiday he would put in the whole afternoon amusing the children and the boys that he knew, by making kites and toys and clockwork steamboats for them.

It was fortunate for the Dean that he had the strange interest and aptitude for mechanical devices[6] which he possessed, or otherwise this kind of thing would have been too cruel an imposition. But the Rev. Mr. Drone had a curious liking for machinery. I think I never heard him preach a better sermon than the one on Aeroplanes (Lo, what now see you on high Jeremiah Two).[7]

So it was that he spent two whole days making a kite with Chinese wings for Teddy Moore, the photographer's son, and closed down the infant class for forty-eight hours so that Teddy Moore should not miss the pleasure of flying it, or rather seeing it flown. It is foolish to trust a Chinese kite to the hands of a young child.

In the same way the Dean made a mechanical top for little Marjorie Trewlaney, the cripple, to see spun: it would have been unwise to allow the afflicted girl to spin it. There was no end to the things that Mr. Drone could make, and always for the children. Even when he was making the sand-clock[8] for poor little Willie Yodel (who died, you know) the Dean went right on with it and gave it to another child with just the same pleasure. Death, you know, to the clergy is a different thing from what it is to us. The Dean and Mr. Gingham used often to speak of it as they walked through the long grass of the new cemetery, the Necropolis. And when your Sunday walk is to your wife's grave, as the Dean's was, perhaps it seems different to anybody.

The Church of England Church, I said, stood close to the rectory, a tall, sweeping church, and inside a great reach of polished cedar beams that ran to the point of the roof. There used to stand on the same spot the little stone church that all the grown-up people in Mariposa still remember, a quaint little building in red and grey stone. About it was the old cemetery, but that was all smoothed out later into the grass plot round the new church, and the headstones laid out flat, and no new graves have been put there for ever so long. But the Mariposa children still walk round and read the headstones lying flat in the grass and look for the old ones—because some of them are ever so old—forty or fifty years back.

Nor are you to think from all this that the Dean was not a man with serious perplexities. You could easily convince yourself of the

6. The copy-text has "advices," as does the *Montreal Daily Star* text, but the manuscript has "devices" (see Spadoni, ed. *Sunshine Sketches of a Little Town*, 311). The fact that, unlike other errors in the 1912 John Lane, The Bodley Head edition, "advices" remained unchanged in subsequent issues may suggest that it is correct, "advices" being communications from a distance of information, intelligence, news, and the like (*OED*).

7. No such text appears in Jeremiah 2, which contains God's remonstration with the Jews for "chang[ing] their gods," "forsaking the Lord," and "turn[ing] into the degenerate plant of a strange vine" (2.11, 19, 21).

8. Traditional and Masonic emblem of the swift passage of time and "human life" (Moore 49).

contrary. For if you watched the Rev. Mr. Drone as he sat reading in the Greek, you would notice that no very long period ever passed without his taking up a sheet or two of paper that lay between the leaves of the Theocritus and that were covered close with figures.

And these the Dean would lay upon the rustic table, and he would add them up forwards and backwards, going first up the column and then down it to see that nothing had been left out, and then down it again to see what it was that must have been left out.

Mathematics, you will understand, were not the Dean's forte. They never were the forte of the men who had been trained at the little Anglican college with the clipped hedges and the cricket ground, where Rupert Drone had taken the gold medal in Greek fifty-two years ago. You will see the medal at any time lying there in its open box on the rectory table, in case of immediate need. Any of the Drone girls, Lilian, or Jocelyn, or Theodora, would show it to you. But, as I say, mathematics were not the rector's forte, and he blamed for it (in a Christian spirit, you will understand) the memory of his mathematical professor, and often he spoke with great bitterness. I have often heard him say that in his opinion the colleges ought to dismiss, of course in a Christian spirit, all the professors who are not, in the most reverential sense of the term, fit for their jobs.

No doubt many of the clergy of the diocese had suffered more or less just as the Dean had from lack of mathematical training. But the Dean always felt that his own case was especially to be lamented. For you see, if a man is trying to make a model aeroplane—for a poor family in the lower part of the town—and he is brought to a stop by the need of reckoning the coefficient of torsion of cast-iron rods, it shows plainly enough that the colleges are not truly filling their divine mission.

· · · · ·

But the figures that I speak of were not those of the model aeroplane. These were far more serious. Night and day they had been with the rector now for the best part of ten years, and they grew, if anything, more intricate.

If, for example, you try to reckon the debt of a church—a large church with a great sweep of polished cedar beams inside, for the special glorification of the All Powerful, and with imported tiles on the roof for the greater glory of Heaven and with stained-glass windows for the exaltation of the All Seeing—if, I say, you try to reckon up the debt on such a church and figure out its interest and its present worth, less a fixed annual payment, it makes a pretty complicated sum.[9] Then if you try to add to this the annual cost of

9. Problem in arithmetic.

insurance, and deduct from it three-quarters of a stipend, year by year, and then suddenly remember that three-quarters is too much, because you have forgotten the boarding-school fees of the littlest of the Drones (including French, as an extra—she must have it, all the older girls did), you have got a sum that pretty well defies ordinary arithmetic. The provoking part of it was that the Dean knew perfectly well that with the help of logarithms he could have done the thing in a moment. But at the Anglican college they had stopped short at that very place in the book. They had simply explained that Logos was a word and Arithmos a number,[1] which, at the time, seemed amply sufficient.

So the Dean was perpetually taking out his sheets of figures, and adding them upwards and downwards, and they never came the same. Very often Mr. Gingham, who was a warden,[2] would come and sit beside the rector and ponder over the figures, and Mr. Drone would explain that with a book of logarithms you could work it out in a moment. You would simply open the book and run your finger up the columns (he illustrated exactly the way in which the finger was moved), and there you were. Mr. Gingham said that it was a caution, and that logarithms (I quote his exact phrase) must be a terror.

Very often, too, Nivens, the lawyer, who was a sidesman,[3] and Mullins, the manager of the Exchange Bank, who was the chairman of the vestry,[4] would come and take a look at the figures. But they never could make much of them, because the stipend[5] part was not a matter that one could discuss.

Mullins would notice the item for a hundred dollars due on fire insurance and would say, as a business man, that surely that couldn't be fire insurance, and the Dean would say surely not, and change it: and Mullins would say surely there couldn't be fifty dollars for taxes, because there weren't any taxes, and the Dean would admit that of course it couldn't be for the taxes. In fact, the truth is that the Dean's figures were badly mixed, and the fault lay indubitably with the mathematical professor of two generations back.

It was always Mullins's intention some day to look into the finances of the church, the more so as his father had been with Dean Drone at the little Anglican college with the cricket ground. But he was a busy man. As he explained to the rector himself, the banking business nowadays is getting to be such that a banker can

1. In Greek, "Arithmos" means "number." "Logos" means "word" in Greek, but in Christian theology the "Logos" is the Word of God incarnate in Jesus Christ.
2. Churchwarden: an elected lay officer who assists in the administration of an Anglican parish and acts as its legal representative.
3. Deputy churchwarden.
4. Committee responsible for parish business.
5. Minister's salary.

hardly call even his Sunday mornings his own. Certainly Henry Mullins could not. They belonged largely to Smith's Hotel, and during the fishing season they belonged away down the lake, so far away that practically no one, unless it was George Duff of the Commercial Bank, could see them.

But to think that all this trouble had come through the building of the new church.

That was the bitterness of it.

For the twenty-five years that Rural Dean Drone had preached in the little stone church, it had been his one aim, as he often put it in his sermons, to rear a larger Ark in Gideon.[6] His one hope had been to set up a greater Evidence, or, very simply stated, to kindle a Brighter Beacon.[7]

After twenty-five years of waiting, he had been able at last to kindle it. Everybody in Mariposa remembers the building of the church. First of all they had demolished the little stone church to make way for the newer Evidence. It seemed almost a sacrilege, as the Dean himself said, to lay hands on it. Indeed it was at first proposed to take the stone of it and build it into a Sunday School, as a lesser testimony. Then, when that proved impracticable, it was suggested that the stone be reverently fashioned into a wall that should stand as a token. And when even that could not be managed, the stone of the little church was laid reverently into a stone pile; afterwards it was devoutly sold to a building contractor, and, like so much else in life, was forgotten.

But the building of the church, no one, I think, will forget. The Dean threw himself into the work. With his coat off and his white shirt-sleeves conspicuous among the gang that were working at the foundations, he set his hand to the shovel, himself guided the road-scraper, urging on the horses, cheering and encouraging the men, till they begged him to desist. He mingled with the stone-masons, advising, helping, and giving counsel, till they pleaded with him to rest. He was among the carpenters, sawing, hammering, enquiring, suggesting, till they besought him to lay off. And he was night and day with the architect's assistants, drawing, planning, revising, till the architect told him to cut it out.

So great was his activity, that I doubt whether the new church would ever have been finished, had not the wardens and the vestry men insisted that Mr. Drone must take a holiday, and sent him on

6. In the Old Testament or Hebrew Bible, the Ark of the Covenant is a symbol of the presence and glory of God and Gideon is the Israelite who, among other things, destroys an altar to Baal and builds one to the Lord (Judges 6.25–27). Dean Drone is confusing him with Gibeon, a city of the Hivites where the Ark (or Tabernacle) was at one time located (1 Kings 3.4; 1 Chronicles 16.39 and 21.29).
7. Isaiah 30.17: "Ye [shall] be left as a beacon on the top of a mountain, and as an ensign [flag] on a hill."

the Mackinaw trip up the lakes,—the only foreign travel of the Dean's life.

• • • • •

So in due time the New Church was built and it towered above the maple trees of Mariposa like a beacon on a hill. It stood so high that from the open steeple of it, where the bells were, you could see all the town lying at its feet, and the farmsteads to the south of it, and the railway like a double pencil line, and Lake Wissanotti spread out like a map. You could see and appreciate things from the height of the new church,—such as the size and the growing wealth of Mariposa,—that you never could have seen from the little stone church at all.

Presently the church was opened and the Dean preached his first sermon in it, and he called it a Greater Testimony,[8] and he said that it was an earnest, or first-fruit of endeavour, and that it was a token or pledge, and he named it also a covenant.[9] He said, too, that it was an anchorage and a harbour and a lighthouse as well as being a city set upon a hill;[1] and he ended by declaring it an Ark of Refuge[2] and notified them that the Bible Class would meet in the basement of it on that and every other third Wednesday.

In the opening months of preaching about it the Dean had called the church so often an earnest and a pledge and a guerdon and a tabernacle, that I think he used to forget that it wasn't paid for. It was only when the agent of the building society and a representative of the Hosanna Pipe and Steam Organ Co. (Limited), used to call for quarterly payments that he was suddenly reminded of the fact. Always after these men came round the Dean used to preach a special sermon on sin, in the course of which he would mention that the ancient Hebrews used to put unjust traders to death,—a thing of which he spoke with Christian serenity.

I don't think that at first anybody troubled much about the debt on the church. Dean Drone's figures showed that it was only a matter of time before it would be extinguished; only a little effort was needed, a little girding up of the loins[3] of the congregation and they

8. In Exodus 25.22, Numbers 1.50, and elsewhere the Ark and Tabernacle are referred to as the "ark of the testimony" and the "tabernacle of testimony," testimony being the declaration of confidence and faith in God required of the righteous.
9. An "earnest" is a sum of money paid as an installment to secure a contract; figuratively, it is a foretaste or pledge of something to be received in greater abundance later. The "first-fruit" is figuratively the earliest product of a person's work, but "first-fruits" were originally the earliest products of the soil in a given season; they were given by custom as an offering to the gods or God (OED). The Ark of the Covenant is described in detail in Exodus 25.10–16.
1. Matthew 5.14: "Ye are as the light of the world. A city that is set on an hill cannot be hid."
2. There are "cities of refuge" in the Bible (see Numbers 35.6) but the Ark is never called the "Ark of Refuge."
3. Ephesians 6.14: "Stand therefore, having your loins girt about with truth, and having on the breastplate of righteousness."

could shoulder the whole debt and trample it under their feet.[4] Let them but set their hands to the plough[5] and they could soon guide it into the deep water.[6] Then they might furl their sails and sit every man under his own olive tree.[7]

Meantime, while the congregation was waiting to gird up its loins, the interest on the debt was paid somehow, or, when it wasn't paid, was added to the principal.

I don't know whether you have had any experience with Greater Testimonies and with Beacons set on Hills. If you have, you will realize how, at first gradually, and then rapidly, their position from year to year grows more distressing. What with the building loan and the organ instalment, and the fire insurance,—a cruel charge,—and the heat and light, the rector began to realize as he added up the figures that nothing but logarithms could solve them. Then the time came when not only the rector, but all the wardens knew and the sidesmen knew that the debt was more than the church could carry; then the choir knew and the congregation knew and at last everybody knew; and there were special collections at Easter and special days of giving, and special weeks of tribulation, and special arrangements with the Hosanna Pipe and Steam Organ Co. And it was noticed that when the Rural Dean announced a service of Lenten Sorrow,[8]—aimed more especially at the business men,—the congregation had diminished by forty per cent.

• • • • •

I suppose things are just the same elsewhere,—I mean the peculiar kind of discontent that crept into the Church of England congregation in Mariposa after the setting up of the Beacon. There were those who claimed that they had seen the error from the first, though they had kept quiet, as such people always do, from breadth of mind. There were those who had felt years before how it would end, but their lips were sealed from humility of spirit. What was worse was that there were others who grew dissatisfied with the whole conduct of the church.

Yodel, the auctioneer, for example, narrated how he had been to

---

4. Psalm 91.13: "Thou shalt tread upon the lion and adder; the young lion and the dragon shalt thou trample under feet." Matthew 7.6: "Give not that which is holy unto the dogs, neither cast ye pearls before swine, lest they trample them under their feet, and turn again and rend you."
5. Luke 9.62: "And Jesus said unto him, No man, having put his hand to the plough, and looking back, is fit for the kingdom of God."
6. Proverbs 20.15: "Counsel in the heart of man is like deep water: but a man of understanding will draw it out."
7. Romans 11.24: "For if thou wert cut out of the olive tree, which is wild by nature, and wert grafted contrary to nature into a good olive tree; how much more shall these, which be the natural branches, be grafted into their own olive tree."
8. Lent is the period from Ash Wednesday to Easter observed as a time of fasting in commemoration of Christ's fast in the wilderness (Matthew 4.2).

the city and had gone into a service of the Roman Catholic church: I believe, to state it more fairly, he had "dropped in,"—the only recognized means of access to such a service. He claimed that the music that he had heard there was music, and that (outside of his profession) the chanting and intoning could not be touched.

Ed Moore, the photographer, also related that he had listened to a sermon in the city, and that if anyone would guarantee him a sermon like that he would defy you to keep him away from church. Meanwhile, failing the guarantee, he stayed away.

The very doctrines were impeached. Some of the congregation began to cast doubts on eternal punishment,—doubts so grave as to keep them absent from the Lenten Services of Sorrow. Indeed, Lawyer Macartney took up the whole question of the Athanasian Creed[9] one afternoon with Joe Milligan, the dentist, and hardly left a clause of it intact.

All this time, you will understand, Dean Drone kept on with his special services, and leaflets, calls, and appeals went out from the Ark of Gideon like rockets from a sinking ship. More and more with every month the debt of the church lay heavy on his mind. At times he forgot it. At other times he woke up in the night and thought about it. Sometimes as he went down the street from the lighted precincts of the Greater Testimony and passed the Salvation Army, praying around a naphtha lamp under the open sky, it smote him to the heart with a stab.

But the congregation were wrong, I think, in imputing fault to the sermons of Dean Drone. There I do think they were wrong. I can speak from personal knowledge when I say that the rector's sermons were not only stimulating in matters of faith, but contained valuable material in regard to the Greek language, to modern machinery and to a variety of things that should have proved of the highest advantage to the congregation.

There was, I say, the Greek language. The Dean always showed the greatest delicacy of feeling in regard to any translation in or out of it that he made from the pulpit. He was never willing to accept even the faintest shade of rendering different from that commonly given without being assured of the full concurrence of the congregation. Either the translation must be unanimous and without contradiction, or he could not pass it. He would pause in his sermon and would say: "The original Greek is 'Hoson,' but perhaps you will allow me to translate it as equivalent to 'Hoyon.' "[1] And they did. So

9. The statement of Christian belief formerly attributed to Athanasius and sometimes used in Anglican services as an alternative to the Apostles' Creed.
1. "Hoson" and "Hoyon" both mean "what" in Greek, but the former (the counterpart of the Latin "quantus") is used to express magnitude and the latter (the counterpart of the Latin "qualis") to express intrinsic nature or character. The Dean is collapsing the distinction between quantity and quality.

that if there was any fault to be found it was purely on the side of the congregation for not entering a protest at the time.

It was the same way in regard to machinery. After all, what better illustrates the supreme purpose of the All Wise than such a thing as the dynamo or the reciprocating marine engine or the pictures in the Scientific American?[2]

Then, too, if a man has had the opportunity to travel and has seen the great lakes spread out by the hand of Providence from where one leaves the new dock at the Sound[3] to where one arrives safe and thankful with one's dear fellow-passengers in the spirit at the concrete landing stage at Mackinaw—is not this fit and proper material for the construction of an analogy or illustration? Indeed, even apart from an analogy, is it not mighty interesting to narrate, anyway? In any case, why should the churchwardens have sent the rector on the Mackinaw trip, if they had not expected him to make some little return for it?

I lay some stress on this point because the criticisms directed against the Mackinaw sermons always seemed so unfair. If the rector had described his experiences in the crude language of the ordinary newspaper, there might, I admit, have been something unfitting about it. But he was always careful to express himself in a way that showed,—or, listen, let me explain with an example.

"It happened to be my lot some years ago," he would say, "to find myself a voyager, just as one is a voyager on the sea of life, on the broad expanse of water which has been spread out to the north-west of us by the hand of Providence, at a height of five hundred and eighty-one feet above the level of the sea,—I refer, I may say, to Lake Huron."

Now, how different that is from saying: "I'll never forget the time I went on the Mackinaw trip." The whole thing has a different sound entirely. In the same way the Dean would go on:

2. American technical magazine founded in 1850. In the period following the Wright brothers' initial flight of December 17, 1903, *Scientific American* was skeptical of reports of their longer flights, but in its issue of December 15, 1906, it "stated its complete acceptance of the facts about the Wright flights," describing " 'the first successful aeroplane flying-machine' " as an " 'epoch-making invention.' . . . From then on *Scientific American* devoted a great deal of space to the rapid progress of aviation and on September 14, 1907, it offered . . . [a] trophy for the first public flight of one kilometer" or more (Sherwood Harris, *The First to Fly: Aviation's Pioneer Days* [New York: Simon and Schuster, 1970], 132). In *Flight in America, 1900–1983: From the Wrights to the Astronauts* (Baltimore: Johns Hopkins UP, 1984), 19, Roger L. Bilstine observes that, "for youngsters with a knack for mechanical devices, clubs for flying model planes appeared as early as 1911" and prompted *Scientific American* to remark that " '[t]he amount of interest that is aroused is impressive to the man who is unfamiliar with the spread of the model-making movement among boys.' " By 1912, the hold of flying on the popular imagination had spawned several books for "youngsters," including *The Boy Aviators* (1910) by Captain Wilbur Lawton, *Aeroplane Boys* (1910) by Ashton Lamar, *Girl Aviators* (1911) by Margaret Burnham, and *The Second Boys' Book of Model Aeroplanes* (1911).

3. Owen Sound, on Georgian Bay, Lake Huron.

"I was voyaging on one of those magnificent leviathans[4] of the water,—I refer to the boats of the Northern Navigation Company,[5]—and was standing beside the forward rail talking with a dear brother in the faith who was journeying westward also—I may say he was a commercial traveller,—and beside us was a dear sister in the spirit seated in a deck chair, while near us were two other dear souls in grace engaged in Christian pastime on the deck,—I allude more particularly to the game of deck billiards."

I leave it to any reasonable man whether, with that complete and fair-minded explanation of the environment, it was not perfectly proper to close down the analogy, as the rector did, with the simple words: "In fact, it was an extremely fine morning."

Yet there were some people, even in Mariposa, that took exception and spent their Sunday dinner time in making out that they couldn't understand what Dean Drone was talking about, and asking one another if they knew. Once, as he passed out from the doors of the Greater Testimony, the rector heard some one say: "The Church would be all right if that old mugwump[6] was out of the pulpit." It went to his heart like a barbed thorn, and stayed there.

You know, perhaps, how a remark of that sort can stay and rankle, and make you wish you could hear it again to make sure of it, because perhaps you didn't hear it aright, and it was a mistake after all. Perhaps no one said it, anyway. You ought to have written it down at the time. I have seen the Dean take down the encyclopædia in the rectory, and move his finger slowly down the pages of the letter M, looking for mugwump. But it wasn't there. I have known him, in his little study upstairs, turn over the pages of the "Animals of Palestine,"[7] looking for a mugwump. But there was none there. It must have been unknown in the greater days of Judea.[8]

• • • • •

So things went on from month to month, and from year to year, and the debt and the charges loomed like a dark and gathering

---

4. In the Bible, Leviathan is a sea monster who represents the power of God and is destroyed by Him (Job 41; Psalm 74.14; Isaiah 27.1).

5. The Northern Navigation Company operated passenger vessels in Lake Huron and Lake Superior.

6. From an Algonquin word for "great chief," a term that gained currency and came to mean "turncoat" in 1884 when it was used to describe Republicans who refused to accept their party's official presidential candidate, James G. Blaine, and sided instead with Grover Cleveland. Thereafter it came to mean someone, particularly but not exclusively a politician, who was either unable or unwilling to come to a decision on an important issue and, thus, "sat on the fence" with his "mug" on one side and his "wump" on the other.

7. There is no such book, but its equivalents are such works as J. G. Wood's *Bible Animals: A Description of the Habits, Structure, and Uses of Every Living Creature Mentioned in the Scriptures* (1875) and the same author's *Bible Animals and the Lessons Taught by Them* (1888).

8. The southern region of Israel and, in Luke 1.5, the entire country.

cloud on the horizon. I don't mean to say that efforts were not made to face the difficulty and to fight it. They were. Time after time the workers of the congregation got together and thought out plans for the extinction of the debt. But somehow, after every trial, the debt grew larger with each year, and every system that could be devised turned out more hopeless than the last.

They began, I think, with the "endless chain" of letters of appeal. You may remember the device, for it was all-popular in clerical circles some ten or fifteen years ago. You got a number of people to write each of them three letters asking for ten cents from three each of their friends and asking each of them to send on three similar letters. Three each from three each, and three each more from each! Do you observe the wonderful ingenuity of it? Nobody, I think, has forgotten how the Willing Workers of the Church of England Church of Mariposa sat down in the vestry room[9] in the basement with a pile of stationery three feet high, sending out the letters. Some, I know, will never forget it. Certainly not Mr. Pupkin, the teller in the Exchange Bank, for it was here that he met Zena Pepperleigh, the judge's daughter, for the first time; and they worked so busily that they wrote out ever so many letters—eight or nine—in a single afternoon, and they discovered that their handwritings were awfully alike, which was one of the most extraordinary and amazing coincidences, you will admit, in the history of chirography.[1]

But the scheme failed—failed utterly. I don't know why. The letters went out and were copied broadcast and recopied, till you could see the Mariposa endless chain winding its way towards the Rocky Mountains. But they never got the ten cents. The Willing Workers wrote for it in thousands, but by some odd chance they never struck the person who had it.

Then after that there came a regular winter of effort. First of all they had a bazaar that was got up by the Girls' Auxiliary and held in the basement of the church. All the girls wore special costumes that were brought up from the city, and they had booths, where there was every imaginable thing for sale—pincushion covers, and chair covers, and sofa covers, everything that you can think of. If the people had once started buying them, the debt would have been lifted in no time. Even as it was the bazaar only lost twenty dollars.

After that, I think, was the magic lantern lecture that Dean Drone gave on "Italy and her Invaders." They got the lantern[2] and the slides up from the city, and it was simply splendid. Some of the slides were perhaps a little confusing, but it was all there,—the

9. Room in which church vestments are stored and meetings are held.
1. Handwriting.
2. Projector.

pictures of the dense Italian jungle and the crocodiles and the naked invaders with their invading clubs. It was a pity that it was such a bad night, snowing hard, and a curling match on, or they would have made a lot of money out of the lecture. As it was the loss, apart from the breaking of the lantern, which was unavoidable, was quite trifling.

• • • • •

I can hardly remember all the things that there were after that. I recollect that it was always Mullins who arranged about renting the hall and printing the tickets and all that sort of thing. His father, you remember, had been at the Anglican college with Dean Drone, and though the rector was thirty-seven years older than Mullins, he leaned upon him, in matters of business, as upon a staff; and though Mullins was thirty-seven years younger than the Dean, he leaned against him, in matters of doctrine, as against a rock.

At one time they got the idea that what the public wanted was not anything instructive but something light and amusing. Mullins said that people loved to laugh. He said that if you get a lot of people all together and get them laughing you can do anything you like with them. Once they start to laugh they are lost. So they got Mr. Dreery, the English Literature teacher at the high school, to give an evening of readings from the Great Humorists from Chaucer to Adam Smith.[3] They came mighty near to making a barrel of money out of that. If the people had once started laughing it would have been all over with them. As it was I heard a lot of them say that they simply wanted to scream with laughter: they said they just felt like bursting into peals of laughter all the time. Even when, in the more subtle parts, they didn't feel like bursting out laughing, they said they had all they could do to keep from smiling. They said they never had such a hard struggle in their lives not to smile.

In fact the chairman said when he put the vote of thanks that he was sure if people had known what the lecture was to be like there would have been a much better "turn-out." But you see all that the people had to go on was just the announcement of the name of the lecturer, Mr. Dreery, and that he would lecture on English Humour All Seats Twenty-five Cents. As the chairman expressed it himself, if the people had had any idea, any idea at all, of what the lecture would be like they would have been there in hundreds. But how could they get an idea that it would be so amusing with practically nothing to go upon?

3. Several of the prose and verse stories in *The Canterbury Tales* by the English writer Geoffrey Chaucer (c. 1343–1400) are humorous, some, such as "The Miller's Tale," in a very bawdy manner. None of the works of the Scottish economist Adam Smith (1723–1790), the best-known and most influential of which is *An Inquiry into the Nature and Causes of the Wealth of Nations* (1776), can be regarded as more than sporadically or unintentionally humourous.

• • • • •

After that attempt things seemed to go from bad to worse. Nearly everybody was disheartened about it. What would have happened to the debt, or whether they would have ever paid it off, is more than I can say, if it hadn't occurred that light broke in on Mullins in the strangest and most surprising way you can imagine. It happened that he went away for his bank holidays, and while he was away he happened to be present in one of the big cities and saw how they went at it there to raise money. He came home in such a state of excitement that he went straight up from the Mariposa station to the rectory, valise and all, and he burst in one April evening to where the Rural Dean was sitting with the three girls beside the lamp in the front room, and he cried out:

"Mr. Drone, I've got it,—I've got a way that will clear the debt before you're a fortnight older. We'll have a Whirlwind Campaign in Mariposa!"

But stay! The change from the depth of depression to the pinnacle of hope is too abrupt. I must pause and tell you in another chapter of the Whirlwind Campaign in Mariposa.

Chapter V

The Whirlwind Campaign in Mariposa

It was Mullins, the banker, who told Mariposa all about the plan of a Whirlwind Campaign and explained how it was to be done. He'd happened to be in one of the big cities when they were raising money by a Whirlwind Campaign for one of the universities, and he saw it all.

He said he would never forget the scene on the last day of it, when the announcement was made that the total of the money raised was even more than what was needed. It was a splendid sight,—the business men of the town all cheering and laughing and shaking hands, and the professors with the tears streaming down their faces, and the Deans of the Faculties, who had given money themselves, sobbing aloud.

He said it was the most moving thing he ever saw.

So, as I said, Henry Mullins, who had seen it, explained to the others how it was done. He said that first of all a few of the business men got together quietly,—very quietly, indeed the more quietly the better,—and talked things over. Perhaps one of them would dine,—just quietly,—with another one and discuss the situation. Then these two would invite a third man,—possibly even a fourth,—to have lunch with them and talk in a general way,—even talk of other things part of the time. And so on in this way things would be discussed and looked at in different lights and viewed from different angles and then when everything was ready they would go at things with a rush. A central committee would be formed and sub-committees, with captains of each group and recorders and secretaries, and on a stated day the Whirlwind Campaign would begin.

Each day the crowd would all agree to meet at some stated place and eat lunch together,—say at a restaurant or a club or at some eating place. This would go on every day with the interest getting keener and keener, and everybody getting more and more excited, till presently the chairman would announce that the campaign had succeeded and there would be the kind of scene that Mullins had described.

So that was the plan that they set in motion in Mariposa.

• • • • •

I don't wish to say too much about the Whirlwind Campaign itself. I don't mean to say that it was a failure. On the contrary, in many ways it couldn't have been a greater success, and yet somehow it didn't seem to work out just as Henry Mullins had said it would. It may be that there are differences between Mariposa and the larger cities that one doesn't appreciate at first sight. Perhaps it would have been better to try some other plan.

Yet they followed along the usual line of things closely enough. They began with the regular system of some of the business men getting together in a quiet way.

First of all, for example, Henry Mullins came over quietly to Duff's rooms, over the Commercial Bank, with a bottle of rye whiskey, and they talked things over. And the night after that George Duff came over quietly to Mullins' rooms, over the Exchange Bank, with a bottle of Scotch whiskey. A few evenings after that Mullins and Duff went together, in a very unostentatious way, with perhaps a couple of bottles of rye, to Pete Glover's room over the hardware store. And then all three of them went up one night with Ed Moore, the photographer, to Judge Pepperleigh's house under pretence of having a game of poker. The very day after that, Mullins and Duff and Ed Moore, and Pete Glover and the judge got Will Harrison, the harness maker, to go out without any formality on the lake on the pretext of fishing. And the next night after that Duff and Mullins and Ed Moore and Pete Glover and Pepperleigh and Will Harrison got Alf Trelawney, the postmaster, to come over, just in a casual way, to the Mariposa House, after the night mail, and the next day Mullins and Duff and—

But, pshaw! you see at once how the thing is worked. There's no need to follow that part of the Whirlwind Campaign further. But it just shows the power of organization.

And all this time, mind you, they were talking things over, and looking at things first in one light and then in another light,—in fact, just doing as the big city men do when there's an important thing like this under way.

So after things had been got pretty well into shape in this way, Duff asked Mullins one night, straight out, if he would be chairman of the Central Committee. He sprung it on him and Mullins had no time to refuse, but he put it to Duff straight whether he would be treasurer. And Duff had no time to refuse.

• • • • •

That gave things a start, and within a week they had the whole organization on foot. There was the Grand Central Committee and six groups or sub-committees of twenty men each, and a captain for every group. They had it all arranged on the lines most likely to be effective.

In one group there were all the bankers, Mullins and Duff and Pupkin (with the cameo pin), and about four others. They had their photographs taken at Ed Moore's studio, taken in a line with a background of icebergs—a winter scene—and a pretty penetrating crowd they looked, I can tell you. After all, you know, if you get a crowd of representative bank men together in any financial deal, you've got a pretty considerable leverage right away.

In the second group were the lawyers, Nivens and Macartney and the rest—about as level-headed a lot as you'd see anywhere. Get the lawyers of a town with you on a thing like this and you'll find you've got a sort of brain power with you that you'd never get without them.

Then there were the business men—there was a solid crowd for you,—Harrison, the harness maker, and Glover, the hardware man, and all that gang, not talkers, perhaps, but solid men who can tell you to a nicety how many cents there are in a dollar. It's all right to talk about education and that sort of thing, but if you want driving power and efficiency, get business men. They're seeing it every day in the city and it's just the same in Mariposa. Why, in the big concerns in the city, if they found out a man was educated, they wouldn't have him,—wouldn't keep him there a minute. That's why the business men have to conceal it so much.

Then in the other teams there were the doctors and the newspaper men and the professional men like Judge Pepperleigh and Yodel the auctioneer.

• • • • •

It was all organized so that every team had its headquarters, two of them in each of the three hotels—one upstairs and one down.

And it was arranged that there would be a big lunch every day, to be held in Smith's caff, round the corner of Smith's Northern Health Resort and Home of the Wissanotti Angler,—you know the place. The lunch was divided up into tables, with a captain for each table to see about things to drink, and of course all the tables were in competition with one another. In fact the competition was the very life of the whole thing.

It's just wonderful how these things run when they're organized. Take the first luncheon, for example. There they all were, every man in his place, every captain at his post at the top of the table. It was hard, perhaps, for some of them to get there. They had very likely to be in their stores and banks and offices till the last minute and then make a dash for it. It was the cleanest piece of team work you ever saw.

You have noticed already, I am sure, that a good many of the captains and committee men didn't belong to the Church of England Church. Glover, for instance, was a Presbyterian, till they ran the picket fence of the manse two feet on to his property, and after that he became a free-thinker. But in Mariposa, as I have said, everybody likes to be in everything and naturally a Whirlwind Campaign was a novelty. Anyway it would have been a poor business to keep a man out of the lunches merely on account of his religion. I trust that the day for that kind of religious bigotry is past.

Of course the excitement was when Henry Mullins at the head of the table began reading out the telegrams and letters and messages. First of all there was a telegram of good wishes from the Anglican Lord Bishop of the Diocese to Henry Mullins and calling him Dear Brother in Grace—the Mariposa telegraph office is a little unreliable and it read: "Dear Brother in grease," but that was good enough. The Bishop said that his most earnest wishes were with them.

Then Mullins read a letter from the Mayor of Mariposa—Pete Glover was mayor that year—stating that his keenest desires were with them: and then one from the Carriage Company saying that its heartiest good will was all theirs; and then one from the Meat Works saying that its nearest thoughts were next to them. Then he read one from himself, as head of the Exchange Bank, you understand, informing him that he had heard of his project and assuring him of his liveliest interest in what he proposed.

At each of these telegrams and messages there was round after round of applause, so that you could hardly hear yourself speak or give an order. But that was nothing to when Mullins got up again, and beat on the table for silence and made one of those cracking, concise speeches—just the way business men speak—the kind of speech that a college man simply can't make. I wish I could repeat it all. I remember that it began: "Now boys, you know what we're here for, gentlemen," and it went on just as good as that all through.

When Mullins had done he took out a fountain pen and wrote out a cheque for a hundred dollars, conditional on the fund reaching fifty thousand. And there was a burst of cheers all over the room.

Just the moment he had done it, up sprang George Duff,—you know the keen competition there is, as a straight manner of business, between the banks in Mariposa,—up sprang George Duff, I say, and wrote out a cheque for another hundred conditional on the fund reaching seventy thousand. You never heard such cheering in your life.

And then when Netley walked up to the head of the table and laid down a cheque for a hundred dollars conditional on the fund reaching one hundred thousand the room was in an uproar. A hundred thousand dollars! Just think of it! The figures fairly stagger one. To think of a hundred thousand dollars raised in five minutes in a little place like Mariposa!

And even that was nothing! In less than no time there was such a crowd round Mullins trying to borrow his pen all at once that his waistcoat was all stained with ink. Finally when they got order at last, and Mullins stood up and announced that the conditional fund had reached a quarter of a million, the whole place was a perfect babel[1] of cheering. Oh, these Whirlwind Campaigns are wonderful things!

• • • • •

I can tell you the Committee felt pretty proud that first day. There was Henry Mullins looking a little bit flushed and excited, with his white waistcoat and an American Beauty rose,[2] and with ink marks all over him from the cheque signing; and he kept telling them that he'd known all along that all that was needed was to get the thing started and telling again about what he'd seen at the University Campaign and about the professors crying, and wondering if the high school teachers would come down for the last day of the meetings.

Looking back on the Mariposa Whirlwind, I can never feel that it was a failure. After all, there is a sympathy and a brotherhood in these things when men work shoulder to shoulder. If you had seen the canvassers of the Committee going round the town that

---

1. In Genesis 11.1–9, Babel is the site of the tower of the same name that was built when "the whole earth was of one language" and with the ambition that its top might "reach heaven." Alarmed by such aspiration, God "confounded" or confused "the language of . . . the earth" and scattered the inhabitants of Babel "upon the face of all the earth."
2. Large hybrid rose renowned for its pink or red flowers.

evening shoulder to shoulder from the Mariposa House to the Continental and up to Mullins's rooms and over to Duff's, shoulder to shoulder, you'd have understood it.

I don't say that every lunch was quite such a success as the first. It's not always easy to get out of the store if you're a busy man, and a good many of the Whirlwind Committee found that they had just time to hurry down and snatch their lunch and get back again. Still, they came, and snatched it. As long as the lunches lasted, they came. Even if they had simply to rush it and grab something to eat and drink without time to talk to anybody, they came.

No, no, it was not lack of enthusiasm that killed the Whirlwind Campaign in Mariposa. It must have been something else. I don't just know what it was but I think it had something to do with the financial, the book-keeping side of the thing.

It may have been, too, that the organization was not quite correctly planned. You see, if practically everybody is on the committees, it is awfully hard to try to find men to canvass, and it is not allowable for the captains and the committee men to canvass one another, because their gifts are spontaneous. So the only thing that the different groups could do was to wait round in some likely place—say the bar parlour of Smith's Hotel—in the hope that somebody might come in who could be canvassed.

You might ask why they didn't canvass Mr. Smith himself, but of course they had done that at the very start, as I should have said. Mr. Smith had given them two hundred dollars in cash conditional on the lunches being held in the caff of his hotel; and it's awfully hard to get a proper lunch—I mean the kind to which a Bishop can express regret at not being there—under a dollar twenty-five. So Mr. Smith got back his own money, and the crowd began eating into the benefactions, and it got more and more complicated whether to hold another lunch in the hope of breaking even, or to stop the campaign.

It was disappointing, yes. In spite of all the success and the sympathy, it was disappointing. I don't say it didn't do good. No doubt a lot of the men got to know one another better than ever they had before. I have myself heard Judge Pepperleigh say that after the campaign he knew all of Pete Glover that he wanted to. There was a lot of that kind of complete satiety. The real trouble about the Whirlwind Campaign was that they never clearly understood which of them were the whirlwind and who were to be the campaign.

Some of them, I believe, took it pretty much to heart. I know that Henry Mullins did. You could see it. The first day he came down to the lunch, all dressed up with the American Beauty and the white waistcoat. The second day he only wore a pink carnation and a grey waistcoat. The third day he had on a dead daffodil and a cardigan undervest, and on the last day, when the high school teachers should have been there, he only wore his office suit and he hadn't even shaved. He looked beaten.

It was that night that he went up to the rectory to tell the news to Dean Drone. It had been arranged, you know, that the rector should not attend the lunches, so as to let the whole thing come as a surprise; so that all he knew about it was just scraps of information about the crowds at the lunch and how they cheered and all that. Once, I believe, he caught sight of the Newspacket with the two-inch headline: A QUARTER OF A MILLION, but he wouldn't let himself read further because it would have spoilt the surprise.

I saw Mullins, as I say, go up the street on his way to Dean Drone's. It was middle April and there was ragged snow on the streets, and the nights were dark still, and cold. I saw Mullins grit his teeth as he walked, and I know that he held in his coat pocket his own cheque for the hundred, with the condition taken off it, and he said that there were so many skunks in Mariposa that a man might as well be in the Head Office in the city.

The Dean came out to the little gate in the dark,—you could see the lamplight behind him from the open door of the rectory,—and he shook hands with Mullins and they went in together.

Chapter VI

The Beacon on the Hill

Mullins said afterward that it was ever so much easier than he thought it would have been. The Dean, he said, was so quiet. Of course if Mr. Drone had started to swear at Mullins, or tried to strike him, it would have been much harder. But as it was he was so quiet that part of the time he hardly seemed to follow what Mullins was saying. So Mullins was glad of that, because it proved that the Dean wasn't feeling disappointed as, in a way, he might have.

Indeed, the only time when the rector seemed animated and excited in the whole interview was when Mullins said that the campaign had been ruined by a lot of confounded mugwumps. Straight away the Dean asked if those mugwumps had really prejudiced the outcome of the campaign. Mullins said there was no doubt of it, and the Dean enquired if the presence of mugwumps was fatal in matters of endeavor, and Mullins said that it was. Then the rector asked if even one mugwump was, in the Christian sense, deleterious. Mullins said that one mugwump would kill anything. After that the Dean hardly spoke at all.

In fact, the rector presently said that he mustn't detain Mullins too long and that he had detained him too long already and that Mullins must be weary from his train journey and that in cases of extreme weariness nothing but a sound sleep was of any avail; he himself, unfortunately, would not be able to avail himself of the priceless boon of slumber until he had first retired to his study to write some letters; so that Mullins, who had a certain kind of social quickness of intuition, saw that it was time to leave, and went away.

It was midnight as he went down the street, and a dark, still night. That can be stated positively because it came out in court afterwards. Mullins swore that it was a dark night; he admitted, under examination, that there may have been the stars, or at least some of the less important of them, though he had made no attempt, as brought out on cross-examination, to count them: there may have been, too, the electric lights, and Mullins was not willing to deny that it was quite possible that there was more or less moonlight. But that there was no light that night in the form of sunlight, Mullins was absolutely certain. All that, I say, came out in court.

But meanwhile the rector had gone upstairs to his study and had seated himself in front of his table to write his letters. It was here always that he wrote his sermons. From the window of the room you looked through the bare white maple trees to the sweeping outline of the church shadowed against the night sky, and beyond that, though far off, was the new cemetery where the rector walked of a Sunday (I think I told you why): beyond that again, for the window faced the east, there lay, at no very great distance, the New Jerusalem.[1] There were no better things that a man might look towards from his study window, nor anything that could serve as a better aid to writing.

But this night the Dean's letters must have been difficult indeed to write. For he sat beside the table holding his pen and with his head bent upon his other hand, and though he sometimes put a line or two on the paper, for the most part he sat motionless. The fact is that Dean Drone was not trying to write letters, but only one letter. He was writing a letter of resignation. If you have not done that for forty years it is extremely difficult to get the words.

So at least the Dean found it. First he wrote one set of words and then he sat and thought and wrote something else. But nothing seemed to suit.

The real truth was that Dean Drone, perhaps more than he knew himself, had a fine taste for words and effects, and when you feel that a situation is entirely out of the common, you naturally try, if you have the instinct, to give it the right sort of expression.

1. City of God described in Revelation 3.12 and 21.2 as "com[ing] down out of heaven from . . . God" at the Last Judgement.

I believe that at the time when Rupert Drone had taken the medal in Greek over fifty years ago, it was only a twist of fate that had prevented him from becoming a great writer. There was a buried author in him just as there was a buried financier in Jefferson Thorpe. In fact, there were many people in Mariposa like that, and for all I know you may yourself have seen such elsewhere. For instance, I am certain that Billy Rawson, the telegraph operator at Mariposa, could easily have invented radium.[2] In the same way one has only to read the advertisements of Mr. Gingham, the undertaker, to know that there is still in him a poet, who could have written on death far more attractive verses than the Thanatopsis of Cullen Bryant,[3] and under a title less likely to offend the public and drive away custom. He has told me this himself.

So the Dean tried first this and then that and nothing would seem to suit. First of all he wrote:

"It is now forty years since I came among you, a youth full of life and hope and ardent in the work before me—" Then he paused, doubtful of the accuracy and clearness of the expression, read it over again and again in deep thought and then began again:

"It is now forty years since I came among you, a broken and melancholy boy, without life or hope, desiring only to devote to the service of this parish such few years as might remain of an existence blighted before it had truly begun—" And then again the Dean stopped. He read what he had written; he frowned; he crossed it through with his pen. This was no way to write, this thin egotistical strain of complaint. Once more he started:

"It is now forty years since I came among you, a man already tempered and trained, except possibly in mathematics—" And then again the rector paused and his mind drifted away to the memory of the Anglican professor that I spoke of, who had had so little sense of his higher mission as to omit the teaching of logarithms. And the rector mused so long that when he began again it seemed to him that it was simpler and better to discard the personal note altogether, and he wrote:

"There are times, gentlemen, in the life of a parish, when it comes to an epoch which brings it to a moment when it reaches a point—"

The Dean stuck fast again, but refusing this time to be beaten went resolutely on:

"—reaches a point where the circumstances of the moment make the epoch such as to focus the life of the parish in that time."

---

2. Radium was not invented but extracted by Pierre and Marie Curie from a ton of uranium.
3. A meditation on death in blank verse, "Thanatopsis" brought recognition to the American poet William Cullen Bryant (1794–1878) when it was first published in 1817. Its title from the Greek word for death means a view of, or reflection on, death.

Then the Dean saw that he was beaten, and he knew that he not only couldn't manage the parish but couldn't say so in proper English, and of the two the last was the bitterer discovery.

He raised his head, and looked for a moment through the window at the shadow of the church against the night, so outlined that you could almost fancy that the light of the New Jerusalem was beyond it. Then he wrote, and this time not to the world at large but only to Mullins:

"My dear Harry, I want to resign my charge. Will you come over and help me?"

· · · · ·

When the Dean at last rose from writing that, I think it was far on in the night. As he rose he looked again through the window, looked once and then once more, and so stood with widening eyes, and his face set towards what he saw.

What was that? That light in the sky there, eastward?—near or far he could not say. Was it already the dawn of the New Jerusalem brightening in the east, or was it—look—in the church itself,— what is that?—that dull red glow that shines behind the stained-glass windows, turning them to crimson? that fork of flame that breaks now from the casement and flashes upward, along the wood—and see—that sudden sheet of fire that springs the windows of the church with the roar of splintered glass and surges upward into the sky, till the dark night and the bare trees and sleeping street of Mariposa are all illumined with its glow!

Fire! Fire! and the sudden sound of the bell now, breaking upon the night.

So stood the Dean erect, with one hand pressed against the table for support, while the Mariposa fire bell struck out its warning to the sleeping town,—stood there while the street grew loud with the tumult of voices,—with the roaring gallop of the fire brigade,—with the harsh note of the gong—and over all other sounds, the great seething of the flames that tore their way into the beams and rafters of the pointed church and flared above it like a torch into the midnight sky.

So stood the Dean, and as the church broke thus into a very beacon kindled upon a hill,—sank forward without a sign, his face against the table, stricken.

· · · · ·

You need to see a fire in a place such as Mariposa, a town still half of wood, to know what fire means. In the city it is all different. To the onlooker, at any rate, a fire is only a spectacle, nothing more. Everything is arranged, organized, certain. It is only once perhaps in a century that fire comes to a large city as it comes to the little wooden town like Mariposa as a great Terror of the Night.

That, at any rate, is what it meant in Mariposa that night in April, the night the Church of England Church burnt down. Had the fire gained but a hundred feet, or less, it could have reached from the driving shed behind the church to the backs of the wooden shops of the Main Street, and once there not all the waters of Lake Wissanotti could stay the course of its destruction. It was for that hundred feet that they fought, the men of Mariposa, from the midnight call of the bell till the slow coming of the day.

They fought the fire, not to save the church, for that was doomed from the first outbreak of the flames, but to stop the spread of it and save the town. They fought it at the windows, and at the blazing doors, and through the yawning furnace of the open belfry; fought it, with the Mariposa engine thumping and panting in the street, itself aglow with fire like a servant demon fighting its own kind, with tall ladders reaching to the very roof, and with hose that poured their streams of tossing water foaming into the flames.

Most of all they fought to save the wooden driving shed behind the church from which the fire could leap into the heart of Mariposa. That was where the real fight was, for the life of the town. I wish you could have seen how they turned the hose against the shingles, ripping and tearing them from their places with the force of the driven water: how they mounted on the roof, axe in hand, and cut madly at the rafters to bring the building down, while the black clouds of smoke rolled in volumes about the men as they worked. You could see the fire horses harnessed with logging chains to the uprights of the shed to tear the building from its place.

Most of all I wish you could have seen Mr. Smith, proprietor, as I think you know, of Smith's Hotel, there on the roof with a fireman's helmet on, cutting through the main beam of solid cedar, twelve by twelve, that held tight still when the rafters and the roof tree were down already, the shed on fire in a dozen places, and the other men driven from the work by the flaming sparks, and by the strangle of the smoke. Not so Mr. Smith! See him there as he plants himself firm at the angle of the beams, and with the full impact of his two hundred and eighty pounds drives his axe into the wood! I tell you it takes a man from the pine country of the north to handle an axe! Right, left, left, right, down it comes, with never a pause or stay, never missing by a fraction of an inch the line of the stroke! At it, Smith! Down with it! Till with a shout from the crowd the beam gapes asunder, and Mr. Smith is on the ground again, roaring his directions to the men and horses as they haul down the shed, in a voice that dominates the fire itself.

Who made Mr. Smith the head and chief of the Mariposa fire brigade that night, I cannot say. I do not know even where he got the huge red helmet that he wore, nor had I ever heard till the night the church burnt down that Mr. Smith was a member of the fire brigade at all. But it's always that way. Your little narrow-chested men may plan and organize, but when there is something to be done, something real, then it's the man of size and weight that steps to the front every time. Look at Bismarck and Mr. Gladstone and President Taft[4] and Mr. Smith,—the same thing in each case.

I suppose it was perfectly natural that just as soon as Mr. Smith came on the scene he put on somebody's helmet and shouted his directions to the men and bossed the Mariposa fire brigade like Bismarck with the German parliament.

The fire had broken out late, late at night, and they fought it till the day. The flame of it lit up the town and the bare grey maple trees, and you could see in the light of it the broad sheet of the frozen lake, snow covered still. It kindled such a beacon as it burned that from the other side of the lake the people on the night express from the north could see it twenty miles away. It lit up such a testimony of flame that Mariposa has never seen the like of it before or since. Then when the roof crashed in and the tall steeple tottered and fell, so swift a darkness seemed to come that the grey trees and the frozen lake vanished in a moment as if blotted out of existence.

· · · · ·

When the morning came the great church of Mariposa was nothing but a ragged group of walls with a sodden heap of bricks and blackened wood, still hissing here and there beneath the hose with the sullen anger of a conquered fire.

Round the ruins of the fire walked the people of Mariposa next morning, and they pointed out where the wreck of the steeple had fallen, and where the bells of the church lay in a molten heap among the bricks, and they talked of the loss that it was and how many dollars it would take to rebuild the church, and whether it was insured and for how much. And there were at least fourteen people who had seen the fire first, and more than that who had given the first alarm, and ever so many who knew how fires of this sort could be prevented.

Most noticeable of all you could see the sidesmen and the wardens and Mullins, the chairman of the vestry, talking in little groups about the fire. Later in the day there came from the city the insurance men and the fire appraisers, and they too walked about the ruins, and talked with the wardens and the vestry men. There

---

4. William Howard Taft (1857–1930) was president of the United States from 1908 to 1912, Otto Edvard Leopold, prince von Bismarck (1815–1998) was the so-called Iron Chancellor of Germany, and William Ewart Gladstone (1809–1898) was three times prime minister of Great Britain during the second half of the nineteenth century. All three were men of great physical as well as political substance.

was such a luxury of excitement in the town that day that it was just as good as a public holiday.

But the strangest part of it was the unexpected sequel. I don't know through what error of the Dean's figures it happened, through what lack of mathematical training the thing turned out as it did. No doubt the memory of the mathematical professor was heavily to blame for it, but the solid fact is that the Church of England Church of Mariposa turned out to be insured for a hundred thousand, and there were the receipts and the vouchers, all signed and regular, just as they found them in a drawer of the rector's study. There was no doubt about it. The insurance people might protest as they liked. The straight, plain fact was that the church was insured for about twice the whole amount of the cost and the debt and the rector's salary and the boarding-school fees of the littlest of the Drones all put together.

· · · · ·

There was a Whirlwind Campaign for you! Talk of raising money,—that was something like! I wonder if the universities and the city institutions that go round trying to raise money by the slow and painful method called a Whirlwind Campaign, that takes perhaps all day to raise fifty thousand dollars, ever thought of anything so beautifully simple as this.

The Greater Testimony that had lain so heavily on the congregation went flaming to its end, and burned up its debts and its obligations and enriched its worshippers by its destruction. Talk of a beacon on a hill! You can hardly beat that one.

I wish you could have seen how the wardens and the sidesmen and Mullins, the chairman of the vestry, smiled and chuckled at the thought of it. Hadn't they said all along that all that was needed was a little faith and effort? And here it was, just as they said, and they'd been right after all.

Protest from the insurance people? Legal proceedings to prevent payment? My dear sir! I see you know nothing about the Mariposa court, in spite of the fact that I have already said that it was one of the most precise instruments of British fair play ever established. Why, Judge Pepperleigh disposed of the case and dismissed the protest of the company in less than fifteen minutes! Just what the jurisdiction of Judge Pepperleigh's court is I don't know, but I do know that in upholding the rights of a Christian congregation—I am quoting here the text of the decision—against the intrigues of a set of infernal skunks that make too much money, anyway, the Mariposa Court is without an equal. Pepperleigh even threatened the plaintiffs with the penitentiary, or worse.

How the fire started no one ever knew. There was a queer story that went about to the effect that Mr. Smith and Mr. Gingham's assistant had been seen very late that night carrying an automobile can of kerosene up the street. But that was amply disproved by the proceedings of the court, and by the evidence of Mr. Smith himself. He took his dying oath,—not his ordinary one as used in the License cases, but his dying one,—that he had not carried a can of kerosene up the street, and that anyway it was the rottenest kind of kerosene he had ever seen and no more use than so much molasses. So that point was settled.

Dean Drone? Did he get well again? Why, what makes you ask that? You mean, was his head at all affected after the stroke? No, it was not. Absolutely not. It was not affected in the least, though how anybody who knows him now in Mariposa could have the faintest idea that his mind was in any way impaired by the stroke is more that I can tell. The engaging of Mr. Uttermost, the curate, whom perhaps you have heard preach in the new church, had nothing whatever to do with Dean Drone's head. It was merely a case of the pressure of overwork. It was felt very generally by the wardens that, in these days of specialization, the rector was covering too wide a field, and that if he should abandon some of the lesser duties of his office, he might devote his energies more intently to the Infant Class. That was all. You may hear him there any afternoon, talking to them, if you will stand under the maple trees and listen through the open windows of the new Infant School.

And, as for audiences, for intelligence, for attention—well, if I want to find listeners who can hear and understand about the great spaces of Lake Huron, let me tell of it, every time face to face with the blue eyes of the Infant Class, fresh from the infinity of spaces greater still. Talk of grown-up people all you like, but for listeners let me have the Infant Class with their pinafores and their Teddy Bears and their feet not even touching the floor, and Mr. Uttermost may preach to his heart's content of the newer forms of doubt revealed by the higher criticism.[5]

So you will understand that the Dean's mind is, if anything, even keener, and his head even clearer than before. And if you want proof of it, notice him there beneath the plum blossoms reading in the Greek: he has told me that he finds that he can read, with the greatest ease, works in the Greek that seemed difficult before. Because his head is so clear now.

And sometimes,—when his head is very clear,—as he sits there reading beneath the plum blossoms he can hear them singing beyond, and his wife's voice.[6]

5. The intensive study of Biblical texts to determine their authorship, date, and place of origin, the results of which had a destabilizing impact on religious beliefs during the nineteenth and twentieth centuries.
6. This sentence is not in the version of the sketch that was published in the *Montreal Daily Star*.

Chapter VII

The Extraordinary Entanglement of Mr. Pupkin

Judge Pepperleigh lived in a big house with hardwood floors and a wide piazza that looked over the lake from the top of Oneida Street.

Every day about half-past five he used to come home from his office in the Mariposa Court House. On some days as he got near the house he would call out to his wife:

"Almighty Moses, Martha! who left the sprinkler on the grass?"

On other days he would call to her from quite a little distance off: "Hullo, mother! Got any supper for a hungry man?"

And Mrs. Pepperleigh never knew which it would be.

On the days when he swore at the sprinkler you could see his spectacles flash like dynamite. But on the days when he called: "Hullo, mother," they were simply irradiated with kindliness.

Some days, I say, he would cry out with a perfect whine of indignation: "Suffering Cæsar! has that infernal dog torn up those geraniums again?" And other days you would hear him singing out: "Hullo, Rover! Well, doggie, well, old fellow!"

In the same way at breakfast, the judge, as he looked over the morning paper, would sometimes leap to his feet with a perfect howl of suffering, and cry: "Everlasting Moses! the Liberals have carried East Elgin." Or else he would lean back from the breakfast table with the most good-humoured laugh you ever heard and say: "Ha! ha! the Conservatives have carried South Norfolk."

And yet he was perfectly logical, when you come to think of it. After all, what is more annoying to a sensitive, highly-strung man than an infernal sprinkler playing all over the place, and what more agreeable to a good-natured, even-tempered fellow than a well-prepared supper? Or, what is more likeable than one's good, old, affectionate dog bounding down the path from sheer delight at seeing you,—or more execrable than an infernal whelp that has torn up the geraniums and is too old to keep, anyway?

As for politics, well, it all seemed reasonable enough. When the Conservatives got in anywhere, Pepperleigh laughed and enjoyed it, simply because it does one good to see a straight, fine, honest fight where the best man wins. When a Liberal got in, it made him mad, and he said so,—not, mind you, from any political bias, for his office forbid it,—but simply because one can't bear to see the country go absolutely to the devil.

I suppose, too, it was partly the effect of sitting in court all day listening to cases. One gets what you might call the judicial temper of mind. Pepperleigh had it so strongly developed that I've seen him kick a hydrangea pot to pieces with his foot because the accursed thing wouldn't flower. He once threw the canary cage clear into the lilac bushes because the "blasted bird wouldn't stop singing." It was a straight case of judicial temper. Lots of judges have it, developed in just the same broad, all-round way as with Judge Pepperleigh.

· · · · ·

I think it must be passing sentences that does it. Anyway, Pepperleigh had the aptitude for passing sentences so highly perfected that he spent his whole time at it inside of court and out. I've heard him hand out sentences for the Sultan of Turkey[1] and Mrs. Pankhurst[2] and the Emperor of Germany[3] that made one's blood run cold. He would sit there on the piazza of a summer evening reading the paper, with dynamite sparks flying from his spectacles as he sentenced the Czar of Russia[4] to ten years in the salt mines— and made it fifteen a few minutes afterwards. Pepperleigh always read the foreign news—the news of things that he couldn't alter— as a form of wild and stimulating torment.

So you can imagine that in some ways the judge's house was a pretty difficult house to go to. I mean you can see how awfully hard it must have been for Mr. Pupkin. I tell you it took some nerve to step up on that piazza and say, in a perfectly natural, off-hand way: "Oh, how do you do, judge? Is Miss Zena in? No, I won't stay, thanks; I think I ought to be going. I simply called." A man who can do that has got to have a pretty fair amount of savoir what do you call it,[5] and he's got to be mighty well shaved and have his cameo pin put in his tie at a pretty undeniable angle before he can tackle it. Yes, and even then he may need to hang round behind the lilac bushes for half an hour first, and cool off. And he's apt to make pretty good time down Oneida Street on the way back.

Still, that's what you call love, and if you've got it, and are well shaved, and your boots well blacked, you can do things that seem almost impossible. Yes, you can do anything, even if you do trip over the dog in getting off the piazza.

Don't suppose for a moment that Judge Pepperleigh was an un-

1. Muhammad (or Mehmet) V (1844–1918) was the Ottoman Sultan of Turkey from 1909, when the Young Turk revolution deposed his brother Abd al-Hamid II, until his death in 1918. He exercised little power, however, and during his reign the influence of Germany on Turkish affairs increased.
2. Emmeline Pankhurst (1858–1928), the founder with her husband of the Women's Social and Political Union (1903) to further the cause of women's suffrage in Britain.
3. Wilhelm II (1859–1941), emperor of Germany and king of Prussia (1888–1918), whose many impulsive actions included sending a congratulatory telegram to the president of the Transvaal in South Africa after the Boers repulsed a British attack in December 1895.
4. Nicholas II (1868–1918), last czar of Russia (1894–1917), whose aggressive foreign policy led to the Russo-Japanese War (1904–1905) and whose autocratic domestic policy exacerbated the social unrest that led to the Russian revolution.
5. Savoir-faire (French): the faculty of knowing just what to do and how to do it.

approachable or a harsh man always and to everybody. Even Mr. Pupkin had to admit that that couldn't be so. To know that, you had only to see Zena Pepperleigh put her arm round his neck and call him Daddy. She would do that even when there were two or three young men sitting on the edge of the piazza. You know, I think, the way they sit on the edge in Mariposa. It is meant to indicate what part of the family they have come to see. Thus when George Duff, the bank manager, came up to the Pepperleigh house, he always sat in a chair on the verandah and talked to the judge. But when Pupkin or Mallory Tompkins or any fellow like that came, he sat down in a sidelong fashion on the edge of the boards and then they knew exactly what he was there for. If he knew the house well, he leaned his back against the verandah post and smoked a cigarette. But that took nerve.

But I am afraid that this is a digression, and, of course, you know all about it just as well as I do. All that I was trying to say was that I don't suppose that the judge had ever spoken a cross word to Zena in his life.—Oh, he threw her novel over the grape-vine, I don't deny that, but then why on earth should a girl read trash like the *Errant Quest of the Palladin Pilgrim*, and the *Life of Sir Galahad*, when the house was full of good reading like *The Life of Sir John A. Macdonald*, and *Pioneer Days in Tecumseh Township*?

• • • • •

Still, what I mean is that the judge never spoke harshly to Zena, except perhaps under extreme provocation; and I am quite sure that he never, never had to Neil. But then what father ever would want to speak angrily to such a boy as Neil Pepperleigh? The judge took no credit to himself for that; the finest grown boy in the whole country and so broad and big that they took him into the Missinaba Horse when he was only seventeen. And clever,—so clever that he didn't need to study; so clever that he used to come out at the foot of the class in mathematics at the Mariposa high school through sheer surplus of brain power. I've heard the judge explain it a dozen times. Why, Neil was so clever that he used to be able to play billiards at the Mariposa House all evening when the other boys had to stay at home and study.

Such a powerful looking fellow, too! Everybody in Mariposa remembers how Neil Pepperleigh smashed in the face of Peter McGinnis, the Liberal organizer, at the big election—you recall it— when the old Macdonald Government went out.[6] Judge Pepperleigh had to try him for it the next morning—his own son. They say there never was such a scene even in the Mariposa court. There was, I believe, something like it on a smaller scale in Roman

6. The government of Sir John A. Macdonald "went out" twice, in 1873 and 1891 (see p. 54 n. 3).

history, but it wasn't half as dramatic. I remember Judge Pepperleigh leaning forward to pass the sentence—for a judge is bound,
you know, by his oath—and how grave he looked and yet so proud
and happy, like a man doing his duty and sustained by it, and he
said:

"My boy, you are innocent. You smashed in Peter McGinnis's
face, but you did it without criminal intent. You put a face on him,
by Jehoshaphat! that he won't lose for six months, but you did it
without evil purpose or malign design. My boy, look up! Give me
your hand! You leave this court without a stain upon your name."

They said it was one of the most moving scenes ever enacted in
the Mariposa Court.

· · · · ·

But the strangest thing is that if the judge had known what
everyone else in Mariposa knew, it would have broken his heart. If
he could have seen Neil with the drunken flush on his face in the
billiard room of the Mariposa House—if he had known, as everyone else did, that Neil was crazed with drink the night he struck
the Liberal organizer when the old Macdonald Government went
out—if he could have known that even on that last day Neil was
drunk when he rode with the Missinaba Horse to the station to join
the Third Contingent for the war,[7] and all the street of the little
town was one great roar of people—

But the judge never knew, and now he never will. For if you
could find it in the meanness of your soul to tell him, it would serve
no purpose now except to break his heart, and there would rise up
to rebuke you the pictured vision of an untended grave somewhere
in the great silences of South Africa.

Did I say above, or seem to imply, that the judge sometimes
spoke harshly to his wife? Or did you gather for a minute that her
lot was one to lament over or feel sorry for? If so, it just shows that
you know nothing about such things, and that marriage, at least as
it exists in Mariposa, is a sealed book to you. You are as ignorant as
Miss Spiffkins, the biology teacher at the high school, who always
says how sorry she is for Mrs. Pepperleigh. You get that impression
simply because the judge howled like an Algonquin Indian when he

7. The Boer or South African War between Great Britain and two Afrikaner republics,
Transvaal and the Orange Free State, began in October 1899 and ended in May 1902.
The third of the three contingents sent by Canada was Strathcona's Horse, a regiment of
mounted riflemen personally funded by the fur trader and railroad financier Donald
Smith, the first Baron Strathcona and Mount Royal, who was Canada's High Commis-
sioner to Great Britain from 1896 to his death in 1914. At the height of the war between
February and August 1900, Canadian troops took part in several engagements, including
the battles of Paardeburg and Bloemfontein and the siege of Mafeking. Numerous
Canadians were decorated for bravery, including four with the Victoria Cross and nine-
teen with the Distinguished Service Medal, and there were nearly two hundred and fifty
Canadian casualties, over half of them from enteric fever and other diseases.

saw the sprinkler running on the lawn. But are you sure you know the other side of it? Are you quite sure when you talk like Miss Spiffkins does about the rights of it, that you are taking all things into account? You might have thought differently perhaps of the Pepperleighs, anyway, if you had been there that evening when the judge came home to his wife with one hand pressed to his temple and in the other the cablegram that said that Neil had been killed in action in South Africa. That night they sat together with her hand in his, just as they had sat together thirty years ago when he was a law student in the city.

Go and tell Miss Spiffkins that! Hydrangeas,—canaries,—temper,—blazes! What does Miss Spiffkins know about it all?

But in any case, if you tried to tell Judge Pepperleigh about Neil now he wouldn't believe it. He'd laugh it to scorn. That is Neil's picture, in uniform, hanging in the dining-room beside the Fathers of Confederation.[8] That military-looking man in the picture beside him is General Kitchener,[9] whom you may perhaps have heard of, for he was very highly spoken of in Neil's letters. All round the room, in fact, and still more in the judge's library upstairs, you will see pictures of South Africa and the departure of the Canadians (there are none of the return), and of Mounted Infantry and of Unmounted Cavalry and a lot of things that only soldiers and the fathers of soldiers know about.

So you can realize that for a fellow who isn't military, and who wears nothing nearer to a uniform than a daffodil tennis blazer, the judge's house is a devil of a house to come to.

I think you remember young Mr. Pupkin, do you not? I have referred to him several times already as the junior teller in the Exchange Bank. But if you know Mariposa at all you have often seen him. You have noticed him, I am sure, going for the bank mail in the morning in an office suit effect of clinging grey with a gold necktie pin shaped like a riding whip. You have seen him often enough going down to the lake front after supper, in tennis things, smoking a cigarette and with a paddle and a crimson canoe cushion under his arm. You have seen him entering Dean Drone's church in a top hat and a long frock coat nearly to his feet. You have seen him, perhaps, playing poker in Peter Glover's room over the hardware store and trying to look as if he didn't hold three aces,—in

<hr>

8. The delegates who attended one or more of the conferences in 1864 and 1866 at which the terms of the Canadian confederation were agreed upon. Among them were John A. Macdonald and Horatio Herbert Kitchener.
9. Horatio Herbert Kitchener (1850–1916), the first earl Kitchener of Khartoum, led British and Egyptian forces to decisive victories against the army of the Khalifa in 1896–98, most notably at the battles of Atbara and Omdurman. He also distinguished himself in the Boer (South African) War, serving in the Paardeberg and Bloemfontein offensives and in the subsequent advance on Pretoria.

fact, giving absolutely no sign of it beyond the wild flush in his face and the fact that his hair stands on end.

That kind of reticence is a thing you simply have to learn in banking. I mean, if you've got to be in a position where you know for a fact that the Mariposa Packing Company's account is over-drawn by sixty-four dollars, and yet daren't say anything about it, not even to the girls that you play tennis with,—I don't say, not a casual hint as a reference, but not really tell them, not, for in-stance, bring down the bank ledger to the tennis court and show them,—you learn a sort of reticence and self-control that people outside of banking circles never can attain.

Why, I've known Pupkin at the Firemen's Ball lean against the wall in his dress suit and talk away to Jim Eliot, the druggist, with-out giving the faintest hint or indication that Eliot's note for twenty-seven dollars had been protested that very morning. Not a hint of it. I don't say he didn't mention it, in a sort of way, in the supper room, just to one or two, but I mean there was nothing in the way he leant up against the wall to suggest it.

But, however, I don't mention that as either for or against Mr. Pupkin. That sort of thing is merely the A B C of banking, as he himself told me when explaining why it was that he hesitated to di-vulge the exact standing of the Mariposa Carriage Company. Of course, once you get past the A B C you can learn a lot that is mighty interesting.

So I think that if you know Mariposa and understand even the rudiments of banking, you are perfectly acquainted with Mr. Pup-kin. What? You remember him as being in love with Miss Lawson, the high school teacher? In love with HER? What a ridiculous idea. You mean merely because on the night when the Mariposa Belle sank with every soul on board, Pupkin put off from the town in a skiff to rescue Miss Lawson. Oh, but you're quite wrong. That wasn't LOVE. I've heard Pupkin explain it himself a dozen times. That sort of thing,—paddling out to a sinking steamer at night in a crazy skiff,—may indicate a sort of attraction, but not real love, not what Pupkin came to feel afterwards. Indeed, when he began to think of it, it wasn't even attraction, it was merely respect,—that's all it was. And anyway, that was long before, six or seven months back, and Pupkin admitted that at the time he was a mere boy.

• • • • •

Mr. Pupkin, I must explain, lived with Mallory Tompkins in rooms over the Exchange Bank, on the very top floor, the third, with Mullins's own rooms below them. Extremely comfortable quarters they were, with two bedrooms and a sitting-room that was all fixed up with snow-shoes and tennis rackets on the walls and dance pro-grammes and canoe clubs badges and all that sort of thing.

Mallory Tompkins was a young man with long legs and check trousers who worked on the Mariposa Times-Herald. That was what gave him his literary taste. He used to read Ibsen and that other Dutch author—Bumstone Bumstone,[1] isn't it?—and you can judge that he was a mighty intellectual fellow. He was so intellectual that he was, as he himself admitted, a complete eggnostic.[2] He and Pupkin used to have the most tremendous arguments about creation and evolution, and how if you study at a school of applied science you learn that there's no hell beyond the present life.

Mallory Tompkins used to prove absolutely that the miracles were only electricity, and Pupkin used to admit that it was an awfully good argument, but claimed that he had heard it awfully well answered in a sermon, though unfortunately he had forgotten how.

Tompkins used to show that the flood was contrary to geology, and Pupkin would acknowledge that the point was an excellent one, but that he had read a book,—the title of which he ought to have written down,—which explained geology away altogether.

Mallory Tompkins generally got the best of the merely logical side of the arguments, but Pupkin—who was a tremendous Christian—was much stronger in the things he had forgotten. So the discussions often lasted till far into the night, and Mr. Pupkin would fall asleep and dream of a splendid argument, which would have settled the whole controversy, only unfortunately he couldn't recall it in the morning.

Of course, Pupkin would never have thought of considering himself on an intellectual par with Mallory Tompkins. That would have been ridiculous. Mallory Tompkins had read all sorts of things and had half a mind to write a novel himself—either that or a play. All he needed, he said, was to have a chance to get away somewhere by himself and think. Every time he went away to the city Pupkin expected that he might return with the novel all finished; but though he often came back with his eyes red from thinking, the novel as yet remained incomplete.

Meantime, Mallory Tompkins, as I say, was a mighty intellectual fellow. You could see that from the books on the bamboo bookshelves in the sitting-room. There was, for instance, the "Encyclopædia Metropolitana"[3] in forty volumes, that he bought on the

---

1. Henrik Ibsen (1828–1906), author of A Doll's House (1879), Hedda Gabler (1890), and other plays was not Dutch but Norwegian, which was also the nationality of the poet, novelist, and dramatist Bjönstjerne Björnson (1832–1910), whose plays include Beyond Our Powers (1883) and Geography and Love (1889).
2. Agnostic.
3. The Encyclopaedia Metropolitana, which contains an Introduction by Samuel Taylor Coleridge, was published in twenty-six volumes between 1817 and 1845. A revised edition in forty volumes was published between 1848 and 1858.

instalment plan for two dollars a month. Then when they took that away, there was the "History of Civilization,"[4] in fifty volumes at fifty cents a week for fifty years. Tompkins had read in it half-way through the Stone Age before they took it from him. After that there was the "Lives of the Painters,"[5] one volume at a time—a splendid thing in which you could read all about Aahrens, and Aachenthal, and Aax and men of that class. After all, there's nothing like educating oneself. Mallory Tompkins knew about the opening period of all sorts of things, and in regard to people whose names began with "A" you couldn't stick him.

I don't mean that he and Mr. Pupkin lived a mere routine of studious evenings. That would be untrue. Quite often their time was spent in much less commendable ways than that, and there were poker parties in their sitting-room that didn't break up till nearly midnight. Card-playing, after all, is a slow business, unless you put money on it, and, besides, if you are in a bank and are handling money all day, gambling has a fascination.

I've seen Pupkin and Mallory Tompkins and Joe Milligan, the dentist, and Mitchell the ticket agent, and the other "boys" sitting round the table with matches enough piled up in front of them to stock a factory. Ten matches counted for one chip and ten chips made a cent—so you see they weren't merely playing for the fun of the thing. Of course it's a hollow pleasure. You realize that when you wake up at night parched with thirst, ten thousand matches to the bad. But banking is a wild life and everybody knows it.

Sometimes Pupkin would swear off and keep away from the cursed thing for weeks, and then perhaps he'd see by sheer accident a pile of matches on the table, or a match lying on the floor and it would start the craze in him. I am using his words—a "craze"—that's what he called it when he told Miss Lawson all about it, and she promised to cure him of it. She would have, too. Only, as I say, Pupkin found that what he had mistaken for attraction was only respect. And there's no use worrying a woman that you respect about your crazes.

· · · · ·

It was from Mallory Tompkins that Pupkin learned all about the Mariposa people, because Pupkin came from away off—somewhere down in the Maritime Provinces—and didn't know a soul. Mallory Tompkins used to tell him about Judge Pepperleigh, and what a wonderfully clever man he was and how he would have been in the

---

4. *A History of Civilization* by Emory Adams Allan was published in four volumes between 1887 and 1889 and in eight volumes in 1909. A work of the same title translated from the French of François Pierre Guillaume Guizot was published in 1846 and reprinted in 1901–02.
5. *The Lives of the Most Excellent Italian Architects, Painters and Sculptors* (1550, 1568) by the Italian painter, architect, and author Giorgio Vasari.

Supreme Court for certain if the Conservative Government had stayed in another fifteen or twenty years instead of coming to a premature end. He used to talk so much about the Pepperleighs, that Pupkin was sick of the very name. But just as soon as he had seen Zena Pepperleigh he couldn't hear enough of them. He would have talked with Tompkins for hours about the judge's dog Rover. And as for Zena, if he could have brought her name over his lips, he would have talked of her forever.

He first saw her—by one of the strangest coincidences in the world—on the Main Street of Mariposa. If he hadn't happened to be going up the street and she to be coming down it, the thing wouldn't have happened. Afterwards they both admitted that it was one of the most peculiar coincidences they ever heard of. Pupkin owned that he had had the strangest feeling that morning as if something were going to happen—a feeling not at all to be classed with the one of which he had once spoken to Miss Lawson, and which was, at the most, a mere anticipation of respect.

But, as I say, Pupkin met Zena Pepperleigh on the 26th of June, at twenty-five minutes to eleven. And at once the whole world changed. The past was all blotted out. Even in the new forty volume edition of the "Instalment Record of Humanity"[6] that Mallory Tompkins had just received—Pupkin wouldn't have bothered with it.

She—that word henceforth meant Zena—had just come back from her boarding-school, and of all times of year for coming back from a boarding-school and for wearing a white shirt waist and a crimson tie and for carrying a tennis racket on the stricken street of a town—commend me to the month of June in Mariposa.

And, for Pupkin, straight away the whole town was irradiated with sunshine, and there was such a singing of the birds, and such a dancing of the rippled waters of the lake, and such a kindliness in the faces of all the people, that only those who have lived in Mariposa, and been young there, can know at all what he felt.

The simple fact is that just the moment he saw Zena Pepperleigh, Mr. Pupkin was clean, plumb, straight, flat, absolutely in love with her.

Which fact is so important that it would be folly not to close the chapter and think about it.

6. No such work has been identified.

Chapter VIII

The Fore-ordained Attachment of Zena Pepperleigh and Peter Pupkin

Zena Pepperleigh used to sit reading novels on the piazza of the judge's house, half hidden by the Virginia creepers. At times the book would fall upon her lap and there was such a look of unstilled yearning in her violet eyes that it did not entirely disappear even when she picked up the apple that lay beside her and took another bite out of it.

With hands clasped she would sit there dreaming all the beautiful day-dreams of girlhood. When you saw that far-away look in her eyes, it meant that she was dreaming that a plumed and armoured knight was rescuing her from the embattled keep of a castle beside the Danube. At other times she was being borne away by an Algerian corsair[1] over the blue waters of the Mediterranean and was reaching out her arms towards France to say farewell to it.

Sometimes when you noticed a sweet look of resignation that seemed to rest upon her features, it meant that Lord Ronald de Chevereux was kneeling at her feet, and that she was telling him to rise, that her humbler birth must ever be a bar to their happiness, and Lord Ronald was getting into an awful state about it, as English peers do at the least suggestion of anything of the sort.

Or, if it wasn't that, then her lover had just returned to her side, tall and soldierly and sunburned, after fighting for ten years in the Soudan[2] for her sake, and had come back to ask her for her answer and to tell her that for ten years her face had been with him even in the watches[3] of the night. He was asking her for a sign, any kind of sign,—ten years in the Soudan entitles them to a sign,—and Zena was plucking a white rose, just one, from her hair, when she would hear her father's step on the piazza and make a grab for the *Pioneers of Tecumseh Township*, and start reading it like mad.

She was always, as I say, being rescued and being borne away, and being parted, and reaching out her arms to France and to

1. Pirate. In *The Corsair* (1814) by Lord Byron, the hero, Conrad, is a raffish but chivalrous pirate chief who rescues a beautiful slave, Gulnara, from a harem. Despite Gulnara's love for him, Conrad disappears at the end of the poem, only to return in *Lara* (1814) accompanied by a page who, of course, is Gulnara in disguise and in whose arms he finally dies.
2. The Soudan (or Sudan) is both the region that extends across the African continent south of the Sahara and Libyan deserts from Senegal in the west to the mountains of Ethiopia in the east and, probably more germanely, the area between Egypt and Uganda where General Charles Gordon and his army were massacred by Sudanese rebels at Khartoum in 1883 and where General Kitchener (see p. 87 n. 9) waged a successful campaign against the same rebels in 1896–98.
3. Waking periods.

Spain, and saying good-bye forever to Valladolid or the old grey towers of Hohenbranntwein.[4]

And I don't mean that she was in the least exceptional or romantic, because all the girls in Mariposa were just like that. An Algerian corsair could have come into the town and had a dozen of them for the asking, and as for a wounded English officer,—well, perhaps it's better not to talk about it outside or the little town would become a regular military hospital.

Because, mind you, the Mariposa girls are all right. You've only to look at them to realize that. You see, you can get in Mariposa a print dress of pale blue or pale pink for a dollar twenty that looks infinitely better than anything you ever see in the city,—especially if you can wear with it a broad straw hat and a background of maple trees and the green grass of a tennis court. And if you remember, too, that these are cultivated girls who have all been to the Mariposa high school and can do decimal fractions, you will understand that an Algerian corsair would sharpen his scimitar at the very sight of them.

Don't think either that they are all dying to get married; because they are not. I don't say they wouldn't take an errant knight, or a buccaneer or a Hungarian refugee, but for the ordinary marriages of ordinary people they feel nothing but a pitying disdain. So it is that each one of them in due time marries an enchanted prince and goes to live in one of the little enchanted houses in the lower part of the town.

I don't know whether you know it, but you can rent an enchanted house in Mariposa for eight dollars a month, and some of the most completely enchanted are the cheapest. As for the enchanted princes, they find them in the strangest places, where you never expected to see them, working—under a spell, you understand,—in drug-stores and printing offices, and even selling things in shops. But to be able to find them you have first to read ever so many novels about Sir Galahad and the Errant Quest[5] and that sort of thing.

• • • • •

Naturally then Zena Pepperleigh, as she sat on the piazza, dreamed of bandits and of wounded officers and of Lord Ronalds

4. Hohenbranntwein (German: Highbrandy) is not a real province or town, but it is evocative of several German locales with historical and romantic associations such as Hohenlinden (the site of a battle during the Napoleonic Wars) and Hohenstaufen (the site of a ruined castle). "Valladolid": a province in Spain and a city in the province with numerous historical and romantic buildings and associations: it was recovered from the Moors in the tenth century, served as the capital of Castile from 1454 to 1598, and contains a seventeenth-century royal palace.

5. Sir Galahad is the most perfect of King Arthur's Knights of the Round Table and the only one to be successful in the quest for the Holy Grail. His story is told by Sir Thomas Malory in Le Morte d'Arthur (1485) and by Alfred, Lord Tennyson in Idylls of the King (1842–91), as well as by numerous other writers.

riding on foam-flecked chargers. But that she ever dreamed of a junior bank teller in a daffodil blazer riding past on a bicycle, is pretty hard to imagine. So, when Mr. Pupkin came tearing past up the slope of Oneida Street at a speed that proved that he wasn't riding there merely to pass the house, I don't suppose that Zena Pepperleigh was aware of his existence.

That may be a slight exaggeration. She knew perhaps, that he was the new junior teller in the Exchange Bank and that he came from the Maritime Provinces, and that nobody knew who his people were, and that he had never been in a canoe in his life till he came to Mariposa, and that he sat four pews back in Dean Drone's church, and that his salary was eight hundred dollars. Beyond that, she didn't know a thing about him. She presumed, however, that the reason why he went past so fast was because he didn't dare to go slow.

This, of course, was perfectly correct. Ever since the day when Mr. Pupkin met Zena in the Main Street he used to come past the house on his bicycle just after bank hours. He would have gone past twenty times a day but he was afraid to. As he came up Oneida Street, he used to pedal faster and faster,—he never meant to, but he couldn't help it,—till he went past the piazza where Zena was sitting at an awful speed with his little yellow blazer flying in the wind. In a second he had disappeared in a buzz and a cloud of dust, and the momentum of it carried him clear out into the country for miles and miles before he ever dared to pause or look back.

Then Mr. Pupkin would ride in a huge circuit about the country, trying to think he was looking at the crops, and sooner or later his bicycle would be turned towards the town again and headed for Oneida Street, and would get going quicker and quicker and quicker, till the pedals whirled round with a buzz and he came past the judge's house again, like a bullet out of a gun. He rode fifteen miles to pass the house twice, and even then it took all the nerve that he had.

The people on Oneida Street thought that Mr. Pupkin was crazy, but Zena Pepperleigh knew that he was not. Already, you see, there was a sort of dim parallel between the passing of the bicycle and the last ride of Tancred the Inconsolable along the banks of the Danube.[6]

I have already mentioned, I think, how Mr. Pupkin and Zena Pepperleigh first came to know one another. Like everything else

---

6. A Norman knight and hero of the Crusades, Tancred appears in several literary works, including Tasso's *Jerusalem Delivered* (1580), where he unknowingly kills his beloved Clorinda, and Benjamin Disraeli's *Tancred; or, the New Crusade* (1847), where he falls in love with a beautiful Jewish woman, Eva, whom his parents prevent him from marrying. The Austrian portion of the Danube River is renowned for its picturesque scenery.

about them, it was a sheer matter of coincidence, quite inexplicable unless you understand that these things are foreordained.

That, of course, is the way with foreordained affairs and that's where they differ from ordinary love.

• • • • •

I won't even try to describe how Mr. Pupkin felt when he first spoke with Zena and sat beside her as they copied out the "endless chain" letter asking for ten cents. They wrote out, as I said, no less than eight of the letters between them, and they found out that their handwritings were so alike that you could hardly tell them apart, except that Pupkin's letters were round and Zena's letters were pointed and Pupkin wrote straight up and down and Zena wrote on a slant. Beyond that the writing was so alike that it was the strangest coincidence in the world. Of course when they made figures it was different and Pupkin explained to Zena that in the bank you have to be able to make a seven so that it doesn't look like a nine.

So, as I say, they wrote the letters all afternoon and when it was over they walked up Oneida Street together, ever so slowly. When they got near the house, Zena asked Pupkin to come in to tea, with such an easy off-hand way that you couldn't have told that she was half an hour late and was taking awful chances on the judge. Pupkin hadn't had time to say yes before the judge appeared at the door, just as they were stepping up on to the piazza, and he had a table napkin in his hand and the dynamite sparks were flying from his spectacles as he called out:

"Great heaven! Zena, why in everlasting blazes can't you get in to tea at a Christian hour?"

Zena gave one look of appeal to Pupkin, and Pupkin looked one glance of comprehension, and turned and fled down Oneida Street. And if the scene wasn't quite as dramatic as the renunciation of Tancred the Troubadour, it at least had something of the same elements in it.

Pupkin walked home to his supper at the Mariposa House on air, and that evening there was a gentle distance in his manner towards Sadie, the dining-room girl, that I suppose no bank clerk in Mariposa ever showed before. It was like Sir Galahad talking with the tire-women of Queen Guinevere[7] and receiving huckleberry pie at their hands.

After that Mr. Pupkin and Zena Pepperleigh constantly met together. They played tennis as partners on the grass court behind Dr. Gallagher's house,—the Mariposa Tennis Club rent it, you remem-

7. Lady's-maids of King Arthur's wife who was also Lancelot's lover. Guinevere's tale is told with varying degrees of sympathy in *Le Morte d'Arthur*, *Idylls of the King*, and numerous other works.

ber, for fifty cents a month,—and Pupkin used to perform perfect prodigies of valour, leaping in the air to serve with his little body hooked like a letter S. Sometimes, too, they went out on Lake Wissanotti in the evening in Pupkin's canoe, with Zena sitting in the bow and Pupkin paddling in the stern and they went out ever so far and it was after dark and the stars were shining before they came home. Zena would look at the stars and say how infinitely far away they seemed, and Pupkin would realize that a girl with a mind like that couldn't have any use for a fool such as him. Zena used to ask him to point out the Pleiades and Jupiter and Ursa minor, and Pupkin showed her exactly where they were. That impressed them both tremendously, because Pupkin didn't know that Zena remembered the names out of the astronomy book at her boarding-school, and Zena didn't know that Pupkin simply took a chance on where the stars were.

And ever so many times they talked so intimately that Pupkin came mighty near telling her about his home in the Maritime Provinces and about his father and mother, and then kicked himself that he hadn't the manliness to speak straight out about it and take the consequences.

Please don't imagine from any of this that the course of Mr. Pupkin's love ran smooth. On the contrary, Pupkin himself felt that it was absolutely hopeless from the start.

There were, it might be admitted, certain things that seemed to indicate progress.

In the course of the months of June and July and August, he had taken Zena out in his canoe thirty-one times. Allowing an average of two miles for each evening, Pupkin had paddled Zena sixty-two miles, or more than a hundred thousand yards. That surely was something.

He had played tennis with her on sixteen afternoons. Three times he had left his tennis racket up at the judge's house in Zena's charge, and once he had, with her full consent, left his bicycle there all night. This must count for something. No girl could trifle with a man to the extent of having his bicycle leaning against the verandah post all night and mean nothing by it.

More than that—he had been to tea at the judge's house fourteen times, and seven times he had been asked by Lilian Drone to the rectory when Zena was coming, and five times by Nora Gallagher to tea at the doctor's house because Zena was there.

Altogether he had eaten so many meals where Zena was that his meal ticket at the Mariposa lasted nearly double its proper time, and the face of Sadie, the dining-room girl, had grown to wear a look of melancholy resignation, sadder than romance.

Still more than that, Pupkin had bought for Zena, reckoning it altogether, about two buckets of ice cream and perhaps half a bushel of chocolate. Not that Pupkin grudged the expense of it. On the contrary, over and above the ice cream and the chocolate he had bought her a white waistcoat and a walking stick with a gold top, a lot of new neckties and a pair of patent leather boots—that is, they were all bought on account of her, which is the same thing.

Add to all this that Pupkin and Zena had been to the Church of England Church nearly every Sunday evening for two months, and one evening they had even gone to the Presbyterian Church "for fun," which, if you know Mariposa, you will realize to be a wild sort of escapade that ought to speak volumes.

• • • • •

Yet in spite of this, Pupkin felt that the thing was hopeless: which only illustrates the dreadful ups and downs, the wild alternations of hope and despair that characterise an exceptional affair of this sort.

Yes, it was hopeless.

Every time that Pupkin watched Zena praying in church, he knew that she was too good for him. Every time that he came to call for her and found her reading Browning[8] and Omar Khayyam[9] he knew that she was too clever for him. And every time that he saw her at all he realized that she was too beautiful for him.

You see, Pupkin knew that he wasn't a hero. When Zena would clasp her hands and talk rapturously about crusaders and soldiers and firemen and heroes generally, Pupkin knew just where he came in. Not in it, that was all. If a war could have broken out in Mariposa, or the judge's house had been invaded by the Germans, he might have had a chance, but as it was—hopeless.

Then there was Zena's father. Heaven knows Pupkin tried hard to please the judge. He agreed with every theory that Judge Pepperleigh advanced, and that took a pretty pliable intellect in itself. They denounced female suffrage one day and they favoured it the next. One day the judge would claim that the labour movement was eating out the heart of the country and the next day he would hold that the hope of the world lay in the organization of the toiling masses. Pupkin shifted his opinions like the glass in a kaleidoscope. Indeed, the only things on which he was allowed to maintain a steadfast conviction were the purity of the Conservative party of Canada and the awful wickedness of the recall of judges.

8. Probably the English poet Robert Browning (1812–1889), the author of such popular works as *Pippa Passes* (1841) and *Men and Women* (1855), but possibly his wife Elizabeth Barrett Browning (1806–1861), the author of such works as *Sonnets from the Portuguese* (1850) and *Aurora Leigh* (1857).
9. *The Rubáiyát of Omar Khayyám* (1859, 1868, 1872, 1879), Edward Fitzgerald's translation of the poems of the eleventh-century Persian poet Omar Khayyam was popular for its combination of hedonism and wisdom.

But with all that the judge was hardly civil to Pupkin. He hadn't asked him to the house till Zena brought him there, though, as a rule, all the bank clerks in Mariposa treated Judge Pepperleigh's premises as their own. He used to sit and sneer at Pupkin after he had gone till Zena would throw down the *Pioneers of Tecumseh Township* in a temper and flounce off the piazza to her room. After which the judge's manner would change instantly and he would re-light his corn cob pipe and sit and positively beam with content-ment. In all of which there was something so mysterious as to prove that Mr. Pupkin's chances were hopeless.

Nor was that all of it. Pupkin's salary was eight hundred dollars a year and the Exchange Bank limit for marriage was a thousand.

I suppose you are aware of the grinding capitalistic tyranny of the banks in Mariposa whereby marriage is put beyond the reach of ever so many mature and experienced men of nineteen and twenty and twenty-one, who are compelled to go on eating on a meal ticket at the Mariposa House and living over the bank to suit the whim of a group of capitalists.

Whenever Pupkin thought of this two hundred dollars he under-stood all that it meant by social unrest. In fact, he interpreted all forms of social discontent in terms of it. Russian Anarchism, German Socialism, the Labour Movement, Henry George, Lloyd George,[1]—he understood the whole lot of them by thinking of his two hundred dollars.

When I tell you that at this period Mr. Pupkin read *Memoirs of the Great Revolutionists*[2] and even thought of blowing up Henry Mullins with dynamite, you can appreciate his state of mind.

· · · · ·

But not even by all these hindrances and obstacles to his love for Zena Pepperleigh would Peter Pupkin have been driven to commit suicide (oh, yes; he committed it three times, as I'm going to tell you), had it not been for another thing that he knew stood once and for all and in cold reality between him and Zena.

He felt it in a sort of way, as soon as he knew her. Each time that he tried to talk to her about his home and his father and mother and found that something held him back, he realized more and more the kind of thing that stood between them. Most of all did he realize it, with a sudden sickness of heart, when he got word that

1. David Lloyd George (1863–1945) was prime minister of Great Britain from 1916 to 1926, but from 1908 to 1915 he was chancellor of the exchequer, in which role he pre-sented a budget in 1909 that advocated the use of land and income taxes to help pay for a system of social insurance. The budget was rejected by the House of Lords, the result being the elimination of Lords' power of veto by the Parliament Act of 1911. Henry George (1839–1937) was an American economist and reformer who achieved world-wide fame for his proposal in *Land and Land Policy* (1871) and *Progress and Poverty* (1879) that a single or flat tax on land would alleviate poverty.
2. No such work has been identified.

his father and mother wanted to come to Mariposa to see him and he had all he could do to head them off from it.

Why? Why stop them? The reason was, simply enough, that Pupkin was ashamed of them, bitterly ashamed. The picture of his mother and father turning up in Mariposa and being seen by his friends there and going up to the Pepperleighs' house made him feel faint with shame.

No, I don't say it wasn't wrong. It only shows what difference of fortune, the difference of being rich and being poor, means in this world. You perhaps have been so lucky that you cannot appreciate what it means to feel shame at the station of your own father and mother. You think it doesn't matter, that honesty and kindliness of heart are all that counts. That only shows that you have never known some of the bitterest feelings of people less fortunate than yourself.

So it was with Mr. Pupkin. When he thought of his father and mother turning up in Mariposa, his face reddened with unworthy shame.

He could just picture the scene! He could see them getting out of their Limousine touring car, with the chauffeur holding open the door for them, and his father asking for a suite of rooms,—just think of it, a suite of rooms!—at the Mariposa House.

The very thought of it turned him ill.

What! You have mistaken my meaning? Ashamed of them because they were poor? Good heavens, no, but because they were rich! And not rich in the sense in which they use the term in Mariposa, where a rich person merely means a man who has money enough to build a house with a piazza and to have everything he wants; but rich in the other sense,—motor cars, Ritz hotels, steam yachts, summer islands and all that sort of thing.

Why, Pupkin's father,—what's the use of trying to conceal it any longer?—was the senior partner in the law firm of Pupkin, Pupkin and Pupkin. If you know the Maritime Provinces at all, you've heard of the Pupkins. The name is a household word from Chedabucto to Chidabecto. And, for the matter of that, the law firm and the fact that Pupkin senior had been an Attorney General was the least part of it. Attorney General! Why, there's no money in that! It's no better than the Senate. No, no, Pupkin senior, like so many lawyers, was practically a promoter, and he blew companies like bubbles, and when he wasn't in the Maritime Provinces he was in Boston and New York raising money and floating loans, and when they had no money left in New York he floated it in London: and when he had it, he floated on top of it big rafts of lumber on the Miramichi and codfish on the Grand Banks and lesser fish in the Fundy Bay. You've heard perhaps of the Tidal Transportation

Company, and Fundy Fisheries Corporation, and the Paspebiac Pulp and Paper Unlimited? Well, all of those were Pupkin senior under other names. So just imagine him in Mariposa! Wouldn't he be utterly foolish there? Just imagine him meeting Jim Eliot and treating him like a druggist merely because he ran a drug store! or speaking to Jefferson Thorpe as if he were a barber simply because he shaved for money! Why, a man like that could ruin young Pupkin in Mariposa in half a day, and Pupkin knew it.

That wouldn't matter so much, but think of the Pepperleighs and Zena! Everything would be over with them at once. Pupkin knew just what the judge thought of riches and luxuries. How often had he heard the judge pass sentences of life imprisonment on Pierpont Morgan[3] and Mr. Rockefeller. How often had Pupkin heard him say that any man who received more than three thousand dollars a year (that was the judicial salary in the Missinaba district) was a mere robber, unfit to shake the hand of an honest man. Bitter! I should think he was! He was not so bitter, perhaps, as Mr. Muddleson, the principal of the Mariposa high school, who said that any man who received more than fifteen hundred dollars was a public enemy. He was certainly not so bitter as Trelawney, the post-master, who said that any man who got from society more than thirteen hundred dollars (apart from a legitimate increase in recognition of a successful election) was a danger to society. Still, he was bitter. They all were in Mariposa. Pupkin could just imagine how they would despise his father!

And Zena! That was the worst of all. How often had Pupkin heard her say that she simply hated diamonds, wouldn't wear them, despised them, wouldn't give a thank you for a whole tiara of them! As for motor cars and steam yachts,—well, it was pretty plain that that sort of thing had no chance with Zena Pepperleigh. Why, she had told Pupkin one night in the canoe that she would only marry a man who was poor and had his way to make and would hew down difficulties for her sake. And when Pupkin couldn't answer the argument she was quite cross and silent all the way home.

• • • • •

What was Peter Pupkin doing, then, at eight hundred dollars in a bank in Mariposa? If you ask that, it means that you know nothing of the life of the Maritime Provinces and the sturdy temper of the people. I suppose there are no people in the world who hate luxury and extravagance and that sort of thing quite as much as the Maritime Province people, and, of them, no one hated luxury more than Pupkin senior.

Don't mistake the man. He wore a long sealskin coat in winter, yes;

3. John Pierpont Morgan (1837–1913), American banker, financier, and art collector.

but mark you, not as a matter of luxury, but merely as a question of his lungs. He smoked, I admit it, a thirty-five cent cigar, not because he preferred it, but merely through a delicacy of the thorax that made it imperative. He drank champagne at lunch, I concede that point, not in the least from the enjoyment of it, but simply on account of a peculiar affection of the tongue and lips that positively dictated it. His own longing—and his wife shared it—was for the simple, simple life—an island somewhere, with birds and trees. They had bought three or four islands—one in the St. Lawrence, and two in the Gulf, and one off the coast of Maine—looking for this sort of thing. Pupkin senior often said that he wanted to have some place that would remind him of the little old farm up the Aroostook where he was brought up. He often bought little old farms, just to try them, but they always turned out to be so near a city that he cut them into real estate lots, without even having had time to look at them.

But—and this is where the emphasis lay—in the matter of luxury for his only son, Peter, Pupkin senior was a Maritime Province man right to the core, with all the hardihood of the United Empire Loyalists[4] ingrained in him. No luxury for that boy! No, sir! From his childhood, Pupkin senior had undertaken, at the least sign of luxury, to "tan it out of him," after the fashion still in vogue in the provinces. Then he sent him to an old-fashioned school to get it "thumped out of him," and after that he had put him for a year on a Nova Scotia schooner to get it "knocked out of him." If, after all that, young Pupkin, even when he came to Mariposa, wore cameo pins and daffodil blazers, and broke out into ribbed silk saffron ties on pay day, it only shows that the old Adam[5] still needs further tanning even in the Maritime Provinces.

Young Pupkin, of course, was to have gone into law. That was his father's cherished dream and would have made the firm Pupkin, Pupkin, Pupkin, and Pupkin, as it ought to have been. But young Peter was kept out of the law by the fool system of examinations devised since his father's time. Hence there was nothing for it but to sling him into a bank; "sling him" was, I think, the expression. So his father decided that if Pupkin was to be slung, he should be slung good and far—clean into Canada (you know the way they use that word in the Maritime Provinces).[6] And to sling Pupkin he called in the services of an old friend, a man after his own heart,

4. Persons loyal to the British Crown during the American War of Independence, many of whom moved to what is now Nova Scotia and New Brunswick during and after the hostilities.
5. The Adam who with Eve bequeathed innate depravity and corruption to his descendants for eating the fruit of the Tree of Knowledge of Good and Evil in Eden (Genesis 2) (as opposed to the new Adam, Christ).
6. Even after Confederation, the word *Canada* continued to be used in New Brunswick, Nova Scotia, and Prince Edward Island to refer specifically to present-day Ontario and Quebec, which had been united as the Province of Canada in 1841.

just as violent as himself, who used to be at the law school in the city with Pupkin senior thirty years ago. So this friend, who happened to live in Mariposa, and who was a violent man, said at once: "Edward, by Jehosephat! send the boy up here."

So that is how Pupkin came to Mariposa. And if, when he got there, his father's friend gave no sign, and treated the boy with roughness and incivility, that may have been, for all I know, a continuation of the "tanning" process of the Maritime people.

Did I mention that the Pepperleigh family, generations ago, had taken up land near the Aroostook, and that it was from there the judge's father came to Tecumseh township? Perhaps not, but it doesn't matter.

But surely after such reminiscences as these, the awful things that are impending over Mr. Pupkin must be kept for another chapter.

Chapter IX

The Mariposa Bank Mystery

Suicide is a thing that ought not to be committed without very careful thought. It often involves serious consequences, and in some cases brings pain to others than oneself.

I don't say that there is no justification for it. There often is. Anybody who has listened to certain kinds of music, or read certain kinds of poetry, or heard certain kinds of performances upon the concertina, will admit that there are some lives which ought not to be continued, and that even suicide has its brighter aspects.

But to commit suicide on grounds of love is at the best a very dubious experiment. I know that in this I am expressing an opinion contrary to that of most true lovers who embrace suicide on the slightest provocation as the only honourable termination of an existence that never ought to have begun.

I quite admit that there is a glamour and a sensation about the thing which has its charm, and that there is nothing like it for causing a girl to realize the value of the heart that she has broken and which breathed forgiveness upon her at the very moment when it held in its hand the half-pint of prussic acid that was to terminate its beating for ever.

But apart from the general merits of the question, I suppose there are few people, outside of lovers, who know what it is to commit suicide four times in five weeks.

Yet this was what happened to Mr. Pupkin, of the Exchange Bank of Mariposa.

Ever since he had known Zena Pepperleigh he had realized that his love for her was hopeless. She was too beautiful for him and too good for him; her father hated him and her mother despised him; his salary was too small and his own people were too rich.

If you add to all that that he came up to the judge's house one night and found a poet reciting verses to Zena, you will understand the suicide at once. It was one of those regular poets with a solemn jackass face, and lank parted hair and eyes like puddles of molasses. I don't know how he came there—up from the city, probably—but there he was on the Pepperleighs' verandah that August evening. He was reciting poetry—either Tennyson's or Shelley's,[1] or his own, you couldn't tell—and about him sat Zena with her hands clasped and Nora Gallagher looking at the sky and Jocelyn Drone gazing into infinity, and a little tubby woman looking at the poet with her head falling over sideways[2]—in fact, there was a whole group of them.

• • • • •

I don't know what it is about poets that draws women to them in this way. But everybody knows that a poet has only to sit and saw the air with his hands and recite verses in a deep stupid voice, and all the women are crazy over him. Men despise him and would kick him off the verandah if they dared, but the women simply rave over him.

So Pupkin sat there in the gloom and listened to this poet reciting Browning[3] and he realized that everybody understood it but him. He could see Zena with her eyes fixed on the poet as if she were hanging on to every syllable (she was; she needed to), and he stood it just about fifteen minutes and then slid off the side of the verandah and disappeared without even saying good-night.

He walked straight down Oneida Street and along the Main Street just as hard as he could go. There was only one purpose in his mind,—suicide. He was heading straight for Jim Eliot's drug store on the main corner and his idea was to buy a drink of chloroform and drink it and die right there on the spot.

As Pupkin walked down the street, the whole thing was so vivid in his mind that he could picture it to the remotest detail. He could even see it all in type, in big headings in the newspapers of the following day:

---

1. The poetry of either Alfred, Lord Tennyson (1809–1892), the British poet laureate from 1850 to his death and for the most part an exemplar of Victorian values, or Percy Bysshe Shelley (1792–1822), an English Romantic poet whose radical ideas starkly distinguish most of his poems from Tennyson's.
2. Coupled with the earlier description of the poet, the presence of his adoring female companion suggests the Canadian poet Bliss Carman (1861–1929) and his close friend and collaborator Mary Perry King (1865–1939) as possible models for the pair.
3. Robert Browning (see p. 97, n. 8).

APPALLING SUICIDE.
PETER PUPKIN POISONED.

He perhaps hoped that the thing might lead to some kind of public enquiry and that the question of Browning's poetry and whether it is altogether fair to allow of its general circulation would be fully ventilated in the newspapers.

Thinking all that, Pupkin came to the main corner.

On a warm August evening the drug store of Mariposa, as you know, is all a blaze of lights. You can hear the hissing of the soda-water fountain half a block away, and inside the store there are ever so many people—boys and girls and old people too—all drinking sarsaparilla[4] and chocolate sundaes and lemon sours and foaming drinks that you take out of long straws. There is such a laughing and a talking as you never heard, and the girls are all in white and pink and cambridge blue,[5] and the soda fountain is of white marble with silver taps, and it hisses and sputters, and Jim Eliot and his assistant wear white coats with red geraniums in them, and it's all just gay as gay.

The foyer of the opera in Paris may be a fine sight,[6] but I doubt if it can compare with the inside of Eliot's drug store in Mariposa—for real gaiety and joy of living.

This night the store was especially crowded because it was a Saturday and that meant early closing for all the hotels, except, of course, Smith's. So as the hotels were shut, the people were all in the drug store, drinking like fishes. It just shows the folly of Local Option and the Temperance Movement and all that. Why, if you shut the hotels you simply drive the people to the soda fountains and there's more drinking than ever, and not only of the men, too, but the girls and young boys and children. I've seen little things of eight and nine that had to be lifted up on the high stools at Eliot's drug store, drinking great goblets of lemon soda, enough to burst them—brought there by their own fathers, and why? Simply because the hotel bars were shut.

What's the use of thinking you can stop people drinking merely by cutting off whiskey and brandy? The only effect is to drive them to taking lemon sour and sarsaparilla and cherry pectoral and caroka cordial[7] and things they wouldn't have touched before. So in

---

4. A beverage made from the roots of certain tropical American plants.
5. Light blue, the colour worn by the sports teams of the University of Cambridge, England.
6. The spectacular foyer of the Opéra (1861–75) is an extravagant example of the Baroque style that uses curvaceous forms and lavish decoration to create a stunning visual display.
7. Cherry-flavoured chest medicine and a medicinal and/or alcoholic drink possibly containing karoka (*Dandanus spp.* or screw pine), a plant whose fruit is an ingredient of some Asian cuisines, or, perhaps more likely, carika (*Carica papaya L.* or papaya), the seeds, fruits, and juices of which have been used as, among other things, laxatives, vermifuges, heart medicines, and aborteficiants.

the long run they drink more than ever. The point is that you can't prevent people having a good time, no matter how hard you try. If they can't have it with lager beer and brandy, they'll have it with plain soda and lemon pop, and so the whole gloomy scheme of the temperance people breaks down, anyway.

But I was only saying that Eliot's drug store in Mariposa on a Saturday night is the gayest and brightest spot in the world.

And just imagine what a fool of a place to commit suicide in!

Just imagine going up to the soda-water fountain and asking for five cents' worth of chloroform and soda! Well, you simply can't, that's all.

That's the way Pupkin found it. You see, as soon as he came in, somebody called out: "Hello, Pete!" and one or two others called: "Hullo, Pup!" and some said: "How goes it?" and others: "How are you toughing it?" and so on, because you see they had all been drinking more or less and naturally they felt jolly and glad-hearted.

So the upshot of it was that instead of taking chloroform, Pupkin stepped up to the counter of the fountain and he had a bromo-seltzer[8] with cherry soda, and after that he had one of those aerated seltzers, and then a couple of lemon seltzers and a bromophizzer.

I don't know if you know the mental effect of a bromo-seltzer.

But it's a hard thing to commit suicide on.

You can't.

You feel so buoyant.

Anyway, what with the phizzing of the seltzer and the lights and the girls, Pupkin began to feel so fine that he didn't care a cuss for all the Browning in the world, and as for the poet—oh, to blazes with him! What's poetry, anyway?—only rhymes.

So, would you believe it, in about ten minutes Peter Pupkin was off again and heading straight for the Pepperleighs' house, poet or no poet, and, what was more to the point, he carried with him three great bricks of Eliot's ice cream—in green, pink and brown layers. He struck the verandah just at the moment when Browning was getting too stale and dreary for words. His brain was all sizzling and jolly with the bromo-seltzer, and when he fetched out the ice cream bricks and Zena ran to get plates and spoons to eat it with, and Pupkin went with her to help fetch them and they picked out the spoons together, they were so laughing and happy that it was just a marvel. Girls, you know, need no bromo-seltzer. They're full of it all the time.

And as for the poet—well, can you imagine how Pupkin felt when Zena told him that the poet was married, and that the tubby little woman with her head on sideways was his wife?

8. Effervescing mineral water containing bromine.

So they had the ice cream, and the poet ate it in bucketsful. Poets always do. They need it. And after it the poet recited some stanzas of his own and Pupkin saw that he had misjudged the man, because it was dandy poetry, the very best. That night Pupkin walked home on air and there was no thought of chloroform, and it turned out that he hadn't committed suicide, but like all lovers he had commuted it.

• • • • •

I don't need to describe in full the later suicides of Mr. Pupkin, because they were all conducted on the same plan and rested on something the same reasons as above.

Sometimes he would go down at night to the offices of the bank below his bedroom and bring up his bank revolver in order to make an end of himself with it. This, too, he could see headed up in the newspapers as:

BRILLIANT BOY BANKER BLOWS OUT BRAINS.

But blowing your brains out is a noisy, rackety performance, and Pupkin soon found that only special kinds of brains are suited for it. So he always sneaked back again later in the night and put the revolver in its place, deciding to drown himself instead. Yet every time that he walked down to the Trestle Bridge over the Ossawippi he found it was quite unsuitable for drowning—too high, and the water too swift and black, and the rushes too gruesome—in fact, not at all the kind of place for a drowning.

Far better, he realized, to wait there on the railroad track and throw himself under the wheels of the express and be done with it. Yet, though Pupkin often waited in this way for the train, he was never able to pick out a pair of wheels that suited him. Anyhow, it's awfully hard to tell an express from a fast freight.

I wouldn't mention these attempts at suicide if one of them hadn't finally culminated in making Peter Pupkin a hero and solving for him the whole perplexed entanglement of his love affair with Zena Pepperleigh. Incidentally it threw him into the very centre of one of the most impenetrable bank mysteries that ever baffled the ingenuity of some of the finest legal talent that ever adorned one of the most enterprising communities in the country.

It happened one night, as I say, that Pupkin decided to go down into the office of the bank and get his revolver and see if it would blow his brains out. It was the night of the Firemen's Ball and Zena had danced four times with a visitor from the city, a man who was in the fourth year at the University and who knew everything. It was more than Peter Pupkin could bear. Mallory Tompkins was away that night, and when Pupkin came home he was all alone in the building, except for Gillis, the caretaker, who lived in the extension at the back.

He sat in his room for hours brooding. Two or three times he picked up a book—he remembered afterwards distinctly that it was *Kant's Critique of Pure Reason*[9]—and tried to read it, but it seemed meaningless and trivial. Then with a sudden access of resolution he started from his chair and made his way down the stairs and into the office room of the bank, meaning to get a revolver and kill himself on the spot and let them find his body lying on the floor.

It was then far on in the night and the empty building of the bank was as still as death. Pupkin could hear the stairs creak under his feet, and as he went he thought he heard another sound like the opening or closing of a door. But it sounded not like the sharp ordinary noise of a closing door but with a dull muffled noise as if someone had shut the iron door of a safe in a room under the ground. For a moment Pupkin stood and listened with his heart thumping against his ribs. Then he kicked his slippers from his feet and without a sound stole into the office on the ground floor and took the revolver from his teller's desk. As he gripped it, he listened to the sounds on the back-stairway and in the vaults below.

I should explain that in the Exchange Bank of Mariposa the offices are on the ground floor level with the street. Below this is another floor with low dark rooms paved with flagstones, with unused office desks and with piles of papers stored in boxes. On this floor are the vaults of the bank, and lying in them in the autumn—the grain season—there is anything from fifty to a hundred thousand dollars in currency tied in bundles. There is no other light down there than the dim reflection from the lights out on the street, that lies in patches on the stone floor.

I think as Peter Pupkin stood, revolver in hand, in the office of the bank, he had forgotten all about the maudlin purpose of his first coming. He had forgotten for the moment all about heroes and love affairs, and his whole mind was focused, sharp and alert, with the intensity of the night-time, on the sounds that he heard in the vault and on the back-stairway of the bank.

Straight away, Pupkin knew what it meant as plainly as if it were written in print. He had forgotten, I say, about being a hero and he only knew that there was sixty thousand dollars in the vault of the bank below, and that he was paid eight hundred dollars a year to look after it.

As Peter Pupkin stood there listening to the sounds in his stockinged feet, his face showed grey as ashes in the light that fell through the window from the street. His heart beat like a hammer against his ribs. But behind its beatings was the blood of four generations of Loyalists, and the robber who would take that sixty

9. *Critique of Pure Reason* (1781) by the German philosopher Immanuel Kant (1724–1804) is a criticism of eighteenth-century empirical philosophy.

thousand dollars from the Mariposa bank must take it over the dead body of Peter Pupkin, teller.

• • • • •

Pupkin walked down the stairs to the lower room, the one below the ground with the bank vault in it, with as fine a step as any of his ancestors showed on parade. And if he had known it, as he came down the stairway in the front of the vault room, there was a man crouched in the shadow of the passage way by the stairs at the back. This man, too, held a revolver in his hand, and, criminal or not, his face was as resolute as Pupkin's own. As he heard the teller's step on the stair, he turned and waited in the shadow of the doorway without a sound.

There is no need really to mention all these details. They are only of interest as showing how sometimes a bank teller in a corded[1] smoking jacket and stockinged feet may be turned into such a hero as even the Mariposa girls might dream about.

All of this must have happened at about three o'clock in the night. This much was established afterwards from the evidence of Gillis, the caretaker. When he first heard the sounds he had looked at his watch and noticed that it was half-past two; the watch he knew was three-quarters of an hour slow three days before and had been gaining since. The exact time at which Gillis heard footsteps in the bank and started downstairs, pistol in hand, became a nice point afterwards in the cross-examination.

But one must not anticipate. Pupkin reached the iron door of the bank safe, and knelt in front of it, feeling in the dark to find the fracture of the lock. As he knelt, he heard a sound behind him, and swung round on his knees and saw the bank robber in the half light of the passage way and the glitter of a pistol in his hand. The rest was over in an instant. Pupkin heard a voice that was his own, but that sounded strange and hollow, call out: "Drop that, or I'll fire!" and then just as he raised his revolver, there came a blinding flash of light before his eyes, and Peter Pupkin, junior teller of the bank, fell forward on the floor and knew no more.

• • • • •

At that point, of course, I ought to close down a chapter, or volume, or, at least, strike the reader over the head with a sandbag to force him to stop and think. In common fairness one ought to stop here and count a hundred or get up and walk round a block, or, at any rate, picture to oneself Peter Pupkin lying on the floor of the bank, motionless, his arms distended, the revolver still grasped in his hand. But I must go on.

By half-past seven on the following morning it was known all

---

1. Fastened with cords rather than buttons.

over Mariposa that Peter Pupkin the junior teller of the Exchange had been shot dead by a bank robber in the vault of the building. It was known also that Gillis, the caretaker, had been shot and killed at the foot of the stairs, and that the robber had made off with fifty thousand dollars in currency; that he had left a trail of blood on the sidewalk and that the men were out tracking him with bloodhounds in the great swamps to the north of the town.

This, I say, and it is important to note it, was what they knew at half-past seven. Of course as each hour went past they learned more and more. At eight o'clock it was known that Pupkin was not dead, but dangerously wounded in the lungs. At eight-thirty it was known that he was not shot in the lungs, but that the ball had traversed the pit of his stomach.

At nine o'clock it was learned that the pit of Pupkin's stomach was all right, but that the bullet had struck his right ear and carried it away. Finally it was learned that his ear had not exactly been carried away, that is, not precisely removed by the bullet, but that it had grazed Pupkin's head in such a way that it had stunned him, and if it had been an inch or two more to the left it might have reached his brain. This, of course, was just as good as being killed from the point of view of public interest.

Indeed, by nine o'clock Pupkin could be himself seen on the Main Street with a great bandage sideways on his head, pointing out the traces of the robber. Gillis, the caretaker, too, it was known by eight, had not been killed. He had been shot through the brain, but whether the injury was serious or not was only a matter of conjecture. In fact, by ten o'clock it was understood that the bullet from the robber's second shot had grazed the side of the caretaker's head, but as far as could be known his brain was just as before. I should add that the first report about the bloodstains and the swamp and the bloodhounds turned out to be inaccurate. The stains may have been blood, but as they led to the cellar way of Netley's store they may have also been molasses, though it was argued, to be sure, that the robber might well have poured molasses over the bloodstains from sheer cunning.

It was remembered, too, that there were no bloodhounds in Mariposa, although, mind you, there are any amount of dogs there.

So you see that by ten o'clock in the morning the whole affair was settling into the impenetrable mystery which it ever since remained.

Not that there wasn't evidence enough. There was Pupkin's own story and Gillis's story, and the stories of all the people who had heard the shots and seen the robber (some said, the bunch of robbers) go running past (others said, walking past), in the night. Apparently the robber ran up and down half the streets of Mariposa before he vanished.

But the stories of Pupkin and Gillis were plain enough. Pupkin related that he heard sounds in the bank and came downstairs just in time to see the robber crouching in the passage-way, and that the robber was a large hulking, villainous looking man, wearing a heavy coat. Gillis told exactly the same story, having heard the noises at the same time, except that he first described the robber as a small thin fellow (peculiarly villainous looking, however, even in the dark), wearing a short jacket; but on thinking it over, Gillis realized that he had been wrong about the size of the criminal, and that he was even bigger, if anything, than what Mr. Pupkin thought. Gillis had fired at the robber; just at the same moment had Mr. Pupkin.

Beyond that, all was mystery, absolute and impenetrable.

By eleven o'clock the detectives had come up from the city under orders from the head of the bank.

· · · · ·

I wish you could have seen the two detectives as they moved to and fro in Mariposa—fine looking, stern, impenetrable men that they were. They seemed to take in the whole town by instinct and so quietly. They found their way to Mr. Smith's Hotel just as quietly as if it wasn't design at all and stood there at the bar, picking up scraps of conversation—you know the way detectives do it. Occasionally they allowed one or two bystanders—confederates, perhaps—to buy a drink for them, and you could see from the way they drank it that they were still listening for a clue. If there had been the faintest clue in Smith's Hotel or in the Mariposa House or in the Continental, those fellows would have been at it like a flash.

To see them moving round the town that day—silent, massive, imperturbable—gave one a great idea of their strange, dangerous calling. They went about the town all day and yet in such a quiet peculiar way that you couldn't have realized that they were working at all. They ate their dinner together at Smith's café and took an hour and a half over it to throw people off the scent. Then when they got them off it, they sat and talked with Josh Smith in the back bar to keep them off. Mr. Smith seemed to take to them right away. They were men of his own size, or near it, and anyway hotel men and detectives have a general affinity and share in the same impenetrable silence and in their confidential knowledge of the weaknesses of the public.

Mr. Smith, too, was of great use to the detectives. "Boys," he said, "I wouldn't ask too close as to what folks was out late at night: in this town it don't do."

When those two great brains finally left for the city on the five-thirty, it was hard to realize that behind each grand, impassible face a perfect vortex of clues was seething.

But if the detectives were heroes, what was Pupkin? Imagine him with his bandage on his head standing in front of the bank and talking of the midnight robbery with that peculiar false modesty that only heroes are entitled to use.

I don't know whether you have ever been a hero, but for sheer exhilaration there is nothing like it. And for Mr. Pupkin, who had gone through life thinking himself no good, to be suddenly exalted into the class of Napoleon Bonaparte and John Maynard[2] and the Charge of the Light Brigade[3]—oh, it was wonderful. Because Pupkin was a brave man now and he knew it and acquired with it all the brave man's modesty. In fact, I believe he was heard to say that he had only done his duty, and that what he did was what any other man would have done: though when somebody else said: "That's so, when you come to think of it," Pupkin turned on him that quiet look of the wounded hero, bitterer than words.

And if Pupkin had known that all of the afternoon papers in the city reported him dead, he would have felt more luxurious still.

That afternoon the Mariposa court sat in enquiry,—technically it was summoned in inquest on the dead robber—though they hadn't found the body—and it was wonderful to see them lining up the witnesses and holding cross-examinations. There is something in the cross-examination of great criminal lawyers like Nivens, of Mariposa, and in the counter examinations of presiding judges like Pepperleigh that thrills you to the core with the astuteness of it.

They had Henry Mullins, the manager, on the stand for an hour and a half, and the excitement was so breathless that you could have heard a pin drop. Nivens took him on first.

"What is your name?" he said.

"Henry Augustus Mullins."

"What position do you hold?"

"I am manager of the Exchange Bank."

"When were you born?"

"December 30, 1869."[4]

---

2. A legendary figure probably based on Luther Fuller, the wheelman on duty on the steamer *Erie* when it caught fire off Buffalo on August 9, 1841, and sank with the loss of some 200 lives, John Maynard is the hero of several short stories and poems in which he is burned to death while steering the steamer to safety. "John Maynard: A Ballad of Lake Erie" (1868) by the American writer Horatio Alger, Jr., was a much-anthologized and frequently recited treatment of the legendary hero that ends with a resounding answer to the question "where is he, that helmsman bold?": "He sank beside the wheel, / The wave received his lifeless corse, / Blackened with smoke and fire. / God rest him! / Never hero had / A nobler funeral pyre!" "Wir ist John Maynard?" (Who is John Maynard?") by the German poet Theodor Fontane carried the legendary hero's fame to Europe.

3. The Charge of the Light Brigade was the disastrous result of a misunderstanding among senior British officers at the Battle of Balaclava during the Crimean War: on October 24, 1854, a brigade of cavalry charged up a valley that was surrounded on three sides by heavily armed Russians. The heroism of the cavalrymen was commemorated by Tennyson in "The Charge of the Light Brigade," which was first published a few weeks later.

4. Leacock's own birthdate (see p. 3).

After that, Nivens stood looking quietly at Mullins. You could feel that he was thinking pretty deeply before he shot the next question at him.

"Where did you go to school?"

Mullins answered straight off: "The high school down home," and Nivens thought again for a while and then asked:

"How many boys were at the school?"

"About sixty."

"How many masters?"

"About three."

After that Nivens paused a long while and seemed to be digesting the evidence, but at last an idea seemed to strike him and he said:

"I understand you were not on the bank premises last night. Where were you?"

"Down the lake duck shooting."

You should have seen the excitement in the court when Mullins said this. The judge leaned forward in his chair and broke in at once.

"Did you get any, Harry?" he asked.

"Yes," Mullins said, "about six."

"Where did you get them? What? In the wild rice marsh past the river? You don't say so! Did you get them on the sit or how?"

All of these questions were fired off at the witness from the court in a single breath. In fact, it was the knowledge that the first ducks of the season had been seen in the Ossawippi marsh that led to the termination of the proceedings before the afternoon was a quarter over. Mullins and George Duff and half the witnesses were off with shotguns as soon as the court was cleared.

• • • • •

I may as well state at once that the full story of the robbery of the bank at Mariposa never came to the light. A number of arrests— mostly of vagrants and suspicious characters—were made, but the guilt of the robbery was never brought home to them. One man was arrested twenty miles away, at the other end of Missinaba County, who not only corresponded exactly with the description of the robber, but, in addition to this, had a wooden leg. Vagrants with one leg are always regarded with suspicion in places like Mariposa, and whenever a robbery or a murder happens they are arrested in batches.

It was never even known just how much money was stolen from the bank. Some people said ten thousand dollars, others more. The bank, no doubt for business motives, claimed that the contents of the safe were intact and that the robber had been foiled in his design.

But none of this matters to the exaltation of Mr. Pupkin. Good fortune, like bad, never comes in small instalments. On that wonderful day, every good thing happened to Peter Pupkin at once. The morning saw him a hero. At the sitting of the court, the judge publically told him that his conduct was fit to rank among the annals of the pioneers of Tecumseh Townships, and asked him to his house for supper. At five o'clock he received the telegram of promotion from the head office that raised his salary to a thousand dollars, and made him not only a hero but a marriageable man. At six o'clock he started up to the judge's house with his resolution nerved to the most momentous step of his life.

His mind was made up.

He would do a thing seldom if ever done in Mariposa. He would propose to Zena Pepperleigh. In Mariposa this kind of step, I say, is seldom taken. The course of love runs on and on through all its stages of tennis playing and dancing and sleigh riding, till by sheer notoriety of circumstance an understanding is reached. To propose straight out would be thought priggish and affected and is supposed to belong only to people in books.

But Pupkin felt that what ordinary people dare not do, heroes are allowed to attempt. He would propose to Zena, and more than that, he would tell her in a straight, manly way that he was rich and take the consequences.

And he did it.

That night on the piazza, where the hammock hangs in the shadow of the Virginia creeper, he did it. By sheer good luck the judge had gone indoors to the library, and by a piece of rare good fortune Mrs. Pepperleigh had gone indoors to the sewing room, and by a happy trick of coincidence the servant was out and the dog was tied up—in fact, no such chain of circumstances was ever offered in favour of mortal man before.

What Zena said—beyond saying yes—I do not know. I am sure that when Pupkin told her of the money, she bore up as bravely as so fine a girl as Zena would, and when he spoke of diamonds she said she would wear them for his sake.

They were saying these things and other things—ever so many other things—when there was such a roar and a clatter up Oneida Street as you never heard, and there came bounding up to the house one of the most marvellous Limousine touring cars that ever drew up at the home of a judge on a modest salary of three thousand dollars. When it stopped there sprang from it an excited man in a long sealskin coat—worn not for the luxury of it at all but from the sheer chilliness of the autumn evening. And it was, as of course you know, Pupkin's father. He had seen the news of his son's death in the evening paper in the city. They drove the car through, so the chauffeur said, in two hours and a quarter, and behind them there was to follow a special trainload of detectives and emergency men, but Pupkin senior had cancelled all that by telegram half way up when he heard that Peter was still living.

For a moment as his eye rested on young Pupkin you would almost have imagined, had you not known that he came from the Maritime Provinces, that there were tears in them and that he was about to hug his son to his heart. But if he didn't hug Peter to his heart, he certainly did within a few moments clasp Zena to it, in that fine fatherly way in which they clasp pretty girls in the Maritime Provinces. The strangest thing is that Pupkin senior seemed to understand the whole situation without any explanations at all.

Judge Pepperleigh, I think, would have shaken both of Pupkin senior's arms off when he saw him; and when you heard them call one another "Ned" and "Phillip" it made you feel that they were boys again attending classes together at the old law school in the city.

If Pupkin thought that his father wouldn't make a hit in Mariposa, it only showed his ignorance. Pupkin senior sat there on the judge's verandah smoking a corn cob pipe as if he had never heard of Havana cigars in his life. In the three days that he spent in Mariposa that autumn, he went in and out of Jeff Thorpe's barber shop and Eliot's drug store, shot black ducks in the marsh and played poker every evening at a hundred matches for a cent as if he had never lived any other life in all his days. They had to send him telegrams enough to fill a satchel to make him come away.

So Pupkin and Zena in due course of time were married, and went to live in one of the enchanted houses on the hillside in the newer part of the town, where you may find them to this day.

You may see Pupkin there at any time cutting enchanted grass on a little lawn in as gaudy a blazer as ever.

But if you step up to speak to him or walk with him into the enchanted house, pray modulate your voice a little—musical though it is—for there is said to be an enchanted baby on the premises whose sleep must not lightly be disturbed.

Chapter X

The Great Election in Missinaba County

Don't ask me what election it was, whether Dominion or Provincial or Imperial or Universal, for I scarcely know.

It must, of course, have been going on in other parts of the country as well, but I saw it all from Missinaba County which, with the town of Mariposa, was, of course, the storm centre and focus point of the whole turmoil.

I only know that it was a huge election and that on it turned issues of the most tremendous importance, such as whether or not
Mariposa should become part of the United States,[1] and whether
the flag that had waved over the school house at Tecumseh Township for ten centuries should be trampled under the hoof of an
alien invader, and whether Britons should be slaves,[2] and whether
Canadians should be Britons, and whether the farming class would
prove themselves Canadians, and tremendous questions of that
kind.

And there was such a roar and a tumult to it, and such a waving
of flags and beating of drums and flaring of torchlights that such
parts of the election as may have been going on elsewhere than in
Missinaba County must have been quite unimportant and didn't really matter.

Now that it is all over, we can look back at it without heat or pas-
sion. We can see,—it's plain enough now,—that in the great election Canada saved the British Empire, and that Missinaba saved
Canada and that the vote of the Third Concession of Tecumseh
Township saved Missinaba County, and that those of us who carried the third concession,—well, there's no need to push it further.
We prefer to be modest about it. If we still speak of it, it is only quietly and simply and not more than three or four times a day.

But you can't understand the election at all, and the conventions
and the campaigns and the nominations and the balloting, unless
you first appreciate the peculiar complexion of politics in Mariposa.

Let me begin at the beginning. Everybody in Mariposa is either a
Liberal or a Conservative or else is both.[3] Some of the people are or
have been Liberals or Conservatives all their lives and are called
dyed-in-the-wool[4] Grits or old-time Tories and things of that sort.
These people get from long training such a swift penetrating insight
into national issues that they can decide the most complicated
questions in four seconds: in fact, just as soon as they grab the city
papers out of the morning mail, they know the whole solution of

1. During the pre- and post-Confederation periods, Canada's national destiny was frequently conceived in variations of three choices: full independence, annexation to the
   United States, or federation with Britain.
2. An allusion to "Rule, Britannia, Britannia rule the waves; / Britons never, never, never
   shall be slaves," an adaptation of the chorus of a song in *Alfred: a Masque* (1740) by the
   British poet James Thomson that was set to music by Thomas Augustine Arne and became a popular patriotic song.
3. The Liberal party of Canada was not constituted until 1873, but the Conservative party
   (or, as it was formally known until 1942, the Liberal-Conservative party) has its origins
   in the 1854 coalition of conservatives, liberals, and moderate reformers of Canada West
   (Ontario) and the "Bleus" (moderate reformers) of Canada East (Quebec). In the late
   1840s, the liberal reformers of Upper Canada (as Canada West then was) were known as
   the Clear Grit party. As distinct from "conservatives," "old-time Tories" were strong supporters of Canada's British connections and strong opponents of liberal reforms to the
   Canadian government system.
4. Complete; thoroughgoing (from wool that is dyed before being woven).

any problem you can put to them. There are other people whose aim it is to be broad-minded and judicious and who vote Liberal or Conservative according to their judgment of the questions of the day. If their judgment of these questions tells them that there is something in it for them in voting Liberal, then they do so. But if not, they refuse to be the slaves of a party or the henchmen of any political leader. So that anybody looking for henches has got to keep away from them.

But the one thing that nobody is allowed to do in Mariposa is to have no politics. Of course there are always some people whose circumstances compel them to say that they have no politics. But that is easily understood. Take the case of Trelawney, the postmaster. Long ago he was a letter carrier under the old Mackenzie Government,[5] and later he was a letter sorter under the old Macdonald Government,[6] and after that a letter stamper under the old Tupper Government,[7] and so on. Trelawney always says that he has no politics, but the truth is that he has too many.

So, too, with the clergy in Mariposa. They have no politics—absolutely none. Yet Dean Drone round election time always announces as his text such a verse as: "Lo! is there not one righteous man in Israel?" or: "What ho! is it not time for a change?"[8] And that is a signal for all the Liberal business men to get up and leave their pews.

Similarly over at the Presbyterian Church, the minister says that his sacred calling will not allow him to take part in politics and that his sacred calling prevents him from breathing even a word of harshness against his fellow man, but that when it comes to the elevation of the ungodly into high places in the commonwealth (this means, of course, the nomination of the Conservative candidate) then he's not going to allow his sacred calling to prevent him from saying just what he thinks of it. And by that time, having pretty well cleared the church of Conservatives, he proceeds to show from the scriptures that the ancient Hebrews were Liberals to a man, except those who were drowned in the flood or who perished, more or less deservedly, in the desert.

There are, I say, some people who are allowed to claim to have no

---

5. Alexander Mackenzie (1822–1892) was prime minister of Canada's first Liberal government from 1873 to 1878.
6. See p. 54, n. 3.
7. Charles Tupper (1821–1915) was Canada's fifth Conservative prime minister for a few months in 1896 after the death of Macdonald and before the Liberals took power under Wilfrid Laurier (1841–1919), who served as prime minister from 1896 to 1911, the year of the election upon which "The Great Election in Missinaba County" is based.
8. Neither of Dean Drone's statements is a quotation from the Bible, but the first echoes several verses such as Ezekiel 3.20 ("When a righteous man doth turn away from his righteousness . . .") and 2 Peter 2.8 ("For that righteous man dwelling among them . . . vexed his righteous soul . . . with their unlawful deeds").

politics,—the office holders, and the clergy and the school teachers and the hotel keepers. But beyond them, anybody in Mariposa who says that he has no politics is looked upon as crooked, and people wonder what it is that he is "out after."

In fact, the whole town and county is a hive of politics, and people who have only witnessed gatherings such as the House of Commons at Westminster[9] and the Senate at Washington and never seen a Conservative Convention at Tecumseh Corners or a Liberal Rally at the Concession school house,[1] don't know what politics means.

So you may imagine the excitement in Mariposa when it became known that King George had dissolved the parliament of Canada[2] and had sent out a writ or command for Missinaba County to elect for him some other person than John Henry Bagshaw because he no longer had confidence in him.

The king, of course, is very well known, very favourably known, in Mariposa. Everybody remembers how he visited the town on his great tour in Canada, and stopped off at the Mariposa station.[3] Although he was only a prince at the time, there was quite a big crowd down at the depôt and everybody felt what a shame it was that the prince had no time to see more of Mariposa, because he would get such a false idea of it, seeing only the station and the lumber yards. Still, they all came to the station and all the Liberals and Conservatives mixed together perfectly freely and stood side by side without any distinction, so that the prince should not observe any party differences among them. And he didn't,—you could see that he didn't. They read him an address all about the tranquillity and loyalty of the Empire, and they purposely left out any reference to the trouble over the town wharf or the big row there had been about the location of the new post-office. There was a general decent feeling that it wouldn't be fair to disturb the prince with these things: later on, as king, he would, of course, *have* to know all about them, but meanwhile it was better to leave him with the idea that his empire was tranquil.

So they deliberately couched the address in terms that were just as reassuring as possible and the prince was simply delighted with it. I am certain that he slept pretty soundly after hearing that

9. Borough of London, England, where the British Parliament Buildings are located.
1. Country, a concession being a parcel of 32, 200-acre lots that constitute a township in Ontario.
2. It is not the monarch but his or her representative, the governor general, that dissolves parliament in preparation for a Canadian federal election. In 1911 (see p. 116, n. 7) parliament was dissolved by Lord Grey, representing George V (see p. 16, n. 9 and p. 41, n. 4), on September 21, but the government of Wilfrid Laurier (see p. 116, n. 7) remained in power until October 6, four days before the Conservative Robert Borden was sworn in as prime minister on October 10.
3. See p. 41, n. 4.

address. Why, you could see it taking effect even on his aides-de-camp and the people round him, so imagine how the prince must have felt!

I think in Mariposa they understand kings perfectly. Every time that a king or a prince comes, they try to make him see the bright side of everything and let him think that they're all united. Judge Pepperleigh walked up and down arm in arm with Dr. Gallagher, the worst Grit in the town, just to make the prince feel fine.

So when they got the news that the king had lost confidence in John Henry Bagshaw, the sitting member, they never questioned it a bit. Lost confidence? All right, they'd elect him another right away. They'd elect him half a dozen if he needed them. They don't mind; they'd elect the whole town man after man rather than have the king worried about it.

In any case, all the Conservatives had been wondering for years how the king and the governor-general and men like that had tolerated such a man as Bagshaw so long.

Missinaba County, I say, is a regular hive of politics, and not the miserable, crooked, money-ridden politics of the cities, but the straight, real old-fashioned thing that is an honour to the country side. Any man who would offer to take a bribe or sell his convictions for money, would be an object of scorn. I don't say they wouldn't take money,—they would, of course, why not?—but if they did they would take it in a straight fearless way and say nothing about it. They might,—it's only human,—accept a job or a contract from the government, but if they did, rest assured it would be in a broad national spirit and not for the sake of the work itself. No, sir. Not for a minute.

Any man who wants to get the votes of the Missinaba farmers and the Mariposa business men has got to persuade them that he's the right man. If he can do that,—if he can persuade any one of them that he is the right man and that all the rest know it, then they'll vote for him.

The division, I repeat, between the Liberals and the Conservatives, is intense. Yet you might live for a long while in the town, between elections, and never know it. It is only when you get to understand the people that you begin to see that there is a cross division running through them that nothing can ever remove. You gradually become aware of fine subtle distinctions that miss your observation at first. Outwardly, they are all friendly enough. For instance, Joe Milligan the dentist is a Conservative, and has been for six years, and yet he shares the same boat-house with young Dr. Gallagher, who is a Liberal, and they even bought a motor boat between them. Pete Glover and Alf McNichol were in partnership in the hardware and paint store, though they belonged on different sides.

But just as soon as elections drew near, the differences in politics became perfectly apparent. Liberals and Conservatives drew away from one another. Joe Milligan used the motor boat one Saturday and Dr. Gallagher the next, and Pete Glover sold hardware on one side of the store and Alf McNichol sold paint on the other. You soon realized too that one of the newspapers was Conservative and the other was Liberal, that there was a Liberal drug store and a Conservative drug store, and so on. Similarly round election time, the Mariposa House was the Liberal Hotel, and the Continental Conservative, though Mr. Smith's place, where they always put on a couple of extra bar tenders, was what you might call Independent-Liberal-Conservative, with a dash of Imperialism[4] thrown in. Mr. Gingham, the undertaker, was, as a natural effect of his calling, an advanced Liberal, but at election time he always engaged a special assistant for embalming Conservative customers.

So now, I think, you understand something of the general political surroundings of the great election in Missinaba County.

John Henry Bagshaw was the sitting member, the Liberal member, for Missinaba County.

The Liberals called him the old war horse, and the old battle-axe, and the old charger and the old champion and all sorts of things of that kind. The Conservatives called him the old jackass and the old army mule and the old booze fighter and the old grafter and the old scoundrel.

John Henry Bagshaw was, I suppose, one of the greatest political forces in the world. He had flowing white hair crowned with a fedora hat, and a smooth statesmanlike face which it cost the country twenty-five cents a day to shave.

Altogether the Dominion of Canada had spent over two thousand dollars in shaving that face during the twenty years that Bagshaw had represented Missinaba County. But the result had been well worth it.

Bagshaw wore a long political overcoat that it cost the country twenty cents a day to brush, and boots that cost the Dominion fifteen cents every morning to shine.

But it was money well spent.

Bagshaw of Mariposa was one of the most representative men of the age, and it's no wonder that he had been returned for the country for five elections running, leaving the Conservatives nowhere.

---

4. Policy favouring the maintenance or strengthening of ties with Great Britain and other parts of the British Empire.

Just think how representative he was. He owned two hundred acres out on the Third Concession and kept two men working on it all the time to prove that he was a practical farmer. They sent in fat hogs to the Massinaba County Agricultural Exposition and World's Fair every autumn, and Bagshaw himself stood beside the pig pens with the judges, and wore a pair of corduroy breeches and chewed a straw all afternoon. After that if any farmer thought that he was not properly represented in Parliament, it showed that he was an ass.

Bagshaw owned a half share in the harness business and a quarter share in the tannery and that made him a business man. He paid for a pew in the Presbyterian Church and that represented religion in Parliament. He attended college for two sessions thirty years ago, and that represented education and kept him abreast with modern science, if not ahead of it. He kept a little account in one bank and a big account in the other, so that he was a rich man or a poor man at the same time.

Add to that that John Henry Bagshaw was perhaps the finest orator in Mariposa. That, of course, is saying a great deal. There are speakers there, lots of them that can talk two or three hours at a stretch, but the old war horse could beat them all. They say that when John Henry Bagshaw got well started, say after a couple of hours of talk, he could speak as Pericles or Demosthenes or Cicero[5] never could have spoken.

You could tell Bagshaw a hundred yards off as a member of the House of Commons. He wore a pepper-and-salt suit to show that he came from a rural constituency, and he wore a broad gold watch-chain with dangling seals to show that he also represents a town. You could see from his quiet low collar and white tie that his electorate were a God-fearing, religious people, while the horse-shoe pin that he wore showed that his electorate were not without sporting instincts and knew a horse from a jackass.

Most of the time, John Henry Bagshaw had to be at Ottawa (though he preferred the quiet of his farm and always left it, as he said, with a sigh). If he was not in Ottawa, he was in Washington, and of course at any time they might need him in London, so that it was no wonder that he could only be in Mariposa about two months in the year.

That is why everybody knew, when Bagshaw got off the afternoon train one day early in the spring, that there must be something very

5. Marcus Tullius Cicero (106–43 B.C.E.) was a Roman politician, a master of oratory and prose style, and the author of *De Oratore* (55 B.C.E.), a treatise on rhetoric. Pericles (c. 500–429 B.C.E.) was a great Athenian statesman and orator. Demosthenes (c. 383–322 B.C.E.) was an Athenian orator who was regarded as the finest prose writer in ancient Greece.

important coming and that the rumours about a new election must be perfectly true.

Everything that he did showed this. He gave the baggage man twenty-five cents to take the check[6] off his trunk, the bus driver fifty cents to drive him up to the Main Street, and he went into Callahan's tobacco store and bought two ten-cent cigars and took them across the street and gave them to Mallory Tompkins of the Times-Herald as a present from the Prime Minister.

All that afternoon, Bagshaw went up and down the Main Street of Mariposa, and you could see, if you knew the signs of it, that there was politics in the air. He bought nails and putty and glass in the hardware store, and harness in the harness shop, and drugs in the drug store and toys in the toy shop, and all the things like that that are needed for a big campaign.

Then when he had done all this he went over with McGinnis the Liberal organizer and Mallory Tompkins, the Times-Herald man, and Gingham (the great Independent-Liberal undertaker) to the back parlour in the Mariposa House.

You could tell from the way John Henry Bagshaw closed the door before he sat down that he was in a pretty serious frame of mind.

"Gentlemen," he said, "the election is a certainty. We're going to have a big fight on our hands and we've got to get ready for it."

"It is going to be on the tariff?"[7] asked Tompkins.

"Yes, gentlemen, I'm afraid it is. The whole thing is going to turn on the tariff question. I wish it were otherwise. I think it madness, but they're bent on it, and we got to fight it on that line. Why they can't fight it merely on the question of graft," continued the old war horse, rising from his seat and walking up and down, "Heaven only knows. I warned them. I appealed to them. I said, fight the thing on graft and we can win easy. Take this constituency,—why not have fought the thing out on whether I spent too much money on the town wharf or the post-office? What better issues could a man want? Let them claim that I am crooked, and let me claim that I'm not. Surely that was good enough without dragging in the tariff. But now, gentlemen, tell me about things in the constituency. Is there any talk yet of who is to run?"

Mallory Tompkins lighted up the second of the Prime Minister's cigars and then answered for the group:

"Everybody says that Edward Drone is going to run."

"Ah!" said the old war horse, and there was joy upon his face, "is

6. Baggage tag.
7. Laurier's signing of a Reciprocity Treaty to reduce customs duties between Canada and the United States split the Liberal party, became a major campaign issue in the election of 1911, and contributed crucially to the defeat of the Liberals by the Conservatives.

he? At last! That's good, that's good—now what platform will he run on?"

"Independent."

"Excellent," said Mr. Bagshaw. "Independent, that's fine. On a programme of what?"

"Just simple honesty and public morality."

"Come now," said the member, "that's splendid: that will help enormously. Honesty and public morality! The very thing! If Drone runs and makes a good showing, we win for a certainty. Tompkins, you must lose no time over this. Can't you manage to get some articles in the other papers hinting that at the last election we bribed all the voters in the county, and that we gave out enough contracts to simply pervert the whole constituency. Imply that we poured the public money into this county in bucketsful and that we are bound to do it again. Let Drone have plenty of material of this sort and he'll draw off every honest unbiassed vote in the Conservative party.

"My only fear is," continued the old war horse, losing some of his animation, "that Drone won't run after all. He's said it so often before and never has. He hasn't got the money. But we must see to that. Gingham, you know his brother well; you must work it so that we pay Drone's deposit and his campaign expenses. But how like Drone it is to come out at this time!"

It was indeed very like Edward Drone to attempt so misguided a thing as to come out an Independent candidate in Missinaba County on a platform of public honesty. It was just the sort of thing that anyone in Mariposa would expect from him.

Edward Drone was the Rural Dean's younger brother,—young Mr. Drone, they used to call him, years ago, to distinguish him from the rector. He was a somewhat weaker copy of his elder brother, with a simple, inefficient face and kind blue eyes. Edward Drone was, and always had been, a failure. In training he had been, once upon a time, an engineer and built dams that broke and bridges that fell down and wharves that floated away in the spring floods. He had been a manufacturer and failed, had been a contractor and failed, and now lived a meagre life as a sort of surveyor or land expert on goodness knows what.

In his political ideas Edward Drone was and, as everybody in Mariposa knew, always had been crazy. He used to come up to the autumn exercises at the high school and make speeches about the ancient Romans and Titus Manlius and Quintus Curtius[8] at the

---

8. Quintus Curtius Rufus wrote a history of Alexander the Great in ten books, the first two of which have not survived. Titus Manlius Imperiosus Torquatus was a Roman who, according to tradition, defeated a gigantic Gaul in hand-to-hand combat while repelling an invasion of Rome by the Gauls in 361 B.C.E.

same time when John Henry Bagshaw used to make a speech about the Maple Leaf and ask for an extra half holiday. Drone used to tell the boys about the lessons to be learned from the lives of the truly great, and Bagshaw used to talk to them about the lessons learned from the lives of the extremely rich. Drone used to say that his heart filled whenever he thought of the splendid patriotism of the ancient Romans, and Bagshaw said that whenever he looked out over this wide Dominion his heart overflowed.

Even the youngest boy in the school could tell that Drone was foolish. Not even the school teachers would have voted for him.

"What about the Conservatives?" asked Bagshaw presently; "is there any talk yet as to who they'll bring out?"

Gingham and Mallory Tompkins looked at one another. They were almost afraid to speak.

"Hadn't you heard?" said Gingham; "they've got their man already."

"Who is it?" said Bagshaw quickly.

"They're going to put up Josh Smith."

"Great Heaven!" said Bagshaw, jumping to his feet; "Smith! the hotel keeper."

"Yes, sir," said Mr. Gingham, "that's the man."

Do you remember, in history, how Napoleon turned pale when he heard that the Duke of Wellington[9] was to lead the allies in Belgium? Do you remember how when Themistocles heard that Aristogiton was to lead the Spartans, he jumped into the sea?[1] Possibly you don't, but it may help you to form some idea of what John Henry Bagshaw felt when he heard that the Conservatives had selected Josh Smith, proprietor of Smith's Hotel.

You remember Smith. You've seen him there on the steps of his hotel,—two hundred and eighty pounds in his stockinged feet. You've seen him selling liquor after hours through sheer public spirit, and you recall how he saved the lives of hundreds of people on the day when the steamer sank, and how he saved the town from being destroyed the night when the Church of England Church burnt down. You know that hotel of his, too, half way down the street, Smith's Northern Health Resort, though already they were beginning to call it Smith's British Arms.

9. Arthur Wellesley (1769–1852), first duke of Wellington, led the Campaigns in France that culminated in the defeat of Napoleon Bonaparte at the Battle of Waterloo (1815) near Brussels, Belgium.
1. Aristogiton was revered by the Athenians as a champion of liberty and Themistocles (d. 459 B.C.E.) (with whom Napoleon compared himself in his formal letter of surrender in 1815) was an Athenian statesman and commander whose intrigues incurred the enmity of the militaristic Greek state of Sparta. Neither "jumped into the sea," an act romantically and falsely attributed to the Greek poet Sappho after she was rejected by Phaon.

So you can imagine that Bagshaw came as near to turning pale as a man in federal politics can.

"I never knew Smith was a Conservative," he said faintly; "he always subscribed to our fund."

"He is now," said Mr. Gingham ominously; "he says the idea of this reciprocity[2] business cuts him to the heart."

"The infernal liar!" said Mr. Bagshaw.

There was silence for a few moments. Then Bagshaw spoke again.

"Will Smith have anything else in his platform besides the trade question?"

"Yes," said Mr. Gingham gloomily, "he will."

"What is it?"

"Temperance and total prohibition!"

John Henry Bagshaw sank back in his chair as if struck with a club. There let me leave him for a chapter.

Chapter XI

The Candidacy of Mr. Smith

"Boys," said Mr. Smith to the two hostlers, stepping out on to the sidewalk in front of the hotel,—"hoist that there British Jack[1] over the place and hoist her up good."

Then he stood and watched the flag fluttering in the wind.

"Billy," he said to the desk clerk, "get a couple more and put them up on the roof of the caff behind the hotel. Wire down to the city and get a quotation on a hundred of them. Take them signs 'American Drinks' out of the bar. Put up noo ones with 'British Beer at all Hours'; clear out the rye whiskey and order in Scotch and Irish, and then go up to the printing office and get me them placards."

Then another thought struck Mr. Smith.

"Say, Billy," he said, "wire to the city for fifty pictures of King George. Get 'em good, and get 'em coloured. It don't matter what they cost."

"All right, sir," said Billy.

"And Billy," called Mr. Smith, as still another thought struck him (indeed, the moment Mr. Smith went into politics you could see these thoughts strike him like waves), "get fifty pictures of his father, old King Albert."[2]

---

2. See p. 121, n. 7.
1. Union Jack: the flag of Great Britain.
2. George V was the son of Albert Edward (later Edward VII) and thus the grandson rather than the son of Prince (not King) Albert (1819–1861), the consort of Queen Victoria.

"All right, sir."

"And say, I tell you, while you're at it, get some of the old queen, Victorina, if you can. Get 'em in mourning, with a harp and one of them lions and a three-pointed prong."

• • • • •

It was on the morning after the Conservative Convention. Josh Smith had been chosen the candidate. And now the whole town was covered with flags and placards and there were bands in the streets every evening, and noise and music and excitement that went on from morning till night.

Election times are exciting enough even in the city. But there the excitement dies down in business hours. In Mariposa there aren't any business hours and the excitement goes on *all* the time.

Mr. Smith had carried the Convention before him. There had been a feeble attempt to put up Nivens. But everybody knew that he was a lawyer and a college man and wouldn't have a chance by a man with a broader outlook like Josh Smith.

So the result was that Smith was the candidate and there were placards out all over the town with SMITH AND BRITISH ALLE-GIANCE in big letters, and people were wearing badges with Mr. Smith's face on one side and King George's on the other, and the fruit store next to the hotel had been cleaned out and turned into committee rooms with a gang of workers smoking cigars in it all day and half the night.

There were other placards, too, with BAGSHAW AND LIBERTY, BAGSHAW AND PROSPERITY, VOTE FOR THE OLD MISSI-NABA STANDARD BEARER, and up town beside the Mariposa House there were the Bagshaw committee rooms with a huge white streamer across the street, and with a gang of Bagshaw workers smoking their heads off.

But Mr. Smith had an estimate made which showed that nearly two cigars to one were smoked in his committee rooms as compared with the Liberals. It was the first time in five elections that the Conservative had been able to make such a showing as that.

One might mention, too, that there were Drone placards out,— five or six of them,—little things about the size of a pocket handkerchief, with a statement that "Mr. Edward Drone solicits the votes of the electors of Missinaba County." But you would never notice them. And when Drone tried to put up a streamer across the

(1819–1901) (Smith's "Victorina"), who reigned from 1837 until her death. One of the music-hall sensations in the years preceding the First World War was the Victorina Troupe, who billed themselves as the "Originators and Presenters of the Most Marvelous Sword Swallowing Act on Earth." Miss Victorina herself swallowed a lighted electric bulb that shone through her body.

Main Street with DRONE AND HONESTY the wind carried it away into the lake.

The fight was really between Smith and Bagshaw, and everybody knew it from the start.

I wish that I were able to narrate all the phases and the turns of the great contest from the opening of the campaign till the final polling day. But it would take volumes.

First of all, of course, the trade question was hotly discussed in the two newspapers of Mariposa, and the Newspacket and the Times-Herald literally bristled with statistics. Then came interviews with the candidates and the expression of their convictions in re gard to tariff questions.

"Mr. Smith," said the reporter of the Mariposa Newspacket, "we'd like to get your views of the effect of the proposed reduction of the differential duties."[3]

"By gosh, Pete," said Mr. Smith, "you can search me. Have a cigar."

"What do you think, Mr. Smith, would be the result of lowering the *ad valorem*[4] British preference and admitting American goods at a reciprocal rate?"

"It's a corker, ain't it?" answered Mr. Smith. "What'll you take, lager or domestic?"

And in that short dialogue Mr. Smith showed that he had instantaneously grasped the whole method of dealing with the press. The interview in the paper next day said that Mr. Smith, while unwilling to state positively that the principle of tariff discrimination was at variance with sound fiscal science, was firmly of opinion that any reciprocal interchange of tariff preferences with the United States must inevitably lead to a serious per capita[5] reduction of the national industry.

· · · · · ·

"Mr. Smith," said the chairman of a delegation of the manufacturers of Mariposa,[6] "what do you propose to do in regard to the tariff if you're elected?"

"Boys," answered Mr. Smith, "I'll put her up so darned high they won't never get her down again."

· · · · · ·

"Mr. Smith," said the chairman of another delegation, "I'm an old free trader—"

3. Preferential duties: lower customs duties imposed on the goods of certain countries but not others.
4. According to value (Latin).
5. Literally, by heads: across the board; shared equally.
6. The Canadian Manufacturers' Association was founded in 1871 and incorporated by Act of Parliament in 1902 with the mandate "to promote Canadian industries and to further the interests of Canadian manufacturers." The CMA was a vocal opponent of reciprocity in the election of 1911.

"Put it there," said Mr. Smith, "so'm I. There ain't nothing like it."

· · · · ·

"What do you think about imperial defence?"[7] asked another questioner.

"Which?" said Mr. Smith.

"Imperial defence."

"Of what?"

"Of everything."

"Who says it?" said Mr. Smith.

"Everybody is talking of it."

"What do the Conservative boys at Ottaway[8] think about it?" answered Mr. Smith.

"They're all for it."

"Well, I'm fer it too," said Mr. Smith.

· · · · ·

These little conversations represented only the first stage, the argumentative stage of the great contest. It was during this period, for example, that the Mariposa Newspacket absolutely proved that the price of hogs in Mariposa was decimal six higher than the price of oranges in Southern California and that the average decennial import of eggs into Missinaba County had increased four decimal six eight two in the last fifteen years more than the import of lemons in New Orleans.

Figures of this kind made the people think. Most certainly.

After all this came the organizing stage and after that the big public meetings and the rallies. Perhaps you have never seen a county being "organized." It is a wonderful sight. First of all the Bagshaw men drove through crosswise in top buggies and then drove through it again lengthwise. Whenever they met a farmer they went in and ate a meal with him, and after the meal they took him out to the buggy and gave him a drink. After that the man's vote was absolutely solid until it was tampered with by feeding a Conservative.

In fact, the only way to show a farmer that you are in earnest is to go in and eat a meal with him. If you can't eat it, he won't vote for you. That is the recognized political test.

But, of course, just as soon as the Bagshaw men had begun to get the farming vote solidified, the Smith buggies came driving through in the other direction, eating meals and distributing cigars and turning all the farmers back into Conservatives.

---

7. Supporters of Canada's connections with Britain and other parts of the British Empire argued that military and naval preparedness was essential to the unity and survival of the Empire in the face of American expansionism and the European armament race.
8. The Conservative Party in Ottawa.

Here and there you might see Edward Drone, the Independent candidate, wandering round from farm to farm in the dust of the political buggies. To each of the farmers he explained that he pledged himself to give no bribes, to spend no money and to offer no jobs, and each one of them gripped him warmly by the hand and showed him the way to the next farm.

After the organization of the county there came the period of the public meetings and the rallies and the joint debates between the candidates and their supporters.

I suppose there was no place in the whole Dominion where the trade question—the Reciprocity question—was threshed out quite so thoroughly and in quite such a national patriotic spirit as in Mariposa. For a month, at least, people talked of nothing else. A man would stop another in the street and tell him that he had read last night that the average price of an egg in New York was decimal ought[9] one more than the price of an egg in Mariposa, and the other man would stop the first one later in the day and tell him that the average price of a hog in Idaho was point six of a cent per pound less (or more,—he couldn't remember which for the moment) than the average price of beef in Mariposa.

People lived on figures of this sort, and the man who could remember most of them stood out as a born leader.

But of course it was at the public meetings that these things were most fully discussed. It would take volumes to do full justice to all the meetings that they held in Missinaba County. But here and there single speeches stood out as masterpieces of convincing oratory. Take, for example, the speech of John Henry Bagshaw at the Tecumseh Corners School House. The Mariposa Times-Herald said next day that that speech would go down in history, and so it will,—ever so far down.

Anyone who has heard Bagshaw knows what an impressive speaker he is, and on this night when he spoke with the quiet dignity of a man old in years and anxious only to serve his country, he almost surpassed himself. Near the end of his speech somebody dropped a pin, and the noise it made in falling fairly rattled the windows.

"I am an old man now, gentlemen," Bagshaw said, "and the time must soon come when I must not only leave politics, but must take my way towards that goal from which no traveller returns."[1]

There was a deep hush when Bagshaw said this. It was understood to imply that he thought of going to the United States.

"Yes, gentlemen, I am an old man, and I wish, when my time comes to go, to depart leaving as little animosity behind me as pos-

9. Nought: zero.
1. In the "To be, or not to be" soliloquy in William Shakespeare's *Hamlet*, death is "The undiscovered country from whose bourne / No traveller returns" (3.1.79–80).

sible. But before I *do* go, I want it pretty clearly understood that there are more darn scoundrels in the Conservative party than ought to be tolerated in any decent community. I bear," he continued, "malice towards none and I wish to speak with gentleness to all, but what I will say is that how any set of rational responsible men could nominate such a skunk as the Conservative candidate passes the bounds of my comprehension. Gentlemen, in the present campaign there is no room for vindictive abuse. Let us rise to a higher level than that. They tell me that my opponent, Smith, is a common saloon keeper. Let it pass. They tell me that he has stood convicted of horse stealing, that he is a notable perjurer, that he is known as the blackest-hearted liar in Missinaba County. Let us not speak of it. Let no whisper of it pass our lips.

"No, gentlemen," continued Bagshaw, pausing to take a drink of water, "let us rather consider this question on the high plane of national welfare. Let us not think of our own particular interests but let us consider the good of the country at large. And to do this, let me present to you some facts in regard to the price of barley in Tecumseh Township."

Then, amid a deep stillness, Bagshaw read off the list of prices of sixteen kinds of grain in sixteen different places during sixteen years.

"But let me turn," Bagshaw went on to another phase of the national subject, "and view for a moment the price of marsh hay in Missinaba County—"

When Bagshaw sat down that night it was felt that a Liberal vote in Tecumseh Township was a foregone conclusion.

But here they hadn't reckoned on the political genius of Mr. Smith. When he heard next day of the meeting, he summoned some of his leading speakers to him and he said:

"Boys, they're beating us on them statissicks. Ourn ain't good enough."

Then he turned to Nivens and he said:

"What was them figures you had here the other night?"

Nivens took out a paper and began reading.

"Stop," said Mr. Smith, "what was that figure for bacon?"

"Fourteen million dollars," said Nivens.

"Not enough," said Mr. Smith, "make it twenty. They'll stand for it, them farmers."

Nivens changed it.

"And what was that for hay?"

"Two dollars a ton."

"Shove it up to four," said Mr. Smith. "And I tell you," he added, "if any of them farmers says the figures ain't correct, tell them to go to Washington and see for themselves; say that if any man wants the proof of your figures let him go over to England and ask,—tell him to go straight to London and see it all for himself in the books."

· · · · ·

After this, there was no more trouble over statistics. I must say though that it is a wonderfully convincing thing to hear trade figures of this kind properly handled. Perhaps the best man on this sort of thing in the campaign was Mullins, the banker. A man of his profession simply has to have figures of trade and population and money at his fingers' ends and the effect of it in public speaking is wonderful.

No doubt you have listened to speakers of this kind, but I question whether you have ever heard anything more typical of the sort of effect that I allude to than Mullins's speech at the big rally at the Fourth Concession.

Mullins himself, of course, knows the figures so well that he never bothers to write them into notes and the effect is very striking.

"Now, gentlemen," he said very earnestly, "how many of you know just to what extent the exports of this country have increased in the last ten years? How many could tell what per cent. of increase there has been in one decade of our national importation?"—then Mullins paused and looked round. Not a man knew it.

"I don't recall," he said, "exactly the precise amount myself,—not at this moment,—but it must be simply tremendous. Or take the question of population," Mullins went on, warming up again as a born statistician always does at the proximity of figures, "how many of you know, how many of you can state, what has been the decennial percentage increase in our leading cities—?"

There he paused, and would you believe it, not a man could state it.

"I don't recall the exact figures," said Mullins, "but I have them at home and they are positively colossal."

But just in one phase of the public speaking, the candidacy of Mr. Smith received a serious set-back.

It had been arranged that Mr. Smith should run on a platform of total prohibition. But they soon found that it was a mistake. They had imported a special speaker from the city, a grave man with a white tie, who put his whole heart into the work and would take nothing for it except his expenses and a sum of money for each speech. But beyond the money, I say, he would take nothing.

He spoke one night at the Tecumseh Corners social hall at the same time when the Liberal meeting was going on at the Tecumseh Corners school house.

"Gentlemen," he said, as he paused half way in his speech,— "while we are gathered here in earnest discussion, do you know what is happening over at the meeting place of our opponents? Do you know that seventeen bottles of rye whiskey were sent out from the town this afternoon to that innocent and unsuspecting school house? Seventeen bottles of whiskey hidden in between the blackboard and the wall, and every single man that attends that meeting,—mark my words, every single man,—will drink his fill of the abominable stuff at the expense of the Liberal candidate!"

Just as soon as the speaker said this, you could see the Smith men at the meeting look at one another in injured surprise, and before the speech was half over the hall was practically emptied.

After that the total prohibition plank was changed and the committee substituted a declaration in favour of such a form of restrictive license as should promote temperance while encouraging the manufacture of spirituous liquors, and by a severe regulation of the liquor traffic should place intoxicants only in the hands of those fitted to use them.

• • • • •

Finally there came the great day itself,[2] the Election Day that brought, as everybody knows, the crowning triumph of Mr. Smith's career. There is no need to speak of it at any length, because it has become a matter of history.

In any case, everybody who has ever seen Mariposa knows just what election day is like. The shops, of course, are, as a matter of custom, all closed, and the bar rooms are all closed by law so that you have to go in by the back way. All the people are in their best clothes and at first they walk up and down the street in a solemn way just as they do on the twelfth of July and on St. Patrick's Day, before the fun begins. Everybody keeps looking in at the different polling places to see if anybody else has voted yet, because, of course, nobody cares to vote first for fear of being fooled after all and voting on the wrong side.

Most of all did the supporters of Mr. Smith, acting under his instructions, hang back from the poll in the early hours. To Mr. Smith's mind voting was to be conducted on the same plan as bear-shooting.

"Hold back your votes, boys," he said, "and don't be too eager. Wait till when she begins to warm up and then let 'em have it good and hard."

In each of the polling places in Mariposa there is a returning officer and with him are two scrutineers, and the electors, I say, peep in and out like mice looking into a trap. But if once the scrutineers get a man well into the polling booth, they push him in behind a little curtain and make him vote. The voting, of course, is by secret

---

2. The election of 1911 was held on September 21.

ballot, so that no one except the scrutineers and the returning officer and the two or three people who may be round the poll can possibly tell how a man has voted.

That's how it comes about that the first results are often so contradictory and conflicting. Sometimes the poll is badly arranged
and the scrutineers are unable to see properly just how the ballots
are being marked and they count up the Liberals and Conservatives
in different ways. Often, too, a voter makes his mark so hurriedly
and carelessly that they have to pick it out of the ballot box and
look at it to see what it is.

I suppose that may have been why it was that in Mariposa the results came out at first in such a conflicting way.

Perhaps that was how it was that the first reports showed that
Edward Drone the Independent candidate was certain to win. You
should have seen how the excitement grew upon the streets when
the news was circulated. In the big rallies and meetings of the Liberals and Conservatives, everybody had pretty well forgotten all
about Drone, and when the news got round at about four o'clock
that the Drone vote was carrying the poll, the people were simply
astounded. Not that they were not pleased. On the contrary. They
were delighted. Everybody came up to Drone and shook hands and
congratulated him and told him that they had known all along that
what the country wanted was a straight, honest, non-partisan representation. The Conservatives said openly that they were sick of
party, utterly done with it, and the Liberals said that they hated it.
Already three or four of them had taken Drone aside and explained
that what was needed in the town was a straight, clean, non-
partisan post-office, built on a piece of ground of a strictly non-
partisan character, and constructed under contracts that were not
tainted and smirched with party affiliation. Two or three men were
willing to show to Drone just where a piece of ground of this character could be bought. They told him too that in the matter of the
postmastership itself they had nothing against Trelawney, the present postmaster, in any personal sense, and would say nothing
against him except merely that he was utterly and hopelessly unfit
for his job and that if Drone believed, as he had said he did, in a
purified civil service, he ought to begin by purifying Trelawney.

Already Edward Drone was beginning to feel something of what
it meant to hold office and there was creeping into his manner the
quiet self-importance which is the first sign of conscious power.

In fact, in that brief half-hour of office, Drone had a chance to
see something of what it meant. Henry McGinnis came to him and
asked straight out for a job as federal census-taker on the ground
that he was hard up and had been crippled with rheumatism all
winter. Nelson Williamson asked for the post of wharf master on

the plea that he had been laid up with sciatica all winter and was absolutely fit for nothing. Erasmus Archer asked him if he could get his boy Pete into one of the departments at Ottawa, and made a strong case of it by explaining that he had tried his cussedest to get Pete a job anywhere else and it was simply impossible. Not that Pete wasn't a willing boy, but he was slow,—even his father admitted it,—slow as the devil, blast him, and with no head for figures and unfortunately he'd never had the schooling to bring him on. But if Drone could get him in at Ottawa, his father truly believed it would be the very place for him. Surely in the Indian Department or in the Astronomical Branch or in the New Canadian Navy there must be any amount of opening for a boy like this? And to all of these requests Drone found himself explaining that he would take the matter under his very earnest consideration and that they must remember that he had to consult his colleagues and not merely follow the dictates of his own wishes. In fact, if he had ever in his life had any envy of Cabinet Ministers, he lost it in this hour.

But Drone's hour was short. Even before the poll had closed in Mariposa, the news came sweeping in, true or false, that Bagshaw was carrying the county. The second concession had gone for Bagshaw in a regular landslide,—six votes to only two for Smith,— and all down the township line road (where the hay farms are) Bagshaw was said to be carrying all before him.

Just as soon as that news went round the town, they launched the Mariposa band of the Knights of Pythias (every man in it is a Liberal) down the Main Street with big red banners in front of it with the motto BAGSHAW FOREVER in letters a foot high. Such rejoicing and enthusiasm began to set in as you never saw. Everybody crowded round Bagshaw on the steps of the Mariposa House and shook his hand and said they were proud to see the day and that the Liberal party was the glory of the Dominion and that as for this idea of non-partisan politics the very thought of it made them sick. Right away in the committee rooms they began to organize the demonstration for the evening with lantern slides and speeches and they arranged for a huge bouquet to be presented to Bagshaw on the platform by four little girls (all Liberals) all dressed in white.

And it was just at this juncture, with one hour of voting left, that Mr. Smith emerged from his committee rooms and turned his voters on the town, much as the Duke of Wellington sent the whole line to the charge at Waterloo. From every committee room and sub-committee room they poured out in flocks with blue badges fluttering on their coats.

"Get at it, boys," said Mr. Smith, "vote and keep on voting till they make you quit."

Then he turned to his campaign assistant. "Billy," he said, "wire down to the city that I'm elected by an overwhelming majority and tell them to wire it right back. Send word by telephone to all the polling places in the county that the hull[3] town has gone solid Conservative and tell them to send the same news back here. Get carpenters and tell them to run up a platform in front of the hotel; tell them to take the bar door clean off its hinges and be all ready the minute the poll quits."

It was the last hour that did it. Just as soon as the big posters went up in the windows of the Mariposa Newspacket with the telegraphic despatch that Josh Smith was reported in the city to be elected, and was followed by the messages from all over the county, the voters hesitated no longer. They had waited, most of them, all through the day, not wanting to make any error in their vote, but when they saw the Smith men crowding into the polls and heard the news from the outside, they went solid in one great stampede, and by the time the poll was declared closed at five o'clock there was no shadow of doubt that the county was saved and that Josh Smith was elected for Missinaba.

· · · · ·

I wish you could have witnessed the scene in Mariposa that evening. It would have done your heart good,—such joy, such public rejoicing as you never saw. It turned out that there wasn't really a Liberal in the whole town and that there never had been. They were all Conservatives and had been for years and years. Men who had voted, with pain and sorrow in their hearts, for the Liberal party for twenty years, came out that evening and owned up straight that they were Conservatives. They said they could stand the strain no longer and simply had to confess. Whatever the sacrifice might mean, they were prepared to make it.

Even Mr. Golgotha Gingham, the undertaker, came out and admitted that in working for John Henry Bagshaw he'd been going straight against his conscience. He said that right from the first he had had his misgivings. He said it had haunted him. Often at night when he would be working away quietly, one of these sudden misgivings would overcome him so that he could hardly go on with his embalming. Why, it appeared that on the very first day when reciprocity was proposed, he had come home and said to Mrs. Gingham that he thought it simply meant selling out the country. And the strange thing was that ever so many others had just the same misgivings. Trelawney admitted that he had said to Mrs. Trelawney that it was madness, and Jeff Thorpe, the barber, had, he admitted, gone home to his dinner, the first day reciprocity was talked of, and

3. Core; central.

said to Mrs. Thorpe that it would simply kill business in the country and introduce a cheap, shoddy, American form of hair-cut that would render true loyalty impossible. To think that Mrs. Gingham and Mrs. Trelawney and Mrs. Thorpe had known all this for six months and kept quiet about it! Yet I think there were a good many Mrs. Ginghams in the country. It is merely another proof that no woman is fit for politics.

· · · · ·

The demonstration that night in Mariposa will never be forgotten. The excitement in the streets, the torchlights, the music of the band of the Knights of Pythias (an organization which is Conservative in all but name), and above all the speeches and the patriotism.

They had put up a big platform in front of the hotel, and on it were Mr. Smith and his chief workers, and behind them was a perfect forest of flags. They presented a huge bouquet of flowers to Mr. Smith, handed to him by four little girls in white,—the same four that I spoke of above, for it turned out that they were all Conservatives.

Then there were the speeches. Judge Pepperleigh spoke and said that there was no need to dwell on the victory that they had achieved, because it was history; there was no occasion to speak of what part he himself had played, within the limits of his official position, because what he had done was henceforth a matter of history; and Nivens, the lawyer, said that he would only say just a few words, because anything that he might have done was now history; later generations, he said, might read it but it was not for him to speak of it, because it belonged now to the history of the country. And, after them, others spoke in the same strain and all refused absolutely to dwell on the subject (for more than half an hour) on the ground that anything that they might have done was better left for future generations to investigate. And no doubt this was very true, as to some things, anyway.

Mr. Smith, of course, said nothing. He didn't have to,—not for four years,—and he knew it.

Chapter XII

L'Envoi. The Train to Mariposa[1]

It leaves the city every day about five o'clock in the evening, the train for Mariposa.

---

1. From the French *en voie* (on the way), an envoi (or envoy) is the concluding part of a poem or book. It is frequently addressed to a person of power or importance. The form with which it is most closely associated is the *ballade*, one of the artificial French forms that were popular on both sides of the Atlantic in the late nineteenth and early twentieth centuries.

Strange that you did not know of it, though you come from the little town—or did, long years ago.

Odd that you never knew, in all these years, that the train was there every afternoon, puffing up steam in the city station, and that you might have boarded it any day and gone home. No, not "home,"—of course you couldn't call it "home" now; "home" means that big red sandstone house of yours in the costlier part of the city. "Home" means, in a way, this Mausoleum Club where you sometimes talk with me of the times that you had as a boy in Mariposa.

But of course "home" would hardly be the word you would apply to the little town, unless perhaps, late at night, when you'd been sitting reading in a quiet corner somewhere such a book as the present one.

Naturally you don't know of the Mariposa train now. Years ago, when you first came to the city as a boy with your way to make, you knew of it well enough, only too well. The price of a ticket counted in those days, and though you knew of the train you couldn't take it, but sometimes from sheer homesickness you used to wander down to the station on a Friday afternoon after your work, and watch the Mariposa people getting on the train and wish that you could go.

Why, you knew that train at one time better, I suppose, than any other single thing in the city, and loved it too for the little town in the sunshine that it ran to.

Do you remember how when you first began to make money you used to plan that just as soon as you were rich, really rich, you'd go back home again to the little town and build a great big house with a fine verandah,—no stint about it, the best that money could buy, planed lumber, every square foot of it, and a fine picket fence in front of it.

It was to be one of the grandest and finest houses that thought could conceive; much finer, in true reality, than that vast palace of sandstone with the porte-cochère[2] and the sweeping conservatories that you afterwards built in the costlier part of the city.

But if you have half forgotten Mariposa, and long since lost the way to it, you are only like the greater part of the men here in this Mausoleum Club in the city. Would you believe it that practically every one of them came from Mariposa once upon a time, and that there isn't one of them that doesn't sometimes dream in the dull quiet of the long evening here in the club, that some day he will go back and see the place.

They all do. Only they're half ashamed to own it.

Ask your neighbour there at the next table whether the partridge

---

2. Large gateway for vehicles leading into a courtyard or large porch for sheltering persons entering or exiting vehicles.

that they sometimes serve to you here can be compared for a moment to the birds that he and you, or he and some one else, used to shoot as boys in the spruce thickets along the lake. Ask him if he ever tasted duck that could for a moment be compared to the black ducks in the rice marsh along the Ossawippi. And as for fish, and fishing,—no, don't ask him about that, for if he ever starts telling you of the chub they used to catch below the mill dam and the green bass that used to lie in the water-shadow of the rocks beside the Indian's Island, not even the long dull evening in this club would be long enough for the telling of it.

But no wonder they don't know about the five o'clock train for Mariposa. Very few people know about it. Hundreds of them know that there is a train that goes out at five o'clock, but they mistake it. Ever so many of them think it's just a suburban train. Lots of people that take it every day think it's only the train to the golf grounds, but the joke is that after it passes out of the city and the suburbs and the golf grounds, it turns itself little by little into the Mariposa train thundering and pounding towards the north with hemlock sparks pouring out into the darkness from the funnel of it.

Of course you can't tell it just at first. All those people that are crowding into it with golf clubs, and wearing knickerbockers[3] and flat caps, would deceive anybody. That crowd of suburban people going home on commutation tickets and sometimes standing thick in the aisles, those are, of course, not Mariposa people. But look round a little bit and you'll find them easily enough. Here and there in the crowd those people with the clothes that are perfectly all right and yet look odd in some way, the women with the peculiar hats and the—what do you say?—last year's fashions? Ah yes, of course, that must be it.

Anyway, those are the Mariposa people all right enough. That man with the two-dollar panama[4] and the glaring spectacles is one of the greatest judges that ever adorned the bench of Missinaba County. That clerical gentleman with the wide black hat, who is explaining to the man with him the marvellous mechanism of the new air brake[5] (one of the most conspicuous illustrations of the divine structure of the physical universe), surely you have seen him before. Mariposa people! Oh yes, there are any number of them on the train every day.

But of course you hardly recognize them while the train is still passing through the suburbs and the golf district and the outlying

3. Wide breeches gathered in below the knee.
4. Hand-plaited hat made of strips of the leaves of a South American plant, or an imitation of such a hat. In 1912, two dollars would be quite expensive for a Panama.
5. Brake, invented in 1868 by the American inventor George Westinghouse, that works on compressed air.

parts of the city area. But wait a little, and you will see that when the city is well behind you, bit by bit the train changes its character. The electric locomotive that took you through the city tunnels is off now and the old wood engine is hitched on in its place. I suppose, very probably, you haven't seen one of these wood engines since you were a boy forty years ago,—the old engine with a wide top like a hat on its funnel, and with sparks enough to light up a suit for damages once in every mile.

Do you see, too, that the trim little cars that came out of the city on the electric suburban express are being discarded now at the way stations, one by one, and in their place is the old familiar car with the stuff cushions in red plush[6] (how gorgeous it once seemed!) and with a box stove set up in one end of it? The stove is burning furiously at its sticks this autumn evening, for the air sets in chill as you get clear away from the city and are rising up to the higher ground of the country of the pines and the lakes.

Look from the window as you go. The city is far behind now and right and left of you there are trim farms with elms and maples near them and with tall windmills beside the barns that you can still see in the gathering dusk. There is a dull red light from the windows of the farmstead. It must be comfortable there after the roar and clatter of the city, and only think of the still quiet of it.

As you sit back half dreaming in the car, you keep wondering why it is that you never came up before in all these years. Ever so many times you planned that just as soon as the rush and strain of business eased up a little, you would take the train and go back to the little town to see what it was like now, and if things had changed much since your day. But each time when your holidays came, somehow you changed your mind and went down to Naragansett or Nagahuckett or Nagasomething, and left over the visit to Mariposa for another time.

It is almost night now. You can still see the trees and the fences and the farmsteads, but they are fading fast in the twilight. They have lengthened out the train by this time with a string of flat cars and freight cars between where we are sitting and the engine. But at every crossway we can hear the long muffled roar of the whistle, dying to a melancholy wail that echoes into the woods; the woods, I say, for the farms are thinning out and the track plunges here and there into great stretches of bush,—tall tamarack and red scrub willow and with a tangled undergrowth of brush that has defied for two generations all attempts to clear it into the form of fields.

Why, look, that great space that seems to open out in the half-dark of the falling evening,—why, surely yes,—Lake Ossawippi, the

---

6. Cushions made of a type of wool that resembles velvet.

big lake, as they used to call it, from which the river runs down to the smaller lake,—Lake Wissanotti,—where the town of Mariposa has lain waiting for you there for thirty years.

This is Lake Ossawippi surely enough. You would know it anywhere by the broad, still, black water with hardly a ripple, and with the grip of the coming frost already on it. Such a great sheet of blackness it looks as the train thunders along the side, swinging the curve of the embankment at a breakneck speed as it rounds the corner of the lake.

How fast the train goes this autumn night! You have travelled, I know you have, in the Empire State Express, and the New Limited and the Maritime Express that holds the record of six hundred whirling miles from Paris to Marseilles. But what are they to this, this mad career, this breakneck speed, this thundering roar of the Mariposa local driving hard to its home! Don't tell me that the speed is only twenty-five miles an hour. I don't care what it is. I tell you, and you can prove it for yourself if you will, that that train of mingled flat cars and coaches that goes tearing into the night, its engine whistle shrieking out its warning into the silent woods and echoing over the dull still lake, is the fastest train in the whole world.

Yes, and the best too,—the most comfortable, the most reliable, the most luxurious and the speediest train that ever turned a wheel.

And the most genial, the most sociable too. See how the passengers all turn and talk to one another now as they get nearer and nearer to the little town. That dull reserve that seemed to hold the passengers in the electric suburban has clean vanished and gone. They are talking,—listen,—of the harvest, and the late election, and of how the local member is mentioned for the cabinet and all the old familiar topics of the sort. Already the conductor has changed his glazed hat for an ordinary round Christie[7] and you can hear the passengers calling him and the brakesman "Bill" and "Sam" as if they were all one family.

What is it now—nine thirty? Ah, then we must be nearing the town,—this big bush[8] that we are passing through, you remember it surely as the great swamp just this side of the bridge over the Ossawippi? There is the bridge itself, and the long roar of the train as it rushes sounding over the trestle work that rises above the marsh. Hear the clatter as we pass the semaphores and the switch lights! We must be close in now!

What? it feels nervous and strange to be coming here again after all these years? It must indeed. No, don't bother to look at the reflection of your face in the window-pane shadowed by the night

7. Bowler hat made in England by the Christie company.
8. Tract of uncleared land.

outside. Nobody could tell you now after all these years. Your face has changed in these long years of money-getting in the city. Perhaps if you had come back now and again, just at odd times, it wouldn't have been so.

There,—you hear it?—the long whistle of the locomotive, one, two, three! You feel the sharp slackening of the train as it swings round the curve of the last embankment that brings it to the Mariposa station. See, too, as we round the curve, the row of the flashing lights, the bright windows of the depôt.

How vivid and plain it all is. Just as it used to be thirty years ago. There is the string of the hotel 'buses,[9] drawn up all ready for the train, and as the train rounds in and stops hissing and panting at the platform, you can hear above all other sounds the cry of the brakesmen and the porters:

"MARIPOSA! MARIPOSA!"

• • • • •

And as we listen, the cry grows fainter and fainter in our ears and we are sitting here again in the leather chairs of the Mausoleum Club, talking of the little Town in the Sunshine that once we knew.

9. See p. 9, n.2.

Editorial Emendations

This list records all editorial emendations in the present text to the second impression of *Sunshine Sketches of a Little Town* as well as the changes between the first and the second impressions of the book. The latter are followed by (2). Thus "16, 37: Edward VII,] Edward VII.," indicates that on page 16 in line 37 of the present text a period has been removed where one was present in the second impression and "4, 22: marriage, which] marriage which (2)" indicates that on page 4 in line 22 of the present text a comma is present that was added in the second impression. For a discussion of the choice of copy-text and editorial principles of this Norton Critical Edition see "The Present Text" section of the Introduction.

In all impressions of the book, the "Contents" page appears between the author's "Preface" and the sketches themselves. In the first impression, the column containing the sketch numbers is headed by "*Chapters*" but in subsequent impressions it is headed by "*Chapter*".

4, 22: marriage, which] marriage which (2)
8, 12: half way] half-way (2)
8, 24: in fact, to] in fact to (2)
9, 1: Rural Dean] rural dean (2)
10, 21: long, sullen] long sullen (2)
12, 4: walk this] walk down this
13, 18: Mariposa court] Mariposa Court
16, 37: Edward VII,] Edward VII.,
18, 2: business-men] business men (2)
19, 28: Times-Herald] Times Herald (2)
23, 5: ago?),] ago?) (2)

34, 7: realize] realise (2)
34, 20: heard] hear (2)
34, 30: recognized] recognised (2)
34, 37: realized] realised (2)
35, 10: thing, because] thing because (2)
37, 14: parentheses] parenthesis (2)
37, 39: County] county
39, 2: (title) Excursion] Excursions
40, 35: else,] else (2)
43, 34: more] more' (2)
43, 35: Oddfellows'] Oddfellows (2)
44, 17: to go."] to go?" (2)
44, 24: Not even] Not ever (2)

45, 11: seven"; and] seven;" and

47, 6: sand-banks] sand banks (2)

50, 24: "O Canada"] "O Can-a-da"

52, 4: realize] realise (2)

55, 9: stuff hemlock] stuff in hemlock

57, 35: recuperate it] recuperate, it (2)

57, 41: not, instead] not instead (2)

58, 2: devices] advices (*Star*)

61, 39: holiday, and] holiday and (2)

62, 13: in it, and] in it and (2)

62, 14: first-fruit] firstfruit

64, 5: profession) the] profession), the (2)

64, 8: like that] like that, (2)

65, 6: American?] American. (2)

66, 3: Company,—] Company— (2)

66, 9: whether, with] whether with (2)

66, 28–29: "Animals of Palestine,"] 'Animals of Palestine,' (2)

69, 12: room, and] room and (2)

71, 35: the city] the city, (2)

75, 29: that, because] that because (2)

77, 1: it was] was (2)

77, 35: brings] bring (2)

79, 42: the shed,] the shed (2)

82, 40: blossoms] blossoms, (2)

85, 1: unapproachable or] unapproachable, or (2)

86, 2: sentence—for] sentence,—for (2)

86, 3: oath—and] oath,—and (2)

86, 16: House—if] House,—if (2)

86, 22: people—] people,— (2)

87, 11: canaries,—temper] canaries—temper (2)

87, 29: all you] all, you (2)

91, 25: year for coming] year coming

92, 20: rise, that] rise that (2)

92, 20: happiness, and] happiness and (2)

92, 31: *Township*] *Townships* (2)

97, 33: country and] country, and (2)

102, 35: half-pint] half pint (2)

107, 31: focused] focussed (2)

108, 14: may be turned] may be sometimes turned (2)

110, 11: robber; just] robber, just (2)

110, 27: strange, dangerous] strange dangerous (2)

112, 33: County] county

115, 5: centuries should] centuries, should (2)

122, 9: makes] make

122, 37: ideas Edward] ideas, Edward (2)

124, 26: *Hours*'; clear] hours;' clear

125, 37: solicits] solicited (2)

134, 17: o'clock there] o'clock, there (2)

135, 26: And, after] And after (2)

136, 2: town—or] town, or (2)

136, 32: conceive; much] conceive, much (2)

138, 39: tamarack] tamerack

138, 43: Ossawippi, the] Ossawippi the (2)

BACKGROUNDS AND CONTEXTS

Genesis

ALBERT MORITZ AND THERESA MORITZ

The Train to Mariposa†

The years 1912 to 1914 form one of Leacock's primary creative moments. In this period he wrote and published *Sunshine Sketches of a Little Town* and *Arcadian Adventures with the Idle Rich*, books in which he explored the two environments he now inhabited simultaneously: small market town with conservative traditions, and mercantile capitalist metropolis of international and up-to-date pretensions. The history of *Sunshine Sketches*, written and published in 1912, goes back to 1911, when Leacock participated in the national election portrayed in the book's last two chapters, "The Great Election in Missinaba County" and "The Candidacy of Mr. Smith." And it goes back further, to the summer of 1908, when he acquired the property, with its spit of land into Lake Couchiching on Orillia's eastern outskirts, which he named Old Brewery Bay, and built there * * * his first cottage. * * *

By 1911, [Leacock's] increased prominence was attracting opportunities in several spheres. * * * That spring and summer, the country's political passions, heightened by French-English tensions and debates about the economy and Canada's relations to the British Empire, came to a boiling point in the famous, and acrimonious, "reciprocity" campaign that resulted in Liberal Prime Minister Wilfrid Laurier's defeat on 21 September by Conservative Robert Borden. During the campaign, Leacock lent his support as a public speaker to Borden's Conservatives, which meant arguing against the Liberal party's free-trade economic position, even though he himself had taught the benefits of a limited free-trade policy to his McGill students. Leacock's seeming inconsistency arose first from his Conservative friendships and his own general conservatism, and second from the complicated issues of the

---

† From Albert Moritz and Theresa Moritz, *Stephen Leacock: His Remarkable Life*. Copyright © 2002 Fitzhenry & Whiteside Limited. Reprinted by permission of Fitzhenry & Whiteside Limited.

election, which associated free trade with a movement toward the United States, while protectionism was associated with closer ties to the Empire.

* * *

The end of the campaign and the election coincided rather neatly with the opening of the 1911–12 academic year at McGill. That fall there arrived to Leacock a request from the *Montreal Star* that he should provide it with a series of sketches. According to B. K. Sandwell, the idea originated with Sandwell's friend Edward Beck, the *Star's* managing editor, who wanted to persuade the humorist to create a specifically Canadian work. * * * [T]he three men decided that the work would take the form of a serial rather than a series of unconnected pieces and that it would have a Canadian setting. In Sandwell's belief, this agreement represented, at the time, "the only really large-scale commission ever received for a fictional job to be done for a purely Canadian audience."[1]

In creating *Sunshine Sketches of a Little Town*, Leacock filled this bare format with the life and charm of the town of Mariposa. It is possible that Leacock already presented the basic concept in the early meetings with Beck and Sandwell. There exist two pages of his notes, dated 7 January 1912, which are headed "Plan and Ideas for a series of sketches about a little country town and the people in it: Each sketch about 4000 words: General title—SUNSHINE SKETCHES OF A LITTLE TOWN."[2] The first page gives the general concept of *Sunshine Sketches* as a whole, and the second outlines the story that became "The Speculations of Jefferson Thorpe." Leacock records the titles for "sketches up to date" (those already conceived): "The Hostelry of Mr. Smith," "The Speculations of Calverly Short" and "The Tidal Wave of Local Option." The last of these was never written, although its subject, prohibition, was to serve Leacock in future essays. He says to himself, "For Calverly try *Madison* Short" and, on the second page, not satisfied with either name, he devises the title "The Speculations of Jefferson." Here he was using, for this tale of a small town barber's adventures on the stock market, the name of his own barber in Orillia, Jefferson Short. But only the first name satisfied him; sometime between 7 January and the appearance of the sketch in the *Star* on 2 March, he arrived at the surname of "Thorpe."

Sunshine Sketches was written at Leacock's * * * house [in Montreal]. Having made his first notes for the project on 7 January, he worked quickly and the first completed sketch appeared on 17 Feb-

1. B. K. Sandwell, "Stephen Leacock, Worst-Dressed Writer, Made Fun Respectable," 17, and "How the 'Sketches' Started," *Saturday Night* (August 1951), 7.
2. [Leacock], photocopy of notes, 7 January 1912 [Stephen Leacock Memorial House and Museum].

ruary. This piece, "Mariposa and its People," and the second, "The Glorious Victory of Mr. Smith" (24 February), were later combined to make the opening chapter of the book version, "The Hostelry of Mr. Smith." Instalments appeared at intervals of one to two weeks, until the series was completed with the twelfth instalment on 22 June. B. K. Sandwell wrote that "the stories were shaped out at the dinner table" of Leacock's home, where the humorist would narrate the ideas he had developed during his early-morning work sessions, thus testing and improving them before committing a final version to paper. His chair was customarily placed well back from the head of the table so he could leap up and move about the room enacting his words when the spirit moved him.

Leacock's notes of 7 January support the oft-repeated claim that characters in the series were based closely upon his Orillia friends and acquaintances. The notes name several of his models: "Jim Smith, Lach Johnson, McCosh, Canon Greene, Jeff Short" and others.[3] He not only knew these people, he counted several of them among his close friends and sporting companions, he frequented their businesses and used their services. The fact that he maintained the associations just as warmly after the book was published as before, together with what testimony can be still gathered from Leacock's Orillia friends and their descendants, indicates that the familiar story of the town's high dudgeon over the book is mainly legendary. * * *

* * *

In creating the book version of *Sunshine Sketches*, Leacock added to it as a preface a lively autobiographical essay he had contributed to the British periodical *Canada: An Illustrated Weekly for All Interested in the Dominion*; this appeared on 23 December 1911 under the title "Stephen Leacock: Professor and Humorist." * * * [T]o create the book's preface he added to his essay three concluding paragraphs that qualify the apparent resemblances between Mariposa and Orillia. * * *

As with characters, so too with incidents: Leacock adapted, combined and transformed actual happenings in Orillia. The burning of Dean Drone's Church of England Church in "The Beacon on the Hill" was based on the burning of Saint James Anglican, whose incumbent, the Reverend Richard Green (rector 1888–1911), was the model of the "Rural Dean." * * * The fire that destroyed Saint James broke out just after nine o'clock in the morning on Sunday, 19 March 1905, and like the fictional fire it left the church "nothing but a ragged group of walls with a sodden heap of bricks and

3. This and subsequent information on the originals of Leacock's characters in [*Sunshine Sketches of a Little Town*] are from research of the SLMH staff in the SLMH files and exhibits.

blackened wood. . . ." Even the financial situation surrounding the fire provided elements for Leacock's fiction, in which the dean, hard-pressed to meet the mortgage payments for the needlessly elaborate church, is rescued as by providence from his financial quandary when the overinsured building burns. Although the insurance on Saint James did not cover the rebuilding costs, it did exceed the value of the mortgage. * * *

Perhaps the best known of his chapters, "The Marine Excursion of the Knights of Pythias," is also the best example of the way in which he modelled his material not only from factual happenings but also from Orillia's institutions and ideas. In narrating the ill-fated excursion of the *Mariposa Belle*,[4] Leacock suggests that its disastrous "sinking" is in fact a customary event. * * * Arthur Lower has traced the origin of "The Marine Excursion" to the sinking of the lake steamer *Enterprise* at its dock in Barrier in August 1902. On the other hand, * * * Ralph Curry points out that the steamer *Islay* sank while skirting the Couchiching shore in a manner similar to that of the *Mariposa Belle*. While the *Enterprise* is probably the physical model of Leacock's steamer, the third of the three boats that served Lake Couchiching around the turn of the century, the *Longford*, has perhaps the strongest claim of all to being his inspiration. It did not sink; one warm afternoon in October 1898, it ran aground on a sandbar, just as the *Mariposa Belle* later did, during a businessmen's outing. At the wheel was Captain Laughlin ("Lockie") Johnson, the original of Leacock's Captain Christie Johnson. The details of this incident * * * [were recorded by] an unnamed *Orillia Times* reporter * * * [o]n 27 October 1898. * * *

* * * In *Sunshine Sketches*, Leacock's imagination was able to combine many forms of humour—wit, satire, verbal play, caricature and exaggeration, understatement, nonsense in plot and in dialogue—to a degree that very few writers have achieved. And yet, the book's tone springs from something more fundamental than its humour: Leacock's comic view of the world, which suffuses his portrait of Mariposa with a kindly but melancholy light in which everything is clear yet subtly muted, softened and distanced. A loving depiction of the present is mysteriously blended with nostalgia, and a tenuous sense of foreboding that perceives fragility and an invisible decay. When Leacock was writing, the small-town Canada he described was in full vigour; he adhered to a real model, yet there is a sense of a lost paradise, of times remembered, in his depiction of Mariposa. In *Sunshine Sketches*, his perfected style— simple yet ever varied, supple, intimate, preserving the accent of

4. Arthur Lower, "The Mariposa Belle," *Queen's Quarterly* LVIII (Summer 1951). 220–7. RC, 99.

speech within his own distinctive version of the essay's sophistication—embodies a vision of an apparently changeless world that in
fact is slowly changing and passing. Mariposa is a benign, privi-
leged mode of existence, but as such it is only an island always
threatened, from within and without, by the corrosive realities of
the great world and of human nature.

Leacock's narrator sees Mariposa from the perspective of an established resident, a community member: Leacock's own perspective as he looked out at Orillia and environs from the home he had
established on Lake Couchiching. The book reveals affectionate
and critical insights into small-town existence that Leacock had
been gathering since childhood, but it does not convey a child's or
adolescent's vision remembered in adulthood. It keeps revealing
facets of the complex attitude of a grown man, a citizen, who is distanced from his fellows by his insight into society and human motives but who nevertheless chooses to belong, even to the point of
closing one eye to folly and ranging himself with those he satirizes:
with their better selves and their hopes, but also with their foolishness and failures. Mariposa is not Orillia but a dissection of Orillia
that is also an imaginative idealization; carrying a great charge of
thanks and praise. * * * Mariposa contains the creative latitude for
a glancing, multivalent, ironic sensibility that can love and mock in
the same breath. Such a sensibility is often viewed with suspicion
in any real town; it is Mariposa where Leacock is actually at home
and a citizen.

True to the nature of comedy, *Sunshine Sketches* shows us a
world in which crises are not of ultimate seriousness, a world that
beyond injustice and disaster renews itself through the always-
repeated rituals of life and the loves and marriages of the younger
generation. Yet the marriage of Peter Pupkin and Zena Pepperleigh
does not have a central, symbolic role; it is not the climax of the
main plot. Leacock was disappointed he had not developed *Sunshine Sketches* as a unified novel; he thought this failure stemmed
from his inability to make the Pupkin-Pepperleigh romance a
thread that ran through the entire book. In fact, the book seems to
indicate that he could not create such a unity because he did not
believe in it. The minor importance of the romance is in tune with
his constant sense, both here and throughout his writings, that motives of self-interest, covetousness and status-seeking underlie romantic sentiments. Like many of his heroines, Zena professes a
love-inspired asceticism, but when she learns of Pupkin's family
wealth, "she bore up as bravely as so fine a girl as Zena would, and
when he spoke of diamonds she said she would wear them for his
sake." Leacock looks at these workings of the human mind mildly
but clearly; his attitude is not condemnatory, but he realizes that

such ready abandonment of avowed principles is what ultimately erodes the human happiness, here represented by Mariposa, that people miraculously manage to find for themselves from time to time. Zena's attitude, magnified, is exactly that of the plutocrat who, in the final essay in the book, "L'Envoi: The Train to Mariposa," sits in the Mausoleum Club in the great city and dreams of going back to his home town, although the journey never will occur. His self-will and acquisitiveness have exiled him and will keep him in exile. Leacock's narrator sits next to this plutocrat in the Mausoleum Club and stage-manages the empty dream of returning. The reader cannot help feeling the ghost presence of Leacock, Montreal professor and political expert, resident and partisan of small-town Canada. Indeed, the narrator had presented himself in these terms, as a sort of parallel to the Mausoleum Club plutocrat, in the "Preface" that balances "L'Envoi" and frames the book. "L'Envoi" is only one of many occasions in *Sunshine Sketches* on which the narrator, who generally distances himself from the foibles under examination, identifies with what he satirizes. In life, Leacock had one foot in Mariposa and one on Plutoria Avenue. He lived a myth of small-town Arcadia and made it more than a myth; at the same time he hungered for, and to a large measure achieved, the success in the climate of the larger "outside" world that is everything to the millionaires, academics and divines of the great city, which he would soon explore in *Arcadian Adventures with the Idle Rich*. Leacock could not be content with the retired, unknown life of a cracker-barrel philosopher. When we read of Peter Pupkin's father, the Maritime millionaire with forestry and real-estate interests and a hand in government and law, we may recall that it was Leacock, of all those on the Orillia scene, who was related by marriage to a similar figure, Sir Henry Pellatt, owner of a magnificent summer estate in Orillia.

It is fitting and effective that *Sunshine Sketches* reaches its climax not in a marriage but in politics. In the election, the falseness of the outside world intrudes most seriously upon Mariposa; the election reveals how prone the people of Mariposa are to be governed by their own foibles. Once the vote is over and this tempest has been stilled into amusing inconsequentiality, the magic power of Mariposa to resist worldly venality and pretension is dramatically confirmed. At the same time, this power is revealed to consist of nothing but the town's ever-vulnerable smallness and harmlessness. The people of Mariposa resemble, in all respects, the people and forces of the outside world. But in them everything that is dangerous has been reduced in scale and placed in a setting where it does not seem to matter. Leacock's melancholy undertone rises from the subtly expressed fact that these dangers do matter, despite appearances. Influences tending towards a more ruthless world do pass into Mariposa. Perhaps they change it for the worse; at any rate, they drive some people out of it to seek a supposedly greater arena, and it is lost to such people, perhaps forever. Even if Mariposa remains always present, always possible, it may move somehow beyond reach, beyond our ability to live in it anymore. This is why the narrator, at the end, is not in Mariposa but seated beside the plutocrat in the Mausoleum Club, dreaming of "the little Town in the Sunshine" but magnetized by the promise of the city. And so the sense that Mariposa's crises and stumbles are not of ultimate seriousness, are always healed in the ongoingness of a small-town Arcadia, must be qualified. In the midst of humour and praise, Leacock's melancholy inscribes a real threat and a real loss.

*　*　*

Reviews

TIMES LITERARY SUPPLEMENT

Sunshine Sketches†

Philosophers have published learned treatises on man's sense of humour—and occasionally with laughable results. Their personal appeal to it has been for the most part unintentional. But if to make other people merry, to supply a comfortable solvent to their too, too solid flesh, is as blessed a thing as to make them wise, then Professor Leacock is indeed a happy man. "Personally," he confesses, "I would sooner have written 'Alice in Wonderland' than the whole 'Encyclopædia Britannica.'" But what if one has pretty nearly achieved both feats, and can still gaily smile and smile! Surely some kind of explanation is necessary. At this conclusion the author of "Literary Lapses" and "Nonsense Novels" has himself arrived. Hence his preface to this new and very welcome volume, SUNSHINE SKETCHES OF A LITTLE TOWN. * * * Prefaces are usually dull, often imprudent. This one is the cream of the book to which it belongs. And yet it is a record of guileless, well-meaning failures, of falls to rise again. Sixteen hours a day Mr. Leacock spent at Toronto University, he tells us, in the acquisition of languages—living, dead, and moribund. "Very soon after graduation I had forgotten the languages, and found myself intellectually bankrupt. In other words, I was what is called a distinguished graduate." He took to school teaching, and school teaching taught him that the laziest and most unbookish boys are the most successful. Theirs is the Kingdom of Mammon. And he gave it up in disgust. Then came a Fellowship in political economy; then the degree of Doctor of Philosophy—life's ultimate cram; for "after that, no new ideas can be imparted." At last fortune began to smile. Mr. Leacock is now head of the Department of Economics and Political Science in McGill University—"the emolument is so high as to place me distinctly above the policemen, postmen, street-car conductors, and

† From *Times Literary Supplement*, 15 August 1912, 320.

other salaried officials of the neighbourhood." And it ensures what a business man can never enjoy—time to think and time to stop thinking—for months on end. The latter of these Mr. Leacock seems to suggest is occupied in writing such trivialities as scientific treatises on the folk-lore of Central China or on the declining population of Prince Edward Island. His real hard work—for which no conceivable emolument would be a fitting reward—is distilling sunshine. This new book is full of it—the sunshine of humour, the thin keen sunshine of irony, the mellow evening sunshine of sentiment. Universal things like these are not intended merely to pamper the pride of Imperialism. Still, we cannot resist a secret joy in the fact that all the queer and crooked characters that flourish in maple-shaded Mariposa—not a real town, but "about seventy or eighty of them"—are British born. Dr. Gallagher and Judge Pepperleigh, Mr. Pupkin and Jefferson Thorpe, and Golgotha Gingham, the undertaker, with his "caskets," who associated with the living, uninteresting though they often appear, to secure the custom of the dead—these gentlemen see stars only when blindly cheering King George's Union Jack. "Jos. Smith, Prop." *might*, we feel, have been made in U.S.A. His views on Reciprocity have a distinctly American flavour. Mark Twain would have enjoyed the inspiration of his "Caff" and his "Rats' Cellar" and the day of his election:—"Get at it boys; vote and keep on voting till they make you quit!" The Rev. Dean Drone, curiously enough, has a distinct flavour of Hawthorne. And Dean Drone did not entirely approve of Mr. Smith. He had once even "led off a sermon on the text: 'Lord be merciful even unto this publican Matthew Six.' " And it was generally understood as an invitation to strike Mr. Smith dead. But Mr. Smith will live for many a long day. Laughter will keep him sweet. And Drone is perfectly happy in his second childhood, with his Theocritus and his infant class. Encyclopædias come and go. It is in their nature to age. Chairs of philosophy grow rickety in time. But humour is immortal. Falstaff makes better bones than Bacon, and Lewis Carroll will sit hob-nobbing with a little group of children under a May-tree long after the stone is letterless that shelters the dust of Dodgson.

THE SPECTATOR

Sunshine Sketches of a Little Town†

Mr. Stephen Leacock, in a delightful autobiographical preface to his new volume, tells us that many of his friends are under the erroneous impression that he writes his humorous nothings in idle moments when the wearied brain is unable to perform the serious labours of the economist. (Mr. Leacock is head of the Department of Economics and Political Science at McGill University, Montreal.) His own experience is exactly the other way. "The writing of solid, instructive stuff, fortified by facts and figures, is easy enough. There is no trouble in writing a scientific treatise on the folk-lore of Central China, or a statistical inquiry into the declining population of Prince Edward's Island. But to write something out of one's own mind, worth reading for its own sake, is an arduous contrivance only to be achieved in fortunate moments, few and far between. Personally I would sooner have written *Alice in Wonderland* than the whole *Encyclopædia Britannica*." Such sentiments are entirely reassuring, and afford a convincing earnest of the joys of perusing these jocund pages. At the same time we demur to Mr. Leacock's estimate of the frequency of his "fortunate moments." This is not the first but the third volume in which he has contributed to the gaiety of the Old as well as the New World, and for a professor of two dismal sciences the contribution strikes us as decidedly liberal.

Hitherto Mr. Leacock has devoted his fortunate moments to irresponsible fantasies and burlesques. Here he breaks new ground as a chronicler of the annals of a small Canadian provincial town. But he is careful to tell us that Mariposa, on the shores of Lake Wissanotti, is not a real town: "on the contrary, it is about seventy or eighty of them." Similarly the characters engaged are not portraits but composite photographs: they represent types, not individuals. We are quite content to accept Mr. Leacock's *caveat*: the important thing, from the point of view of the reader, is that they combine certain local characteristics with a great deal of essential humanity—freshness with familiarity. The peculiar attribute of the Mariposans is their youth and hopefulness. He does well to call his chapters "Sunshine Sketches," for they have a most welcome freedom from the fashionable pessimism of old-world fiction. The Mariposans have their ups and downs, but they have an invincible resilience; an unquenchable belief in their town and its future; an inexhaustible fund of public spirit. They combine ferocious political partisanship with a complete social solidarity. When the Knights

† From *The Spectator*, 24 August 1912, 277–78.

of Pythias—a society nominally devoted to the Temperance cause—give their annual picnic everybody joins in. [Here follows a quotation of "The Marine Excursion of the Knights of Pythias," from "In Mariposa practically everybody belongs . . ." to ". . . that pretty well settled the question."]

* * * In one sense the Mariposans recall the attitude of the Irishman who said, "I love action, but I hate work." Their social, convivial, and political activities are immense, but they seem to have no regular business hours. The centre of the town is Josh Smith's Hotel, and the central figure of these pages is Josh Smith himself, a man who started life as a cook in the lumber shanties, who could not read, and who looked like an overdressed pirate. His methods were Napoleonic in their unscrupulousness, but underneath a rough exterior he concealed a kind heart. In any emergency Smith took command and inspired universal confidence. He was at once lavish and shrewd: "never drunk, and, as a point of chivalry to his customers, never quite sober"; finally, as a political candidate, he was irresistible. [Here follows a quotation of "The Candidacy of Mr. Smith," from "I wish that I were able to relate . . ." to " 'Well, I'm fer it too,' said Mr. Smith."] Most of the characters in these pages are engaged in trade or business, but there is one charming exception in the person of the Rev. Dean Drone, the incumbent of the Anglican Church, a gentle old scholar, whose only grievance was that his early instructors had never taught him enough mathematics to grapple with the intricacies of church finance. The failure of his various schemes to extricate himself from the burden of debt—the result of an over-lavish expenditure on bricks and mortar—culminating in a "Whirlwind Campaign," exhibits Mr. Leacock in the new light of a humorist who combines a keen sense of the ludicrous with a genuine gift of pathos. Another most engaging character is the local Judge, of whose judicial temper we get many diverting examples. [Here follows a quotation of "The Entanglement of Mr. Pupkin," from "When the Conservatives . . ." to "as with Judge Pepperleigh."] * * * The speculations of Jeff Thorpe, the little barber, who made a small fortune in the mining boom and fell a speedy prey to some Cuban flat-catchers; and the romance of Mr. Pupkin, the little bank clerk, who was afraid to tell his sweetheart that his father was a millionaire, afford congenial scope for Mr. Leacock's skill in handling sentiment in a spirit of kindly satire. There is no bitterness in his laughter, and the epilogue, in which he pictures the dream visit of an exiled Mariposan to the Little Town in the Sunshine, closes an exhilarating volume on a note of tender reminiscence rare in a modern humorist.

NEW YORK TIMES

Amusing Sketches†

You would never guess, from these chuckling little sketches, that Stephen Leacock is a professor of "the dreary science." It is evident that his position as head of the department of economics and political science at McGill University has had not the least depressing effect upon his own temperament. His previous books have won for him the sobriquet of "the Canadian Mark Twain." But that he hardly deserves, quaintly amusing though he is and skillful user sometimes of a method that is something like Mark Twain's own distinctive process for the inspiration of laughter. He himself has too keen a sense of humor not to know that in comparison with the beloved American his own blade of wit is dull and the sparkle of his humor a faint glimmer. Nevertheless, in this series of sketches of the people and the incidents in a little Canadian town there are refined humor and a deep underlying human kindliness. But their chief characteristic is the disguised, tolerant sarcasm with which, with perfect equanimity, he recognizes the weaker and the baser streaks in human nature, and, instead of sneering at them, is moved only to chuckling amusement. It is the distinctive feature of Mr. Leacock's humor and the one that he will do best to cultivate—that and the faculty for unexpected, facetious, Mark Twain-like turns of thought and expression with which he embellishes his entertaining preface.

CANADIAN MAGAZINE

Sunshine Sketches of a Little Town‡

Setting the works of Sam Slick [Thomas Chandler Haliburton] apart for the moment, we know of nothing that could be classed as Canadian humour that equals the first three chapters of this volume. Here we have excellent humour intermixed with wholesome satire. It is wholesome satire, because Mr. Leacock makes good fun out of peculiarities that are common to many Ontario towns. Those of us who have lived in a town like Orillia, for instance, know very well the types personified in Boniface Smith, the barber Thorpe, the undertaker Gingham, and the Reverend Mr. Drone, rural dean.

† From *New York Times*, 29 September 1912, 540.
‡ From *Canadian Magazine*, November 1912, 89–90.

Perhaps it would be not fair to make of Orillia a single instance, for the author may have had in mind such a place as Barrie. Or he may have thought of Fergus. But we suspect that the picture is composite, its application is so general. It is like the sins the evangelist (not Rural Dean Drone) depicts so cunningly that they seem always to fit one's own very self. Still, Mr. Leacock lifts the veil in one or two places, for we know that Glover's hardware store is in Aylmer, even if he does try to locate it in Mariposa. And, again, the banker Mullins used to be in Seaforth, whence he went to Montreal, and then "out West," where he settled down in Vancouver, after first marrying a girl who had sung one season with the Francis Wilson Opera Company. However, humourists should have licence as well as poets, and we do not blame Mr. Leacock for making, to use an expression much abused by lawyers, a change of venue. But we just wish him to know that liberties like this cannot be taken with the *locale* of well-known Ontario business men and nobody say a word about it. No doubt other readers will discover changes of venue, but these two instances show that the author is sufficiently artistic to make a satisfactory composition from all the material within range of his observation. His observation has been enough to see that in many Ontario towns and villages the main street is remarkable for false fronts and telegraph poles of colossal thickness. Furthermore, as he himself writes:

> "To the careless eye the scene on the main street of a summer afternoon is one of deep and unbroken peace. * * *
>
> * * *
>
> * * * Ask any of its inhabitants if Mariposa isn't a busy, hustling, thriving town. * * * [A]sk any of them if they ever knew a more rushing, go-a-head town than Mariposa?"

But what bothers us about this town of Mariposa is the lake. We can fit the maple trees on the side streets, the Oddfellows' Hall, the Knights of Pythias, the brass band, the fire hall, and the Young Men's Christian Association into any number of towns, but the lake fits into only one here and there. Even the population which starts with the census returns at about 5,000, and goes up to various estimates until the bartender at the Mariposa House offers to bet the whole room that there are 9,000 people in Mariposa—even the population fits in. Likewise do the seasons. Dark enough and dull it seems of a winter night, with the lights burning dim behind the shop windows. But in time the snow melts and the ice goes out of the lake (we wish he had left the lake out), "the sun shines high and the shantymen come down from the lumber woods and lie around drunk on the sidewalk outside of Smith's Hotel—and that's springtime." Before we know it, "the sun shines warmer, and the maple trees come out and Lawyer Macartney puts on his tennis trousers, and that's summer time." Later on, "the evening closes dark and still, and in the gloom of the main corner of Mariposa the Salvation Army around a naphtha lamp lift up the confession of their sins—and that is autumn." The eagerness to buy mining stocks was as marked at Peterborough as at Orillia, and everybody everywhere "went in." In Bobcaygeon, just the same as at Mariposa, "Jim Eliot mortgaged the inside of the drug store and jammed it into Twin Temagami. Pete Glover at the hardware store bought Nippewa stock at thirteen cents, and sold it to his brother at seventeen, and bought it back in less than a week at nineteen. They took a chance. Judge Pepperleigh put the rest of his wife's money into Temiskaming common, and Lawyer Macartney got the fever, too, and put every cent that his sister possessed into Tulip preferred." But to know how Jefferson Thorpe, the barber, held his shares in Northern Star one must read Chapter II. And the point of importance about it all is that Mr. Leacock has made to the literature of Canada a contribution of permanent value. He has hit home, and at the same time he has "hit off" many distinctive characteristics of Ontario town life.

CRITICISM

Critical Views

DESMOND PACEY

Leacock as a Satirist†

*   *   *

Leacock's satire is seen most clearly in his three best books: *Literary Lapses, Sunshine Sketches of a Little Town,* and *Arcadian Adventures with the Idle Rich.* The satire is not, however, confined to these books: it occurs intermittently throughout his work, but before we examine other examples, it may be well to consider the basis on which his satire rests.

The satirist is one who makes fun of the follies and foibles of mankind, and who does this by relating men's behaviour to some ideal standard or norm from which they depart. Has Leacock any such satiric norm, or is he, as some suggest, a mere writer of nonsense? I believe that a fundamental unity of outlook underlies all of Leacock's best work. He is, to put it briefly, a country squire of the eighteenth century who revolts against the unbridled acquisitiveness and arrogant commercialism of the early twentieth century. His values are eighteenth century ones: common sense, benevolence, moderation, good taste, His method of presenting these values, however, is the genial one of Addison rather than the savage one of Swift.

For proof that this is Leacock's attitude we may go to both his life and his books. We see the instinct of the country squire in his dress: he wore good tweeds and serges, but wore them carelessly, chose sizes too large, and deliberately eschewed the elegant and the up-to-date. We see it also in the maintenance of his country home at Orillia, to which he retreated after each academic session. There he was a modern Squire Allworthy. "He liked entertaining in Orillia particularly," his niece tells us in her preface to *Last Leaves,* "to fill the house with week-end guests, friends from everywhere. He liked to look down the broad table and proudly point out that every-

† From *Queen's Quarterly* 58 (Summer 1951): 208–19. Reprinted by permission of *Queen's Quarterly.*

thing was 'off the farm', except the can of sardines in the hors d'oeuvres."

But we see all this even more clearly in his books. In *The Unsolved Riddle of Social Justice* (1920), we see it directly, without the mask of irony. This book is the attempt of a benevolent man of the eighteenth century to restore some semblance of decency and order to the chaos of an industrial society. "The tattered outcast dozes on his bench while the chariot of the wealthy is drawn by. The palace is the neighbour of the slum." Here Leacock's effect is less like that which we might expect from a contemporary economist, and more like the probable reaction of Sir Roger de Coverley suddenly confronted with twentieth century London. It is the sturdy common sense of an eighteenth century squire dismissing socialism as "a mere beautiful dream, possible only for the angels". It is an eighteenth century instinct which would patch up the present social order rather than destroy it in favour of a new one. And the patching which Leacock suggests is just that which a benevolent squire of that period would have devised. Let us, says Leacock in effect, look after the children, the workless, the aged and the infirm as those people were looked after in the village by the squire and his lady.

In his greatest book of humour, *Sunshine Sketches of a Little Town* (1912), Leacock uses gentle irony to suggest the same general outlook. Here he creates an idyll of a small community based on the farming life of the surrounding area, and for the closest approach to the picture which emerges we must go again to the eighteenth century—to the 'sweet Auburn' whose passing Goldsmith so movingly lamented. In Mariposa, life moves at a snail's pace, and there is time for the courtesy and contemplation which have been crowded out in the industrial world. Dean Drone, sitting in his garden over a book of Theocritus, is more like the parson of Auburn than the modern 'go-getting' cleric whom Leacock was later to pillory in *Arcadian Adventures with the Idle Rich*. Josh Smith, with his "chequered waistcoat of dark blue with a flowered pattern", "his shepherd's plaid trousers", "his grey spats and patent leather boots", is an innkeeper whom Fielding would have recognised or Dickens seized upon as a survivor from an earlier and more ample day.

Mariposa, however, is not merely an eighteenth century English or Irish village transferred to twentieth century Canada: it is also recognisably a Canadian small town. There were, and happily there still are, such communities in which the noises of the contemporary industrial era are heard only as a faint and distant murmur, and out of them, at this very period, many Canadian regional novelists were shaping their tales. Leacock could write as nostalgically, as sentimentally, as any of them about the beauties of his region. He was not joking when he wrote, in 'The Marine Excursion of

the Knights of Pythias', that "You may talk as you will about the intoning choirs of your European cathedrals, but the sound of
'O Canada' borne across the waters of a silent lake at evening is
good enough for those of us who know Mariposa."

Or was he joking? It is the ambiguity, the subtle irony, of *Sunshine Sketches* which make it so fascinating. Leacock was aware of
the sunshine of Mariposa, but also of its littleness—for there is
irony even in the title. In contrast with big cities like Montreal and
New York, Mariposa is a Utopia, a blessed spot which the tide of in-
dustrialism has almost completely passed by. When 'The Whirlwind
Campaign in Mariposa' fails to produce the results that a similar financial drive had achieved in the city, Leacock drily comments: "It
may be that there are differences between Mariposa and the larger
cities that one doesn't appreciate at first sight." And the flaws in
Mariposa life are chiefly things which, like the whirlwind campaign, arise from a misguided desire to ape the cities. Mariposa
isn't content to be a sleepy small town: it wants to become a
metropolis. * * *

                              *   *   *

SILVER DONALD CAMERON

Ironist†

                              *   *   *

Critical discussions of *Sunshine Sketches* revolve about two central
questions, each of which sharply divides the critics. The first of
these is the book's general flavour: is it sharply satiric, or is it kind
and fundamentally affectionate? The second question is concerned
more with characterization and structure, and with the mind and
motives of Leacock himself: is this a tentative, exploratory step in
the direction of the fully articulated novel and therefore, did Leacock achieve his full potential as a writer?

Obviously, the two questions are logically related. The first turns
on Leacock's relation to his material, on the way he saw the material and intended his reader to see it. Essentially, so does the second: the novelist's concern is with plot and character handled
within a set of conventions for which Ian Watt has suggested the
term "formal realism."[1] Those who feel that Leacock could never
have been a novelist say in effect that Leacock did not see his

---

† From *Faces of Leacock*. Toronto: Ryerson, 1967, 122–37. Reprinted by permission of the
   author.
1. Ian Watt, *The Rise of the Novel* (Berkeley and Los Angeles: University of California
   Press, 1957), 32.

characters, or their actions, in terms of formal realism—in other words, that his type of approach to his material is incompatible with the novel form. The whole question of Leacock's possibilities as a novelist is taken up below. The nature of *Sunshine Sketches* itself is the point at issue at the moment, the way in which Leacock sees the people who inhabit his book and their actions. What is the characteristic quality of his vision?

* * *

Perhaps by looking closely at specific passages one can come to some conclusions about Leacock's general approach. If it is satirical Leacock will distinguish sharply between himself and his characters; if it is intended to be pathetic, he will attempt less to judge his characters than to understand them and to identify himself with them. The ironist displays both attitudes at once. Seeing the characters both from within and without, the ironist simultaneously observes and forgives his weaknesses; he combines the viewpoints of satire and pathos.

Moreover, the ironist's view of character implies an awareness of a duality in the human condition: man is at once both social and individual. As a social being he has a relationship with his fellows, and the relationship carries responsibilities. When he fails to live up to those responsibilities he is a legitimate object of satire. On the other hand he is an individual; seen in terms of his own makeup and the forces acting upon it, his failings in the social sphere are understandable, and he may even take on a kind of nobility. The ironic view of character reflects the complexity of this dual condition.

Although Leacock's vision in *Sunshine Sketches* appears at first to be satiric, and although a large element of the book is undoubtedly satiric, its overall vision is ironic, and in its best passages the reader must be aware, however indistinctly, that he is in the presence of basic questions about the nature of truth and the nature of man. Leacock usually begins with an external view of his characters and comes gradually to suggest their inner lives as well; he begins in satire but he ends in irony. Pathos and humour Leacock considered an ideal blend: "United, each tempers and supports the other: pathos keeps humour from breaking into guffaws and humour keeps pathos from subsiding into sobs. It is like the union of two metals, one too hard, the other too soft for use alone." (*Humour and Humanity*, 233)

* * *

Perhaps the best illustration of Leacock's irony is afforded by the Reverend Rupert Drone, Dean of the Anglican Church. Dean Drone at first appears to be no more than a caricature of the simple

country cleric. His name suggests this; so does his first appearance
in the book, just after Josh Smith has begun his flamboyant career
as proprietor of the old Royal Hotel:

> When the Rev. Dean Drone led off with a sermon on the text
> "Lord be merciful even unto this publican Matthew Six," it
> was generally understood as an invitation to strike Mr. Smith
> dead. (SS 12)

Throughout the first four chapters, Dean Drone remains a figure
who appears only occasionally, and then for satiric purposes. (He
goes on the Marine Excursion of the Knights of Pythias, for instance, with "a trolling line in case of maskinonge, and a landing
net in case of pickerel, and with his eldest daughter, Lilian Drone,
in case of young men.") In the fourth chapter he becomes individualized; we discover that he loves to read Greek, though he refuses
to translate any; he cannot do mathematics; he is much impressed
by such mechanical contrivances as the airplane. And he has had
his great dream: the building of a new church.

But now that the new church has been built, Dean Drone finds it
difficult to pay the debt. Various attempts to raise money all result
in comic catastrophes. Some members of the congregation begin to
blame Mr. Drone, and we discover that he can be hurt. Leacock
records the incident with a sympathy which, though it is flecked
with humour, is remarkably unequivocal:

> Once . . . the rector heard someone say: "The Church would
> be all right if that old mugwump was out of the pulpit." It went
> to his heart like a barbed thorn, and stayed there.
>
> You know, perhaps, how a remark of that sort can stay and
> rankle, and make you wish you could hear it again to make
> sure of it, because perhaps you didn't hear it aright, and it was
> a mistake after all. Perhaps no one said it, anyway. You ought
> to have written it down at the time. I have seen the Dean take
> down the encyclopaedia in the rectory, and move his finger
> slowly down the pages of the letter M, looking for mugwump.
> But it wasn't there. I have known him, in his little study up-
> stairs, turn over the pages of the "Animals of Palestine," look-
> ing for a mugwump. But there was none there. It must have
> been unknown in the greater days of Judea. (SS 65–66)

The Dean's gentleness, his respect for scholarship and his unworld-
liness all unite to evoke his pain, and Leacock's direct reference to
the reader ("*You* know, perhaps . . .") is an appeal for sympathy.
From this point on, Dean Drone is never again the simple figure of
fun he once was.

When the term "mugwump" comes up again its effect is terrible. The climax of the Church's fund-raising efforts is the Whirlwind Campaign, which is another financial failure, and Mullins, the chairman of the Campaign, comes to give the Dean one hundred dollars which Mullins has himself contributed. Mullins later reports that the rector was very quiet:

> Indeed, the only time when the rector seemed animated and excited in the whole interview was when Mullins said that the campaign had been ruined by a lot of confounded mugwumps. Straight away the Dean asked if those mugwumps had really prejudiced the outcome of the campaign. Mullins said there was no doubt of it, and the Dean inquired if the presence of mugwumps was fatal in matters of endeavour, and Mullins said that it was. Then the rector asked if even one mugwump was, in the Christian sense, deleterious. Mullins said that one mugwump would kill anything. After that the Dean hardly spoke at all. (SS 78)

The serious discussion of mugwumps is comic, but something dreadful is happening to the Dean. Soon he excuses himself on the ground that he has some letters to write, but:

> The fact is that Dean Drone was not trying to write letters, but only one letter. He was writing a letter of resignation. If you have not done that for forty years it is extremely difficult to get the words. (SS 79)

The flat simplicity and the understatement are heartbreaking. They are succeeded by a passage equally heartbreaking, in which Leacock's irony reaches perhaps its peak in the whole book; only the "Envoi" can compare with it. The Dean's efforts to write the letter lead him into some hilarious thickets of syntax and meaning. The sense of the letter keeps changing; each draft contradicts the previous one, and finally the letter looks like this:

> "There are times, gentlemen, in the life of a parish, when it comes to an epoch which bring it to a moment when it reaches a point . . . where the circumstances of the moment make the epoch such as to focus the life of the parish in that time." (SS 80)

Yet the context in which this comedy occurs is the moment of final defeat for a good old man who has given his whole life to the charge he is now resigning; who has striven to serve both his gentle God and the community of which he is a devoted member; who has tried in his humble, unworldly, rather bumbling way to leave the world a better place than he found it. Leacock snaps this essentially bitter moment into perspective by showing that the Dean has met defeat even on the ground of his pride in his use of language. It has always been an ill-founded pride, and the source of a good deal of fun. At last the Dean, too,

> . . . saw that he was beaten, and he knew that he not only couldn't manage the parish but couldn't say so in proper English, and of the two the last was the bitterer discovery. (*SS* 80–81)

Leacock concludes the scene:

> He raised his head, and looked for a moment through the window at the shadow of the church against the night, so outlined that you could almost fancy that the light of the New Jerusalem was beyond it. Then he wrote, and this time not to the world at large but only to Mullins:
> "My dear Harry, I want to resign my charge. Will you come over and help me?"

In that last passage the irony twists again. First, of course, the church is seen through the rector's eyes: "the light of the New Jerusalem" is an example of the comically elaborate religious terms and images through which he sees the world. But the deeper irony arises from the fact that there really *is* a light behind the church, though it is not the light of the New Jerusalem. It is the light of flames: the church is burning at the hands of an arsonist—Josh Smith, as later events reveal. In order to solve its financial problems, the congregation fires its church; the irony of this act is complex. It defeats the moral, religious and unworldly virtues of Dean Drone— and for what? To solve a problem which is financial and worldly. Men, Leacock seems to be saying, do not even understand, let alone obey, religious codes of conduct. The fire destroys all the Dean's illusions about the instruction he has given his flock in moral and ethical matters. Not only does the fire destroy the substance of the Dean's achievement as a Christian leader, but also the physical church which was its symbol. By a further irony the Dean himself has caused the fire, however inadvertently, through his own mismanagement. And, in a final ironic twist we discover that the destruction of this church, which is heavily over-insured, will completely finance a new one. The Dean's symbol is thus secured, but the fire which allows Mariposa to secure it obliterates its meaning and spirit.

The Dean realizes something of what the burning of the church implies—or perhaps his reaction is simply one of shock:

> So stood the Dean, and as the church broke thus into a very beacon kindled upon a hill—sank forward without a sign, his face against the table, stricken. (*SS* 81–82)

The Dean recovers from his stroke but is never fully sane again; still a gentle old man, but remote from the world, he suffers from hallucinations, and Leacock takes leave of him in a passage which, though coloured with humour, is suffused with compassion:

> So you will understand that the Dean's mind is, if anything, even keener, and his head even clearer than before. And if you want proof of it, notice him there beneath the plum blossoms reading in the Greek: he has told me that he finds that he can read, with the greatest ease, works in the Greek that seemed difficult before, because his head is so clear now.
>
> And sometimes—when his head is very clear—as he sits there reading beneath the plum blossoms, he can hear them singing beyond, and his wife's voice. (SS 86)

Once again there is direct reference to the reader, too: "you will understand." Looking back over these various passages, one is struck by the number of such references, and by the fact that there are two extra characters in each scene: the narrator and the reader. Quite clearly, neither is exempt from Leacock's humorous scrutiny. In fact, much of the humour of the book is based on the interplay among the inhabitants of Mariposa, the narrator (who is evidently not Leacock), and the reader.

The narrator is naive, unsophisticated, baffled by such abstractions as election issues; a Mariposan to the core, even something of a Booster, he usually seems quite unaware of moral issues. Like Gulliver at the court of Brobdingnag, he often tells a true story which he expects will display the glories of his home, but which instead exposes its hypocrisy, immorality and pettiness. Such a character is an ideal vehicle of satire, and indeed the narrator does quite unconsciously direct a good deal of the book's satiric thrust. But he is balanced by the reader, and the "real" truth constantly passes back and forth between the two.

This reader-narrator interplay begins the book. The narrator, who knows what Mariposa is "really" like, shows the reader around the town, demonstrating that the surface impression is not the actual truth. ("But this quiet is mere appearance. In reality, and to those who know it, the place is a perfect hive of activity." SS 2) Is the narrator right in this and in his other comments on Mariposa? Perhaps—and perhaps not. In the first and last chapters, Leacock's equivocating irony is brought to bear on both the city and the little town. Each has virtues which the other cannot share; each has shortcomings to which the other is immune. The wider scope the city offers is necessarily accompanied by cold impersonality, while the small town, which provides warmth and community, lacks privacy and tends to stifle initiative. The Mariposan view of the city is instructive here. The town usually sees the city as treacherous and malign. Mullins reflects, after the Whirlwind Campaign has failed, that there are "so many skunks in Mariposa that a man might as well be in the Head Office in the city" (SS 77), and similar remarks are made throughout the book. Yet, as Desmond Pacey has pointed out, Mariposa spends a great deal of energy in trying to become a metropolis; the narrator's comment that the town is "a hive of activity"—SS 2) Is the narrator right in this and in his other Mariposa's view of the city, an irony which reflects the town's simultaneous rejection of and longing for city values? The overall effect of *Sunshine Sketches* is to leave us with a similarly complex awareness of the way of life symbolized by Mariposa.

To a considerable extent, the relation between reader and narrator is responsible for this awareness. That relation begins the book and it carries the same theme throughout. It emerges most clearly in the last chapter, where once again the difference between the outsider's view (this time of the entire town) and the insider's view forms the basis of an ironic coda which comments on a whole rural way of life.

Here the irony turns, to a considerable extent, on our new knowledge that both the reader and the narrator are, like the rest of the members of the Mausoleum Club, originally from Mariposa, and on their inability really to go back. We leave them, after our "mad career" on the train to Mariposa, sitting in armchairs in their club in the city. They have done well in the city; the reader owns a "vast palace of sandstone . . . in the costlier part of the city." (SS 149) Neither of them can ever fully be part of Mariposa again; they notice such things as its out-of-style clothing. The city values of both reader and narrator make them see the town from the outside.

Yet as the train thunders north through the woods, we come to identify with Mariposa, with the way of life represented by the people on the train. The excitement of home-coming mounts; the train becomes the fastest, finest and most sociable train in the world; and finally we arrive at the station, while brakemen and porters cry "MARIPOSA! MARIPOSA!"

At that climactic moment Leacock ends the book by pulling us back again to our actual positions, outside the town, smiling at it a little, and yet filled with a sense of lost youth and innocence. The reader and the narrator have paid a heavy price for their success. Mariposa has more than its share of stupidity and hypocrisy; it also has simplicity and vigour.

And yet life in Mariposa is more complicated, more equivocal than it seems. The narrator has discovered this as he has matured, and the ironic vision rests partly on his recognition both that Mariposa was a good place to be a child and that it would be a bad place to be an adult. He is nostalgic for Mariposa, but he does not leave the Mausoleum Club.

This recognition, however, seems to imply a contradiction in the narrator. I have said that throughout the book he has appeared to be a naive, rather unintelligent Mariposan. Yet in the "Envoi" he is evidently a city dweller of considerable penetration and insight. Does this indicate a flaw in Leacock's conception of him? No: Leacock evidently conceived of the narrator as an intelligent man feigning simplicity. This explains a good deal: the speed with which the narrator moves from cowardice to courage when the steamer sinks, for instance, is both attractive and credible if the narrator is only pretending to be unaware of the inconsistency.

*   *   *

W. H. MAGEE

Stephen Leacock: Local Colourist†

Most of Stephen Leacock's surprisingly few durable pieces of humour gain their solidity from characters and themes of the type prominent in the tradition of local colour fiction. In turn, his unique blend of humour, as well as a rare insight into life, make his version of local colour memorable. Both the local colour tradition and his special strengths contribute, for example, to the success of "My Financial Career", the first story in his first volume of humour, *Literary Lapses* (1910). The timid young man who momentarily loses his wits during his first visit to a bank reflects the small town dread of big city sophistication which underlay both American and Canadian local colour at the turn of the century. Henceforth he will save money, but he will keep his savings in a sock. He represents all the virtues admired by the tradition, which treated naiveté as innocence, stubbornness as perseverance, dullness as sobriety, and moral conformity as integrity. Consequently Leacock does not look on the hero as a fool at all. Instead he presents him to us as a friend, a companion for genial humour rather than a target for satire.

*   *   *

Sunshine Sketches of a Little Town contains all the familiar ingredients of typical local colour, although in this version they look a little strange because the most memorable characters are more elaborated and more integrated into a larger purpose than usual. Yet in the background there are several quaint characters who have

† From *Canadian Literature* 39 (Winter 1969): 34–42. Reprinted by permission.

not been developed. The village drunk—here schoolteacher Diston who never gets a raise—is a staple of local colour fiction; and the undertaker Golgotha Gingham is similarly extraneous to plot and and theme. More developed but still peripheral vignettes include Yodel the auctioneer, Mullins the banker, and fiery Judge Pepperleigh. A local custom which comes right out of the tradition appears in the opening chapter, when the steam merry-go-round comes to Mariposa town and the calculating innkeeper Josh Smith treats all the children. Such characters and incidents justify the claim of the opening sentence that there are "a dozen towns just like it", but they also recall Canadian literature as much as Canadian life. They help to evoke the familiar golden atmosphere of "a land of hope and sunshine", as Leacock put it in his preface. But the atmosphere gains much more strength from the more developed incidents, which are all Leacock's own.

From the first Leacock presents Mariposa not so much in the usual formless collection of odd characters and bizarre incidents as through a pervading sense of a whole life. With a typical sense of being at the centre of the universe, the townsfolk talk of "main street" and the "lake" from the first page on, ignoring the proper Indian names. They display their self-centred pride even more actively by comparing the width of Main Street favourably with that of Wall Street. These mannerisms are merely amusing, but Leacock uses other special customs and features of the environment to help define the four seasons of the year in Mariposa. By winter the electric light is as strong as coal oil lamps, by spring the farmers from Missanaba County stroll through Mariposa like dangerous lumbermen, by summer the seven cottages on the lake are rented, and by autumn the Salvation Army sings on street corners under naphtha lamps. In such a description Leacock goes beyond typical local colour, and beyond his typical humour too, using both as a means of comprehending a whole society.

In terms of characterization, the simply quaint figures like Diston the drunk schoolteacher merely lurk in the background of the stories. For the two bank clerks, in contrast, Leacock uses a sort of inverted quaintness by stressing their city-like similarity (the one with the cameo pin and the face of a horse, and the other one with the other cameo pin and the face of another horse). A central figure like Josh Smith may look at first like "a character" (and "an overdressed pirate"), but he quickly becomes a rounded, vigorous and amiable representative of the small town at its best. Most unexpected of all, the town barber Jefferson Thorpe plunges right through the layers of quaintness and reveals a pathetic man of high principles who automatically assumes the money losses of townsfolk who have speculated foolishly on his advice.

This example of exceptional integrity indicates both a final trait which Leacock shares with the lesser local colourists and at the same time the insight which makes his version great. Like them he assumes that no evil or tragedy worth of the label is possible in the small town of the story. Leacock can be funny or this topic too, putting the perspective of humour between himself and the small town. When the *Mariposa Belle* sinks in six feet of mud in the "lake", he tells us that disasters such as mass drownings never occur in Mariposa. The quip sounds satiric, but in effect it is whimsical. Leacock clung to his love of the small towns for a lifetime just because dreadful things really did not happen in the "land of hope and sunshine". Yet he had the insight to recognize that men can be double-faced in Mariposa just as they can be anywhere. The most successful citizens are in fact hypocrites: Judge Pepperleigh orders the tavern shut down because he was kept out after hours, and Josh Smith ensures that it keeps operating by banqueting the leading citizens daily in his restaurant until his liquor license is renewed. Leacock laughs at both men, but he laughs with kindness. He recognizes human traits which almost every local colourist pretended did not exist in his town, yet they do not infuriate him as they do most humourists, who unlike him are satirists. To him they do not, cannot, constitute evil.

*   *   *

INA FERRIS

The Face in the Window:
Sunshine Sketches Reconsidered†

In the final chapter of *Sunshine Sketches of a Little Town*, the narrator turns to a "you" who is simultaneously himself and the reader and offers this advice: "No, don't bother to look at the reflection of your face in the window-pane shadowed by the night outside. Nobody could tell you now after all these years. Your face has changed. . . ."[1] This act of self-scrutiny, implicating both narrator and reader, is the central event of *Sunshine Sketches*. Through his anonymous but intimate narrator Leacock generalizes less the collective, external experience of small-town life than the individual, internal experience of recognizing and attempting to integrate a self

† From *Studies in Canadian Literature* 3.2 (Summer 1978): 78–85. Reprinted by permission.
1. Stephen Leacock, *Sunshine Sketches of a Little Town*, New Canadian Library (Toronto: McClelland & Stewart, 1960), p. 152. Further references will be incorporated in the text.

fragmented through time. "L'Envoi" redefines the focus of the entire narrative, exposing the internal nature of its ostensibly external
journey and firmly establishing the narrator as the locus of concern. Through the ending Leacock builds into his narrative its own
reinterpretation by providing the cue to the rereading that must
now take place if his imaginative exploration is to be understood
fully. And such a rereading demands that we take seriously the interiorization of fiction in the final pages.

Despite being widely read and taught, Sunshine Sketches remains
one of the most underestimated narratives in our literature. A recent biographer of Leacock has dismissed it as "a parochial treatment of parochialism."[2] Certainly, the surface naivete, crudity, and
shallowness of the book encourage underestimation, and its light
tone discourages critical seriousness. Reinforcing such discourage-
ment is the formidable voice of Robertson Davies declaring that
Leacock "would have laughed at a critic who grew too serious
about his work."[3] But it is also Davies, we remember, who insists on
the deep vein of melancholy in Leacock and who chooses the darkness of "L'Envoi" to represent Sunshine Sketches in his Feast of
Stephen. Moreover, the hybrid nature of the work itself creates a
confusion that muddies discussion and flattens the narrative. The
ongoing (and rather tired) debate about its generic status, for instance, continues to invoke a tradition of formal realism inap-
propriate to Leacock's book.[4] By recognizing that the formative
impulse of Sunshine Sketches is a psychological one, rooted in the
narrator's knowledge of his changed face, we can not only uncover
a different and deeper coherence than commonly recognized but
also locate Leacock's narrative in the mainstream of modern Canadian writing. This is not to say that Leacock is a conscious literary
innovator or a significant precursor of more recent fiction. He is
not. But Sunshine Sketches—largely unintentionally perhaps—is a
more modern and serious work than commonly perceived. By iso-
lating some of its neglected resonances, we can account more satis-
factorily for its enduring power.

The memorable final chapter suggests that the source of that
power lies in the narrative voice that here assumes centre stage.
Through the internalization of landscape and action in "L'Envoi,"
the narrator stands revealed as the weary, disillusioned inhabitant
of the city we had suspected him of being. The imagery surrounding him points to the underlying impetus for the journey into the

2. David M. Legate, Stephen Leacock: A Biography (Toronto: Doubleday, 1970), p. 63.
3. Stephen Leacock (Toronto: McClelland & Stewart, 1970), p. 7.
4. Donald Cameron, for example, leans heavily on Ian Watt's paradigm for the novel in his
   argument for Leacock's potential as a novelist. See Faces of Leacock (Toronto: Ryerson
   Press, 1967).

past that has constituted the main narrative line. Images of night, autumn, and the Mausoleum Club evoke the problems of time and death that haunt the narrator's present, accentuating the psychological urgency of his imaginative return. Time has eroded his sense of a coherent self, and the creation of Mariposa signals an attempt to rediscover a past self lost "in these long years of money-getting in the city." Through memory and imagination, he may be able to reintegrate the self and so make sense of the moments of his existence before death cuts off the possibility of meaning. By referring to himself as "you," he not only draws the reader into this process but underlines the internal split, the self-alienation, that "L'Envoi" as a whole dramatizes and accepts finally as irreparable. Between Mariposa and the Mausoleum Club, as the typography itself emphasizes, there can be no permanent bridge. The train connecting past and present cannot forge the final link, and the selves of then and now remain irretrievably separate. Sitting in the Mausoleum Club, the narrator is left with an empty present and a past that is a nostalgic memory rather than a sustaining presence. Unlike Margaret Laurence, whose *A Bird in the House* recalls *Sunshine Sketches*, Leacock cannot find a way to affirm a continuity of the self through time. But in focusing on this problem of the continuity of the self and formulating it in terms of an experienced disjunction between past and present, Leacock's work draws on impulses close to those animating not only Laurence's fiction but also that of other contemporary writers as diverse as Robertson Davies, Mordecai Richler, and Margaret Atwood. "You have to go home again," asserts Morag Gunn.[5] Leacock's narrator tries to do so, but, like the speaker in Al Purdy's "The Country North of Belleville," he has lost his way.

The melancholy awareness of time as separation and disintegration that surfaces so dramatically in the final chapter informs the whole narrative structure of *Sunshine Sketches*. But in rereading the whole in light of the final interiorization of fiction, the private dimension of this awareness emerges more clearly. Details interpreted previously in terms of social theme assume a psychological significance, generating a new level of narrative coherence. Thus the disposal of Mariposa's small stone church, recorded in the fourth section, becomes emblematic of psychological process in the narrator. Faced with the question of what to do with this symbol of its past, the town initially decides to incorporate the stone into a new structure. When this proves "impracticable," it contemplates refashioning the stone into a wall as a "token." Eventually, the town abandons entirely the idea of retention, selling off the stone to a

---

5. Margaret Laurence, *The Diviners* (Toronto: Bantam, 1975), p. 302.

building contractor, and the old church," like so much else in life, was forgotten" (p. 61). Despite its light, satiric touch, the passage has a peculiar poignancy, an emotional resonance exceeding that required by its social theme. The explanation lies in its personal significance for the narrator as an image of his own relationship to the past. The actions of the Mariposans—their gradual discarding of the past and choice of money in exchange—mirror his own actions and suggest how the changed face of "L'Envoi" came into being. Contemplating his reflection here, the narrator posits a relationship between the self-fragmentation he now recognizes and his repression of his past: "Perhaps if you had come back now and again . . . it [the changed face] wouldn't have been so" (p. 152).

This is not to deny the public, social level of *Sunshine Sketches* as a humorous exposure of small-town consciousness, but it is to suggest that *Sunshine Sketches* operates simultaneously and skilfully on several levels. The narrator's Mariposan pose, for example, constitutes an essential strategy in rendering both the social theme and the explorative private journey. Its role in shaping the satiric public vision is well-known and need not be discussed explicitly; our concern is with its function in articulating the psychological theme. In this effort to discover an authentic continuity of the self, the narrator forges a complex voice that mingles the perspective of a Mariposan with that of the city-dweller and so endeavours to fuse the two central experiences of his life. By adopting the tone of a Mariposan, he reactivates the perspective of his youth, capturing through language the values of Mariposa and his own youthful sense of the town as the boundary of the universe. This naive and confident voice is overlaid with the sophisticated adult voice of experience as language modulates from the folksy rhythms of "Anyway, they were fair and straight, this Cuban crowd" to the educated cadence of "it seemed to spoil one's idea of Jeff" (pp. 30, 33). The voice that stumbles over "eggnostic" and "Gothey" can also handle "theodolite" with ease and casually slip in reference to the *Iliad*. But the very transparency of the Mariposan pose *as* pose suggests that in bringing to bear upon a single image the divergent perspectives of youth and maturity, the narrator has succeeded less in integrating the selves than in reinforcing his sense of their disjunction. This is particularly apparent in his use of mock-heroic techniques where the double perspective operates most strongly. Josh Smith, for instance, prompts a sequence of Napoleonic allusions that serves simultaneously to recreate the view of childhood and to undercut Mariposa's pretentious self-image. Irony is both indulgence and exposure: the narrator participates in the imaginative world of childhood even as his adult self performs the critical act of judgment. But no significant relationship between the two modes of the self emerges. Rather, they remain juxtaposed, thus only underlining the gap between then and now. Such is the typical pattern of the mock-heroic strain in *Sunshine Sketches*. Whether it takes the form of a reference to the "colossal thickness" of the telegraph poles or to the "enchanted princes" of Mariposa, irony tests the self as much as the town and exposes the hollowness in both.

There are moments, however, when the technique becomes more problematic, when irony apparently changes direction as the voices of innocence and experience merge briefly. The voice of experience mingles a critical awareness of the limitations of youth and of Mariposa with a deep yearning for its own lost innocence and simplicity of feeling. Such a yearning permeates the evocative description of Lake Wissanotti on the morning of the ill-fated excursion of the Knights of Pythias. Lingering over the "last thin threads of the mist" and the "long call of the loon," the narrator conjures into being "the land of the silent pine and the moving waters" (p. 36). The utter simplicity of scene calls forth a corresponding simplicity of response and implies a lost relationship to landscape now possible only in memory and the imagination. Immediately following the passage, the ironic mask of the cantankerous provincial returns: "Don't talk to me of the Italian lakes, or the Tyrol or the Swiss Alps. Take them away. Move them somewhere else. I don't want them." Here the mock-heroic does not yield its usual deflation of the Mariposan sensibility. The moment stands as one in which the selves of then and now achieve a temporary fusion of perspective, their values merging as the experienced adult voice meets the ignorant youthful voice in response to Lake Wissanotti. The comic dismissal of the European Sublime is meant seriously. Such moments are rare and rarely unambiguous, marked by a tentativeness apparent even in the above instance where the nervous rhythms of the provincial voice indicate an underlying uneasiness. Uncertainty of tone marks a similar moment when the narrator asserts that the "foyer of the opera in Paris may be a fine sight, but I doubt if it can compare with the inside of Eliot's drug store." Having set up the expected deflation, he disorders the pattern by pausing and adding, "for real gaiety and joy of living" (p. 111). He may well mean what he says. But we cannot be certain. Such passages, with their blurring of the direction of the irony, raise the possibility of achieving a coherent perspective rooted in a coherent self. But they are only transitory moments, constituting glimpses and guesses. More typically, the pattern is one of the separation of past and present, of juxtaposition rather than integration, culminating in the bleak recognition that "Your face has changed."

*   *   *

Mariposa is a static world rendered in terms of timeless fictional modes, but it is enclosed by a framework of reminiscence, a form which acknowledges the inescapability of time. The collision of Mariposa with the world of time in the final chapter accounts for the curious emotional impact of recognizing the Mariposans on the train. At this moment, as Donald Cameron points out, the narrator seems to have grown older, while the Mariposans "are perfectly unchanged by the passage of time."[6] These final pages force the direct recognition of Mariposa as refuge from a relentless chronicity and clarify its role as a wish-fulfilling dream for both narrator and reader. Drawing together the psychological strains of the narrative, the last chapter generates a powerful impact and thus suggests that the enduring appeal of *Sunshine Sketches* has less to do with its social function as collective memory than with its indulgence of the private, subliminal self. This use of fiction as a way out of time contains literary as well as psychological implications, developing not only the theme of the self but also the related theme of fiction. Fiction, Frank Kermode reminds us, endows time with a human shape, provides a meaningful order.[7] The narrator, conscious of himself as a story-teller, is well aware of this function. "I am afraid that this is no way to tell a story," he announces when, in violation of chronological sequence, he reveals the fact of the Mariposa Belle's accident. The revelation, he explains, has been triggered by his pondering "the contrast between the excursion crowd in the morning and the scene at night" (p. 42). Contrast prompts the desire to discover cause, to connect rationally the antithetical moments. Here he identifies the basic impulse of fiction to provide connections and to transform mere successiveness into significant sequence. A story, he implies, is a rational construct of chronological time, imitating and making sense of its linearity.

The tales of the Mariposans imagine different ways of structuring personal time through different literary modes. But whether time appears as the downward curve of disillusionment (as for Jeff Thorpe) or as the rising curve of fulfillment (as for Josh Smith), it possesses a rational shape and coherence. Such sense making, however, as the narrator seems to realize in his comment on his own narration, is a fiction, "a story." Scepticism about the authenticity and adequacy of fiction underlies *Sunshine Sketches* and accounts for its obvious literariness that keeps constantly before the reader the conventionality and fictionality of its resolutions. Romance, pastoral, and picaresque provide the patterns of reconciliation and meaning. Even as the patterns are mocked, they are realized—but only in Mariposa. Time here has been turned into timeless literary convention, and Mariposa differentiated sharply from the real world. While narrative stress on the artificiality of

6. *Faces of Leacock*, p. 145.
7. *The Sense of an Ending* (London: Oxford Univ. Press, 1967).

the creation signals a recognition of the inadequacy of traditional modes as models for contemporary experience, no new model emerges. The narrator has not found a fiction that will suffice: his time remains unreconciled.

The distrust of literary convention in *Sunshine Sketches* goes beyond its traditional function as a strategy of comedy and realism and points to a basic distrust of the imagination itself. Throughout *Sunshine Sketches*, as both theme and shaping force of the narrative, the operation of the imagination is identified with fantasy, retreat, delusion. Within the stories it appears as snare and distortion—Jeff Thorpe dazzled by the imaginative appeal of Cuba, his daughter deluded by visions of an acting career, Zena Pepperleigh falsifying the world through the lens of romance. For the narrator, as we have seen, it functions primarily as retreat from a painful reality. The train of the imagination may be "the fastest train in the whole world," but it can offer no sustaining insight into the narrator's existential condition. Even when *Sunshine Sketches* acknowledges the sustaining power of fiction, as in the case of Judge Pepperleigh and his son, it stresses the falsehood involved. Indulging in the freedom and release that the imagination offers, Leacock yet exposes these as illusory. The view of the imagination implicit in *Sunshine Sketches* is thus sceptical and limited. Leacock identifies the imagination with fantasy, unable or unwilling to distinguish between the two. The distinction, as Leacock's much admired Dickens well knew, is crucial. Aware as Dickens is of the real dangers of the uncontrolled imagination and of the ease with which it can be debased into fantasy, he nevertheless affirms its genuine creativity and essential truth. But Leacock lacks this confidence. And it is this, finally, that lies at the root of his failure to develop the complex artistic potential tantalizingly present in *Sunshine Sketches*. While Davies is doubtless correct in identifying Leacock's social insecurity, his desire to be liked, as contributing to the decline after *Sunshine Sketches*, this insecurity but masks a deeper, more crippling uncertainty—the distrust of his own imaginative power.

BEVERLY J. RASPORICH

Charles Dickens and Stephen Leacock: A Legacy of Sentimental Humour†

I know my Dickens as a Scottish divine knows his Bible.
Stephen Leacock, *My Remarkable Uncle*[1]

The influence of Charles Dickens on the Canadian imagination has been a marked one.[2] More to the point, the influence of Dickens on Leacock was remarkable. Not only do Dickensian references and tributes to the "master"[3] inundate Leacock's essays but he was inspired to write two major books on Dickens: *The Greatest Pages of Charles Dickens* and *Charles Dickens, His Life and Work*, as well as articles, essays, reviews and an introduction to a special American edition of *A Christmas Carol*. Leacock was so involved with the work and intrigued by the character of Dickens that his brother George Leacock is reputed to have remarked with tongue in cheek at a Leacock memorial dinner that he [George] "couldn't write very well about Dickens because he had never met him. Judging by Stephen's books, he must have been on very friendly terms with Dickens."[4]

Obviously, no writer creates as an isolated genius in a cultural or literary vacuum and no writer was more aware of this than Stephen Leacock. In the volume *How to Write* he boldly proposes to student writers: "Cultivate an admiration of other people's words and phrases. Soon you will write your own. In a certain sense all literature begins with imitation. Divergence comes later."[5] With these words, Leacock throws down the glove; the challenge being to unravel those often elusive threads of literary connection between

---

† From *Thalia* 3 (Fall/Winter 1980–81): 17–24. Reprinted by permission.
1. Stephen Leacock, *My Remarkable Uncle* (New York: Dodd, Mead and Co., 1942), p. 43.
2. Another Canadian humorist, Paul Hiebert, explains that as a child "one winter I read the complete works of Charles Dickens." See Paul Hiebert, *Doubting Castle* (Winnipeg: Queenston House, 1976), p. 28. The Western Canadian historian Henry Klassen in "Life in Frontier Calgary" mentions the influence of British Victorian writers, including Dickens, in the 1890s in Calgary. See *Western Canada Past and Present*, ed. A. W. Rasporich (Calgary: McClelland and Stewart West, 1975), pp. 48–49. For the influence of nineteenth-century writers in Canada, see also Gordon Roper, "New Forces: New Fiction, 1880–1920," in *Literary History of Canada*, ed. Carl F. Klinck (Toronto: University of Toronto Press, 1965), p. 277.
3. In the preface of *The Greatest Pages of Charles Dickens* Leacock explains "It is hoped that such a work may be of service not only to readers of fiction, but also to those who approach the work of Dickens as students of literature and disciples of a master." See Stephen Leacock, *The Greatest Pages of Charles Dickens* (New York: Doubleday, Doran and Co., 1934), preface.
4. "Highlights of Speeches at Leacock Memorial Dinner," Clipping from Leacock collection in Redpath Library, McGill University.
5. Stephen Leacock, *How to Write* (New York: Dodd, Mead & Co., 1943), p. 29.

himself and Dickens. Even more intriguing and challenging is to comprehend the divergence in the light of the imitation.

The most important Dickensian influence on Leacock resides in the very concept of humour. Leacock's philosophy or theory of humour, largely expressed in his two major critical books *Humour and Humanity* and *Humour: Its Theory and Technique*, was nineteenth century in origin, conceived from his reading of Dickens and, to some extent, from Mark Twain. Although Leacock often made a critical distinction between the excessive sentimentalism of the Victorian period and "true sentiment," he was a great believer in the tear as complimentary, even fundamental, to the laugh. For Leacock, the theorist, the most artistic and "sublime" form of humour was that created primarily by Dickens "when humor and pathos become one, and the eyes of laughter brim with tears."[6] Romantic and ideal, this was the sort of humour inherited and interpreted by Leacock—a humour which celebrated the standards of geniality, kindness and sympathy, particularly as they applied to comic characterization. Leacock considered the creation of ideal character types as one of humour's highest forms and Charles Dickens the master of this art.[7] It was not the Dickens of epic novel or masterful literary style he best appreciated but the humorous Dickens, the creator of the vast gallery of "immortal" comic eccentrics. From Leacock's point of view, the greatest comic characters of all times were those from Dickens's early farce, the *Pickwick Papers*, because here, exclaimed Leacock, was

> that extraordinary magic by which he [*Dickens*] turns a cheat and a crook into a charming character, a criminal imposter into a thing of delight—that is Dickens, and that is no one else. . . . It is as if the world itself were transformed and its worst sins seen in the light of a kindly and amused tolerance that is higher than humanity itself.[8]

For Leacock, comic characterization meant interpreting man sympathetically in the best Dickensian manner.

In a broader sense, this humour of sentiment, as understood by Leacock, transcended character entirely. The pinnacle of the humorist's art was the creation of an atmosphere which projected a heightened awareness of life, in the fact of the passage of time and the finality of death. As he expressed it:

> There is, as has been said, a still higher plane to which humour can attain. This is seen when the contrasts and incon-

6. Stephen Leacock, *Humor: Its Theory and Technique* (Toronto: Dodd, Mead and Co., 1935, p. 125.
7. Stephen Leacock, *Humor and Humanity* (New York: Henry Holt and Co., 1938), p. 125.
8. Stephen Leacock, *Charles Dickens: His Life and Work* (New York: Doubleday and Co. Ltd., 1936), pp. 32–33.

gruities and misfits upon which humor rests are those of life itself: the contrast between what we might be and what we are,
between the petty cares and anxieties of today and the nothingness to which they fade to-morrow, between the fever and
the fret of life and the final calm of death.[9]

For Leacock, humour was celebration, the best of the fever and fret
of life: Christmas at Dingley Dell or the spirit of the fête recovered
by a Scrooge in *A Christmas Carol*, and brought into high relief
by the melancholy and pathos of the human condition, by, for example, the "poignant sympathy that Dickens felt for oppressed
childhood in the person of the crippled Tiny Tim."[1] Leacock's notion of the most artistic form of humour was decidedly that of the
romantic Victorian, of human sympathy and somewhat graveyard
sensibility.

Although Leacock as a philosopher of humour was obviously the
student of Dickens, his critical interpretations of the Victorian
writer's works were highly subjective and single-minded, revealing
Leacock to be less an astute reader of Dickens than an independent creative humorist sanctifying personally inspiring comic
modes. His most telling judgement was his choice of Dickens's nostalgic comedy of a lost golden age, the *Pickwick Papers*, as possibly
the best work of the Victorian writer. While Dickensian critics will
argue that this choice is, at best, debatable, the *Pickwick Papers*
nonetheless provided an inspiring model for Leacock's *Sunshine
Sketches of a Little Town*.

While the Pickwickian fantasy and its sentimental comedy of a
lost Eden has a universal resonance, it is also a particularly Canadian topic. In *Butterfly on Rock*, Doug Jones identifies the Canadian immigrant's desperate and ambivalent longing for the old
country, for paradise lost, as the foremost pattern of serious Canadian literature.[2] Although B. K. Sandwell in his description of the
"appalling miasma of nostalgia for the homeland, which clings
about all of nineteenth-century Canadian literature" exempts Leacock from longing "for a lost land and lost country,"[3] the humorist's
love of Dickens and the genial utopia of the *Pickwick Papers* suggests a similar quest for British roots. In point of fact, Leacock's
constant delight in the Pickwickian mythology was born in the familiar pattern of the genteel British settler looking to the old country for culture while roughing it in the bush. Leacock's mother,

9. Stephen Leacock, *Humor: Its Theory and Technique*, p. 125.
1. Stephen Leacock, Introduction to *A Christmas Carol* by Charles Dickens (Boston: Merrymount Press, 1934), x.
2. Doug Jones, *Butterfly on Rock* (Toronto: University of Toronto Press, 1970), p. 15.
3. B. K. Sandwell, "He Made Humour Almost Respectable," *Canadian Author and Book-man*, 23, (Fall, 1947), pp. 13–16.

Agnes Leacock, in typical immigrant fashion, had included text-books and a "good supply of reading for a young mind" in her baggage from England, out of which *Pickwick Papers* had made a notable impression on the youthful Leacock.[4] Furthermore, as Northrop Frye has pointed out, this romantic caste of mind which seeks solace in the past—and most particularly, in the pastoral past—is an integral part of the Canadian, and Leacock's, literary imagination:

> The pastoral myth . . . The nostalgia for a world of peace and protection, with a spontaneous response to the nature around it, with a leisure and composure not to be found today, is particularly strong in Canada. It is overpowering in our popular literature, from *Anne of Green Gables* to Leacock's Mariposa, and from *Maria Chapdelaine* to *Jake and the Kid*.[5]

The pastoral ideal is not of course exclusively Canadian; it is as old as Theocritus and Virgil's *Eclogues*; but the concept of the New Eden has been used to define the meaning of America since its discovery. In the history of Western literature the pastoral design has traditionally reasserted itself in response to change and with the most momentous change of all, the industrial revolution, the conflict between pastoral and anti-pastoral forces (often represented by machine technology) has concerned a great many writers. At the turn of the twentieth century, Canadians were faced with a growing industrial nation and an unstable age of transition. Like many other Canadian intellectuals of the time Leacock struggled for optimism in the face of change.[6] The direction of his particular search for an ideal lay largely in romantic humour, with its celebration of a better past. *Pickwick Papers* was such a celebration, which not only satisfied Leacock's fantasy of his lost homeland, but also offered the same comic relief and flight from the awesome machine future just as it had to nineteenth-century British Victorians.

While the pastoral dream as the central, informing myth of Dickens's sentimental humour in the *Pickwick Papers* was "borrowed" by Leacock, it was, at the same time, an archetypal resource of his own Canadian literary perspective. In assessing the impact of Dickens's humour on Leacock, it is important to consider how Leacock was able to reshape what he had absorbed from Dickens's work into a unique and private expression in his *Sunshine Sketches of a Little Town*. In this comic fiction, one does discover what Leacock loved best in Dickens, the sentimental comic pastoral tradition of *Pick-*

---

4. David Legate, *Stephen Leacock* (Toronto: Doubleday and Co. Ltd., 1970), p. 13.
5. Northrop Frye, Conclusion, *Literary History of Canada*, ed. Carl F. Klinck (Toronto: University of Toronto Press, 1965), p. 840.
6. See S. E. D. Shortt, *The Search for an Ideal: Six Canadian Intellectuals and Their Convictions in an Age of Transition* (Toronto: University of Toronto Press, 1976).

wick Papers, and its forerunner, the less integrated narrative of parish life, *Sketches by Boz.* In his own novel, too, Leacock manages that "peculiar medium of make-believe," that humorous *atmosphere* of which Leacock believed "Charles Dickens was the greatest master"[7] and into which sentiment and pathos were clearly infused. In this sense, *Sunshine Sketches of a Little Town* belongs to what David Daiches calls that "true English humour which involves sentiment and romance, which laughs gently at its own tears and has more than half a tear for its own laughter."[8] In *Sunshine Sketches of a Little Town* Stephen Leacock appeared to pour old country wine into new bottles. He married the charm and atmosphere of the pastoral sentimental comedy with the Canadian environment. He created for Canadians a Mariposa myth, a genial native paradise equal to that of Mr. Pickwick's world. Yet the connoisseur will appreciate the private, special vintage of the humour of sentiment which is fermented in *Sunshine Sketches of a Little Town.* As compared to Dickens's romantic brand, its bouquet is subtler, its colour more optimistic, its flavour suggestively native.

In a general sense, the shape of *Sunshine Sketches of a Little Town* is very like that of Dickens's early work. The comic celebration of a passing provincial age discoverable in Dickens's *Sketches* and the arcadian sporting life of Mr. Pickwick and the Nimrod Club also characterizes the village life of Mariposa. Here the epic panorama of the English countryside, illumined by Pickwick and company, is synthesized in the collective psychology and ritual of the Canadian small town. Despite the self-contained geographic and imaginative landscape of Mariposa as village, characters and action are broadly the same. Replacing the original masculine confederacy of Pickwick, Winkle, Snodgrass and Tupman exercising good cheer and fellowship, are Mr. Smith and his hostelers—Jefferson Thorpe, Golgotha Gingham, and the various members of the Knights of Pythias. George I. Ford suggests that *Pickwick Papers* provides for the reader "an intoxicated sense of being on an endless spree."[9] Leacock's work is similarly bibulous. In *Sunshine Sketches of a Little Town* the idyll comprises the sensuous pleasures of eating and drinking in male company, of water parties and Whirlwind Campaigns. This is an ideal world which both authors delineate, and one which depends very much for its idealism on the active pursuit of pleasure. In this sense both novels are reminiscent of what Northrop Frye calls in his analysis of literary utopias, the

7. Stephen Leacock, *Humor and Humanity* (New York: Henry Holt and Co., 1938), p. 109.
8. David Daiches, *Critical Approaches to Literature* (New Jersey: Prentice Hall, 1956), p. 282.
9. George H. Ford, *Dickens and His Readers* (New Jersey: Princeton University Press, 1955), p. 11.

"land of Cockayne, the fairy tale where all desires can be instantly gratified."[1]

The land of Cockayne, however, "as an ideal between the paradisal and the pastoral" is seldom taken seriously; the reason, says Frye, "is that it does not derive from any analysis of the writer's present society but is primarily a dream or wish-fulfillment fantasy." Leacock understood Dickens's work to be that of a comedy of escape and along with his friend, G. K. Chesterton, he delightedly proselytized the fanciful and unrealizable aspect of the *Pickwick Papers*. For Leacock, "Mr. Pickwick walks through life conveying with him the contrast between life as it might be and life as it is."[2] Moreover, those roseate spectacles through which Pickwick peers are synonymous with the unjaded innocence, the beautiful naiveté of youth. In *Sunshine Sketches of a Little Town* "the peculiar medium of make-believe" is also synonymous with the illusion of perfect innocence and perfect pleasure. In Jefferson Thorpe's barber shop with its faded cardboard signs, *Turkish Shampoo* and *Roman Massage*, the reader is transported into such an ideal atmosphere of dream and magic. The most unforgettable fantasy of all is, of course, that standing marvel of Mariposa—Mr. Smith's grand illusion—the French Café. The comic pleasure of "half the people of Mariposa crowded at the little tables; crockery rattling, glasses tinkling on trays, corks popping, the waiters in their white coats flying to and fro, Alphonse whirling the cutlets and pancakes in the air, and in and through it all, Mr. Smith, in a white flannel suit and a broad crimson sash about his waist"[3] is very like the well-known Christmas celebration at Dingley Dell. Both are the land of Cockayne. They are comic because we know them to be only illusions of ideal harmony and pleasure.

Both Dickens and Leacock convey the understanding to their reader of the Land of Cockayne, of the fictional world as fantasy, through their similar sense of the theatre—a sensibility and a perspective which contribute to the pathetic element of sentimental humour. It is as true of *Sunshine Sketches of a Little Town* as it is of *Sketches by Boz* and the *Pickwick Papers* that the people are actors, human action is merely comic drama and everyplace seems a stage. The sense of stage is often accomplished by the pastoral scenery, which is really only the backdrop for the comic action. Leacock, in fact, with a director's skill, introduces us to Mariposa as a series of seasonal sets complete with changes in lighting: "The days shorten.

1. Northrop Frye, "Varieties of Literary Utopias" in *Utopias and Utopian Thought*, ed. Frank E. Manuel (Boston: Houghton and Mifflin Co., 1966), p. 41.
2. Stephen Leacock, *Humor: Its Theory and Technique*, p. 122.
3. Stephen Leacock, *Sunshine Sketches of a Little Town* (London: John Lane, The Bodley Head, Eighth impression, 1912), p. 29.

The visitors disappear. The golden rod beside the meadow droops and withers on its stem. The maples blaze in glory and die. The evening closes dark and chill, and in the gloom of the main corner of Mariposa, the Salvation Army around a naptha lamp light up the confession of their sins—and that is autumn" (p. 9). In the *Pickwick Papers* too, the comic players are often highlighted against their backdrops. A typical and very famous scene is that of Mr. Tracy Tupman making hilarious love to the spinster aunt, Miss Wardle, framed against a pastoral bower of "honeysuckle, jessamine and creeping plants."[4] In *Sunshine Sketches of a Little Town* we have a similar stage-view of Zena Pepperleigh in a pastoral frame. As a small-town Eve, she is posed on her father's piazza, dreaming romantic dreams and eating apples among the Virginia creepers (p. 167). Through this distanced stage perspective, the reader implicitly understands that human action is self-conscious posturing, that the expectations of pastoral harmony and perfection are only stage illusions, and ultimately that man on his stage merely plays an insignificant and ironic comic role.

With this stage illusion, Leacock manages to celebrate life even as he dispels the grand dream; by so doing he juxtaposes the laugh with the tear and proves his own romantic theory that humour in its highest plane is based on the incongruity of "the Fever and the Fret of life and the Final calm of death."[5] Leacock obviously learned the effectiveness of such theatrical presentation from Dickens and from the tradition of Victorian melodrama, which boldly and crudely alternated pathos with comedy. Indeed, it seems that he may even have been directly indebted to the Victorian writer for theatrical situations, in that the parish political election and the steam-boat excursion from the early pastoral comedy *Sketches by Boz* reappear in the Canadian environment in *Sunshine Sketches of a Little Town.*

In truth, the steam-boat excursion was not foreign to Canadian waters. Arthur Lower bears witness to Leacock's "good humoured satire" on the sinking of the *Mariposa Belle* as a Canadian actuality, which, he explains, in Leacock's fictionalized account signified the "passing of the epoch—that period between the early pioneer days and our modern urban civilization, when the primitive methods of getting about had been superseded and the ubiquitous gas engine had not come into being."[6] Historically, for Dickens and Leacock, the steam-boat excursion was a natural subject for romantic humour, but Leacock had the advantage of Dickens's example: the

---

4. Charles Dickens, Vol. 1. *The Posthumous Papers of the Pickwick Club* (London: The Caxton Pub. Co., n.d.), p. 75.
5. Stephen Leacock, *Humor: Its Theory and Technique*, p. 125.
6. Arthur Lower, "The Mariposa Belle," *Queen's Quarterly*, 58 (Summer 1951), p. 220.

sinking of the *Endeavour* from *Sketches by Boz*. It was an example
well taken in Canada in the first decade of the twentieth century
where the anxiety for Canada's national future as an industrial society was uppermost in the thoughts of Canadian intellectuals. The
comedy of the *Mariposa Belle* was, and still is, one of Canada's
most popular comic anecdotes and has, in effect, achieved a mythic
proportion.

Despite the Canadian reality of the *Mariposa Belle*, the steam-
boat excursions in Leacock and Dickens are remarkably similar
sketches in their evocation of the laugh with the tear. In both
sketches the initial mood is that of childish exhilaration and exu-
berant play before the ship's departure. In Leacock's book we rediscover the child's perspective in such a simple description as that of
the *Mariposa Belle*:

> why, look at all the decks on her! There's the deck you walk on
> to, from the wharf, all shut in, with windows along it, and the
> after cabin with the long table, and above that the deck with
> all the chairs piled upon it, and the deck in front where the
> band stand round in a circle, and the pilot house is higher
> than that, and above the pilot house is the board with the gold
> name and the flag pole and the steel ropes and the flags.
> (p. 69)

In both sketches that peculiar magic of comic fantasy is conveyed
through the pleasurable expectation of an ideal celebration. On
stage, this is demonstrated by the physical joy of confused prepara-
tions. In *Sketches by Boz*,

> the people shouted, and porters ran down the steps with lug-
> gage that would crush any men but porters; and sloping boards
> with bits of wood nailed on them were placed between the out-
> side boat and the inside boat; and the passengers ran along
> them and looked like many fowls coming out of an area; and
> then the bell ceased, and the boards were taken away, and the
> boats started, and the whole scene was one of most delightful
> bustle and confusion.[7]

On the *Mariposa Belle* too, "everybody was running up and down
all over the boat with deck chairs and camp stools and baskets and
found places, splendid places to sit, and then got scared that there
might be better ones and chased off again" (p. 74).

This "atmosphere of exhilaration," which Leacock found a positive feature in *Pickwick Papers*,[8] soon gives way to a more sombre
tone. The "atmosphere of exhilaration" proceeds from the charac-

---

7. Charles Dickens, *Sketches by Boz*. Vol. II (London: The Caxton Publishing Co., n.d.),
   p. 489.
8. Stephen Leacock, *Charles Dickens: His Life and Work*, p. 32.

ters' grandiose expectations—expectations which are understood to
be sadly unrealistic. The hopes of the unmarried women, for example, for romantic excitement on the steamships (Lilian Drone, Miss
Cleghorn and Miss Lawson on the *Mariposa Belle*, and the Misses
Tauton on the *Endeavour*) are humorous because we know these
dreams to be illusions. In fact, on the steamboat excursions, that
incongruity between expectation and result, which is the very
essence of sentimental humour, is fully demonstrated. While Dickens brings in a squall and a dramatic bout of unpleasant seasick-
ness for his revellers, Leacock punctures the idyll with a mock
sinking. While Dickens's contrast is passionate—even vengeful—
Leacock's is more pathetic. The tone of his account of the disori-
ented Mariposans in their mock disaster is that of wistful,
affectionate recollection: "But when you write about Mariposa, or
hear of it, if you know the place, it's all so vivid and real that a thing
like the contrast between the excursion crowd in the morning and
the scene at night leaps into your mind and you must think of it"
(p. 73).

Yet the essential humour of both writers is the same. It is that
humour of romantic despair born from an overwhelming sadness at
the passage of time and human mortality. As the *Endeavor* pulls
away from the dock to its potential celebration in *Sketches by Boz*,
the old gentlemen are seen walking up and down in pairs on the
deck, marching "as if they were doing a match against time for an
immense stake" (p. 491). They are perfectly symbolic of both authors' romantic conception of the awful brevity of the human condition, an awareness which demands both laughter and copious
tears.

In *Sunshine Sketches of a Little Town*, Leacock's genius in de-
signing sentimental humour was of a more singular and ultimately
more genial variety than Dickens's was. In *Pickwick Papers* the
grand mythological innocence of Pickwick is a dominating factor in
the humour, but in both the *Pickwick Papers* and *Sketches by Boz*
humour is also generated by a gothic touch—by the incongruous
exposure of the slightly malicious or unseemly aspects of the human psyche as a contrast to its genial side. In "The Steamboat Excursion" children are the butt of a devious humour as they are
thumped and whacked about. In Leacock's world there are no such
infant comic butts. Instead, everyone is child-like and seemingly
still in a state of original innocence. Leacock's most successful
comic method in *Sunshine Sketches of a Little Town* does not depend on mythic characterization as much as *Pickwick Papers* does
and certainly does not depend on a grotesque exposure of the unpleasant side of man. It depends mainly on a melodramatic comic
tempo which is inspired by the theatrical Dickens, but which is less

obvious and more up-beat than Dickens's violent juxtapositions of contrary emotions. Although Leacock was fascinated by Dickens's art of managing melodrama he was critical and anxious about its artistic respectability. *Oliver Twist* particularly elicited his worried comment:

> In other words, that peculiar tone of *Oliver Twist*, the distinctive style of narration, is something like the "comic relief" of the melodrama, with which Dickens was only too well acquainted. Here the audience were saved from the humiliation of tears by the reappearance of the comic character of the play. In melodrama the hysteria of tears heightens the hysteria of laughter, each sentiment reacts upon the other. But everyone knows that the effect is inartistic and unworthy. It is a nice point to decide how far such a method of narration may be carried.[9]

Leacock's best sentimental humour was much less melodramatic than the sharp contrast between the hysteria of tears and the hysteria of laughter which the Dickens reader discovers in *Oliver Twist* and the *Pickwick Papers*.

In *Sunshine Sketches of a Little Town* the "hysteria of tears" which Dickens presents in *Pickwick Papers* through Dismal Jemmy's tale (p. 27) is suppressed as mere melancholy for the ravages of time and is implicitly conveyed through a highly theatrical and imagistic technique. This successful technique depends on description of static portraits which the author telescopes for the reader, and then exuberantly vitalizes through a "new standard of vision," speeding up the images to a point of comic exhilaration. The Main Street of Mariposa introduced to the reader as frozen in a death-like attitude of deep and unbroken peace is comically revived through the "reality" of excessive action, of men working on the sausage machines in the basement of Netley's butcher shop and the "four distracting girls on high stools wearing steel caps and talking incessantly" (p. 4). Similarly, the immobilized world of the violet-eyed Zena Pepperleigh is interrupted and thrown into motion by the junior teller of a daffodil blazer, riding past on his bicycle, pedalling faster and faster: "In a second he had disappeared in a buzz and a cloud of dust, and the momentum of it carried him clear out into the country for miles and miles, before he ever dared to pause or look back" (p. 171). The "match against time for an immense stake" is implicit in this technique much as it is in Keats's famous metaphor of the Grecian urn with its frozen symbolic figures of permanent, ideal and expectant life. The tableau of the dentists and lawyers in Macartney's Block "with their coats off ready

---

9. Stephen Leacock, *Charles Dickens: His Life and Work*, pp. 46–47.

to work at any moment" (p. 4) satisfies the desire of the romantic artist for perfection and immortality. Yet the comic impossibility and even the undesirability of this desire is fully reckoned in *Sunshine Sketches of a Little Town* as the author injects movement and life. Thus Leacock manages to maintain throughout his fiction, a brilliant comic tempo of exhilaration which approaches melancholy but which never succumbs to the kind of excessive despair one knows in Dickens's fiction.

For Leacock, the ultimate ideal was in romantic/sentimental humour—in humour with a humanity and optimism that would surpass even Dickens's. This highest form of humour was sublime and temperately pathetic, not passionately morose, nor aggressive in spirit. In *Sunshine Sketches of a Little Town*, Leacock placed his Mariposans in the sunshine and treated them gently, with decorum. It was a touch which was suggestively Canadian. Like Archibald McMechan and Andrew McPhail, Leacock was schooled as a "perfect Christian gentleman." In Leacock's comic recollection of the struggle to make him a gentleman at Upper Canada College, he reveals that what this education encouraged was piety, ethics, dignity and toleration. "Slowly," he recollects, "we learned the qualifications of a gentleman . . . A gentleman would not chew gum in St. George's Church, nor imitate the voice of an Anglican Bishop. A gentleman, it seemed, *couldn't* tell a lie—not wouldn't, just *couldn't*.[1] Most important, a gentleman disregarded the unpleasantries of life. He held to a greater idealism that superseded miserable reality. Leacock gives us an example of such a creature, discovered in "the vast Australian empty country that you are not allowed to call a desert:"

> . . . The only place where there was no hair was the part of the head where hair usually grows. That part was as bald as an egg. He had elastic-side boots but no socks. He had trousers but neither braces nor belt. The trousers were loose about the waist-band, and whilst he talked, when standing, he spent most of the time grabbing them and hitching them up just as they were on the point of falling down. . . .
> But the odd thing is that when they came to talk to this man, there is no mistaking from their narrative that he was a gentleman. It was not only his contempt of a tailor that showed it. . . . He still talked like a gentleman and, like a gentleman, had no word of complaint against a little thing like twenty years of sand. (pp. 30–31)

For all of his mockery of the gentleman, it was a role that Leacock took to heart; it was a system of values which determined

---

1. Stephen Leacock, "The Struggle to Make Us Gentlemen," *My Remarkable Uncle*, p. 28.

his ideal and pleasant treatment of the Mariposans in this early humour.

Interestingly, Leacock's Christian education as an Upper Canadian gentleman also affected his somewhat less than tolerant attitude towards Dickens and his indecorous excesses. Although Leacock understood that his link with Dickens was Protestant and Anglo-Saxon,[2] he exercised his excessively conservative "moral imagination" in his criticism of what he considered as profane or indecorous in Dickens's conduct and writing. For Leacock, Dickens's separation from his wife was a failure in moral responsibility and in publicly defending such a separation, Dickens, said Leacock, showed "atrocious bad taste."[3] As a Canadian Christian gentleman, Leacock even took issue with Dickens's audacious imitation of the New Testament, which the latter had written for his children:

> Not even Charles Dickens could improve the marvellous language of King James translations, hallowed by these hundred years; not even Charles Dickens could replace with other words the chapters and the verses that for three hundred years, on land and sea, at the pulpit, at the altar and the deathbed had been the treasured heritage of our race. Not even Charles Dickens could re-ëdit Jesus Christ.[4]

For Leacock, temperance, kindliness and the preservation of innocence were important ideals, particularly in his early humour. Dickens's gothicism was a particular anathema to him and, as he saw it, an anathema to the Canadian consciousness and to Canadian humour. He commented, for example, on the brutalizing effect on children of *A Child's History of England* with its extravagant gory details, the execution of Lady Jane Grey and the burning of Bishop Hooper, "as an affliction on little children."[5] For Leacock, Dickens's "own strange absorption with the horrors of crime and cruelties of the criminal law led him to intrude them too brutally on the minds of his readers; at times it goes beyond what is wholesome and becomes morbid" (p. 167). In humour too, the gothic spirit suggested to Leacock primitive and uncivilized forms. The best of Dickensian humour—indeed of British humour—was of the genial variety. The genial pages of *Punch*, for example, "represented the highest type of English humour," particularly when its serious

2. Stephen Leacock, *Charles Dickens: His Life and Work.* Here Leacock explains, "We are Protestants. . . . (p. 188) He [Dickens] was utterly and absolutely respectable and orthodox. He turned his Christianity round to get the bright side out, and he turned sinfulness the other way to make it look black. We English are still all like that" (p. 189).
3. Stephen Leacock, *Charles Dickens: His Life and Work*, p. 209.
4. Stephen Leacock, *The Greatest Pages of Charles Dickens*, p. 149.
5. Stephen Leacock, *Charles Dickens, His Life and Work*, p. 169.

undercurrent was the "vanity of human life."[6] Those jokes which depended on brutality and which were a part of British culture were not natural to the Canadian imagination. The "dear old huntsman" joke, for example, which evolved out of the British aristocracy, was cruel and uncivilized to the Canadian.

> To us hunting is cruel. Running an animal to death by bursting its lungs from over-exertion or being torn to pieces by dogs when overtaken seems to us a hideous thing. If a fox has to be killed to prevent damage to the poultry, kill it with a shotgun . . . An Ontario farmer, thus musing in the moonlight as he waits for a ground-hog, is a romantic, a poetic sight—a piece of still life far beyond the noise and dirt of a fox-hunt. (p. 206)

In his attitude towards Dickens and his humour, then, Leacock was always the Canadian gentleman who professed his faith in good taste, good sense and ideal human relationships. The black romanticism—the grotesquerie of the human spirit—which shaped so much of Dickens's humour was foreign to Leacock's comic imagination and contrary to his Christian idealism and the hopeful spirit of his Canadian times. Unlike Dickens, who was driven to dramatize his angry protest against social evil and repressive conventions through passionate and grotesque comedy, Leacock was a decorous humanist who preferred a position of civilized and selective romantic retreat, of consistent comic aloofness. Leacock understood that a character like the bizarre and horrific Vholes from *Bleak House* was an unconscious comic manifestation of the dark side of the unconscious but he would not, indeed, could not, create his kind. His own melancholy undertaker, Golgotha Gingham of *Sunshine Sketches of a Little Town*, typifies the Leacock brand of romantic humour. For Stephen Leacock the Canadian humorist, comedy was sublime through sentiment and tears, but never through horror.

Leacock's romantic idealism in *Sunshine Sketches of a Little Town* was encouraged too by his relatively positive attitude in 1912 towards the machine. Unlike Dickens, who was preserving for his countrymen in *Pickwick Papers* the delightful romantic past of provincial life and the pleasurable travel of stage-coach and inn, in the light of an industrial urban future, Leacock in *Sunshine Sketches of a Little Town* succumbed to his own nation's hopeful industrial expectations. Significantly, this is imagized in the single most romantic myth of the Canadian historical experience, the railway. Later, in 1937, in *The Greatest Pages of American Humour*, Leacock indicates his sympathetic understanding of the railway as an evil industrial agent in early nineteenth-century American

6. Stephen Leacock, *Humor: Its Theory and Technique*, p. 205.

writers. Arguing that Washington Irving and Nathaniel Hawthorne
were not native American writers at all, but that "they belonged
with the British in common stock," he makes this peripheral reference to the evil machine:

> In their humour they came together. In each case it is based
> on the polished models of England and France. There is noth-
> ing 'native' about it. Hawthorne's "Celestial Railroad," repro-
> duced in the next chapter, an adaptation of Bunyan's *Pilgrim's
> Progress* to the wicked, clattering world of railways and ma-
> chinery, runs closely parallel to Irving's work.[7]

In *Sunshine Sketches of a Little Town* the world had not yet become
a wicked, clattering one for the Canadian writer. Instead, the glory
and the excitement of the train on the Canadian frontier are revived in the positive remembrance of time past. The Mariposa local
driving hard to its home, "its engine whistle shrieking out its warning into the silent woods and echoing over the dull still lake"
(p. 262), is that grand rather whimsical myth which dominates the
Canadian historical consciousness.

Leacock's vision of the Mariposa local is a far cry from the "fiery
dragon" of Thoreau or the "juggernaut" of Dickens which "brings
rushing doom and ashen death upon the trembling earth."[8] Unlike
those nineteenth century British and American writers who saw in
the image of the railway the potential chaos of civilization out of
control, Leacock's interpretation of the Mariposa local, and even
the modern suburban trolley cars, is not that of malicious energy
but of physical luxury and, in the instance of the former, happy social intercourse. For Leacock, the Mariposa local is a confederation
symbol, the human link between "woods" and "farms" and "great
stretches of bush,—tall tamerack and red scrub willow and with a
tangled undergrowth of brush that has defied for two generations
all attempts to clear it into the form of fields" (p. 261). The Mariposa locale is primarily a genial meeting place and as such a mythic
articulation of a country which, because of vast geography and isolated population, knew the value of human companionship and the
railway as a progressive human instrument. Like *Pickwick Papers,
Sunshine Sketches of a Little Town* is an interpretation of nation as
village but linked, not by romantic stagecoach, but by romantic railroad, by a "marvelous mechanism" which continues to promise the
future "in the trim little cars that came out of the city on the electric suburban express" (p. 259).

7. Stephen Leacock, *The Greatest Pages of American Humour* (London: Methuen and Co.,
1937), p. 26.
8. Quoted from *Dombey and Sons* in R. G. Collins, "Nineteenth Century Literary Humour," *Mosaic* 9, No. 4 (1976), p. 13.

Although Leacock as the sentimental humorist of *Sunshine Sketches of a Little Town* was very much inspired by Dickens's early work, the locale of his fiction and the special nature of his hopeful, ideal humour was very much his own and, for that matter, very much Canadian. For all the geniality and ideal temper which Leacock celebrated in the *Pickwick Papers*, Dickens never entirely extinguished his grotesque consideration of the human psyche even as he upheld sentiment and humanism. His character, Gabriel Grub, for example, in the *Pickwick Papers*, experiences a moral awakening when he understands that "men like himself, who snarled at the mirth and cheerfulness of others, were the foulest weeds on the fair surface of the earth" (p. 307), but before he does so, Dickens indulges in the bizarre, sadistic comedy of the goblin penance. As poor Grub is force-fed a blazing liquid, the whole assembly of goblins screech with laughter at his choking and coughing. Significantly, Leacock chose to overlook the violent and sanguine disposition of this Pickwickian humour. Indeed, that macabre strain of British Victorian humour in general, where oysters were "et" in Lewis Carroll and ships' crews devoured in W. S. Gilbert, worried him. Leacock preferred, instead, mirth and cheerfulness of an ideal kind. By diverging in such a way from a special thrust of Dickens's comic imagination, Leacock curiously proved himself to be a Canadian writer who was more sentimental than his mentor.

While it is obvious that Leacock learned from Dickens, he proved to be a man of his own time and place in his attraction to and interpretation of the nineteenth-century comic mode of the humour of sentiment. It is quite obvious too that sentimental humour derives from what we have come to label, somewhat pejoratively I think, in the twentieth century as a "romantic frame of mind." The modern reader, schooled in contemporary modes of biting satire and black comedy may be inclined to laugh at sentimental humour, rather than with it. It is good to remember, though, that sentimental humour means celebrating humanity, treating people kindly in the sunlight because underneath the cherishing of the life experience is the sad recognition that joy in living is transitory and that life is brief. This is the condition which all of us share; it is the condition, after all, of being human.[9]

9. Stephen Leacock, *The Greatest Pages of American Humour*, p. 174.

FRANK BIRBALSINGH

Stephen Leacock and the Canadian Literary Sensibility†

The subject of nationality in relation to Canadian politics, economics, history, and literature has received more attention than it probably deserves. This is partly because definite conclusions arc never reached, and may in fact be unreachable; so the subject returns. As far as literature is concerned, the subject has returned many times, in the form particularly of efforts to show a connection between Canadian culture, or social conditions, and the imaginative writing that has been produced in Canada. Northrop Frye has commented variously on an 'obliterated environment' in Canadian history, on the presence of a 'garrison mentality' in Canada, and on a Canadian sensibility that is 'profoundly disturbed'. Although he is skeptical of any 'causal relation' between 'social conditions' and 'great literature',[1] Frye seems to hint at some connection between Canadian culture and the kind of literature produced in Canada, at least up to the end of World War Two. And ten years ago, when she claimed 'survival' as the 'single unifying and informing symbol'[2] of Canadian culture, Margaret Atwood was also pointing to some relationship between Canadian culture and Canadian literature.

Although other commentators have gone so far as to claim that Stephen Leacock's humour expresses a cultural outlook or sensibility that is uniquely Canadian, this claim has not been widely accepted. If it had been, the periodical *Mosaic* may not have been so willing, only a year ago, to publish an essay under the title, "The Leacock Persona and the Canadian Character",[3] which argues that Leacock's humour expresses a specific Canadian—rather than American or broader North American—sensibility. But the essay does not attempt to show the extent to which Leacock's Canadian literary sensibility is shared by other writers in English-speaking Canada—those among his contemporaries, as well as some who preceded him before his birth in 1869, and the many others who followed after his death in 1944.

Since this claim—that Leacock's writing is the product of a sen-

† From *Canadian Literary Review* 1 (Fall/Winter 1982): 73–84. Reprinted by permission.

1. For 'obliterated environment' see Northrop Frye, "In Quest of Identity and Unity," *Globe Magazine* (20 February 1971), p. 9. The remaining excerpts, in order, are from Frye's "Conclusion," in Carl Klinck, ed., *Literary History of Canada*, vol. 2, 2nd ed. (Toronto, 1976), p. 338; p. 342; p. 335.
2. Margaret Atwood, *Survival* (Toronto, 1972), pp. 31–32.
3. Beverly J. Rasporich, "The Leacock Persona and the Canadian Character," *Mosaic* 14:2 (Spring 1981).

sibility shared by other Canadian writers—forms my main argument, I note with curiosity that toward the end of a long and distinguished writing career, Leacock himself explicitly denied the Canadianness of writing (presumably including his own) in Canada:

> Nor is it possible to say that there was in the nineteenth century a "Canadian" literature, meaning literature written in Canada in a Canadian way which others may admire but did not originate. Most people would agree that there is still none . . . Nor is there similarly a Canadian humour, nor any particularly Canadian way of being funny. Nor is there, apart from varying accents, any Canadian language. We use English for writing, American for conversation and slang and profanity, and Scottish morals for moral philosophy and solemnity.[4]

The non-existence of a 'Canadian' literature implies that, in Leacock's view at any rate, there was no distinctively Canadian literary sensibility at the time he made his statement. Yet the argument here is not only that his writing expresses a distinct sensibility, one that had emerged collectively among English-speaking Canadian writers by the early 1900s, but also that Leacock's role in the evolution of this Canadian literary sensibility is such that it would be hard to imagine Canadian literature being what it is today without his writing and its example.

If "literary sensibility" is taken as a characteristic, recurring attitude or point of view to be found in the writing of any given period, and if, so far as this essay is concerned, "Canada" is defined as "English-speaking Canada", then the writing of British expatriates like Frances Brooke and Thomas Cary, in the second half of the eighteenth century, may be reliably taken as the first recognizable examples of cultural attitudes in Canadian literature. During the nineteenth century, clearer attitudes can be detected in the poetry and fiction of such writers as Thomas Chandler Haliburton, John Richardson, and Charles Sangster. And by the early decades of this century, particular attitudes had begun to recur often enough to suggest the emergence of a distinct outlook, as shared by writers like Sara Jeannette Duncan, Stephen Leacock, and Duncan Campbell Scott, among others.

Although it is less true in Frances Brooke's time, when in terms of culture Canada was no more than a provincial outpost of Great Britain, and more true in Leacock's period, when Canada was regarded as a 'colonial nation', it is possible to identify fairly distinctive cultural attitudes recurring among the writers of each period of Canadian literary history, as well as between writers from different

4. Stephen Leacock, *Canada: the Foundation of its Future* (Montreal, 1941), p. 215.

periods. But this essay offers no more than a general sketch of its subject, and it is not possible to make detailed reference to each writer concerned. In any case, it is not particularly revealing to examine pre-1867 stages in the expression of cultural attitudes in Canadian literature. Suffice it to say that by the time Leacock's *Sunshine Sketches of a Little Town* appeared in 1912, a good deal of Canadian writing reflected an outlook on life characteristic enough to stand as a literary sensibility.

In the forementioned essay on Leacock's persona, Beverly Rasporich acknowledges that 'Leacock was not remote from changing continental American comic mythology', but she successfully argues that his persona 'nonetheless remains very much an expression of the Upper Canadian frontier and a rural mythology'.[5] This argument need not be repeated here except to illustrate essential features of Leacock's writing which will help to make clear his literary sensibility. The two most important of these are his zeal for documenting social manners, especially those that are still not fully formed or stabilized by settled culture or custom, and the mild-mannered, ambivalent outlook which sustains his persona, and which is best recognized, in Claude Bissell's words, by its 'willing suspension of conviction'.

That Leacock's writing expresses this combination of documentary fidelity and ambivalence will surely not be disputed by anyone familiar with Mariposa, the fictional town that forms the setting of *Sunshine Sketches*. In his preface to the original edition of the book, Leacock emphasizes the composite character of Mariposa and its citizens, giving the impression that *Sunshine Sketches* is based on observation of actual towns and people in Canada. Also in his preface, Leacock claims to take the inspiration for the book from 'a land of hope and sunshine'. However, the incongruity between this description and the actual behaviour of Mariposans cannot be more striking. As the reader discovers and re-discovers with unceasing and growing delight, Mariposa radiates instead of 'hope' or 'sunshine', a large assortment of peccadilloes: naiveté, self-importance, ignorance, vanity, hypocrisy, prudery and gullibility. These and other failings form the dominant mores of Mariposa's townspeople who, alone in the world, are convinced of the spacious 'width' of their streets, the 'extraordinary importance' of their buildings, and the 'mad round of gaiety' in their 'busy, hustling thriving town'.

Whether it is Jos. Smith, 'the natural king of the hotel business', who executes 'one of the most brilliant and daring strokes in the history of licensed liquor', or Mr. Golgotha Gingham the under-

5. *Ibid.*, pp. 79, 83.

taker, who in 'the true spirit of his profession' never uttered such a word as 'funeral' or 'coffin' or 'hearse', but spoke always of 'interments', of 'caskets' and 'coaches', Mariposa is full of people whose actions contradict their stated intentions as well as the motives acknowledged by both themselves and their fellow citizens. Needless to say, there is little genuine integrity or simple good sense to be found in Mariposa. All is affectation and simulation, contradiction and incongruity. Whatever latent virtue or dignity may exist is obscured by misguided intentions and unreal expectations, aided and abetted by fallible human nature.

The sermons of the Rev. Dr. Drone, rural dean of the Church of England, deal not only with 'matters of faith, but contained valuable material in regard to the Greek language, to modern machinery and to a variety of things that should have proved of the highest advantage to the congregation'. As for more sophisticated intellectual or literary activity, none can compare with Mallory Tompkins who 'had read all sorts of things and had half a mind to write a novel himself—either that or a play'. He wrote nothing, of course. But as Leacock describes him, Tompkins 'was a mighty intellectual fellow', proof of which was to be found in his books, 'the Encyclopaedia Metropolitania in forty volumes' and 'the History of Civilization, in fifty volumes', both of which were bought on the installment plan and taken back when Tompkins did not pay; although he had read the second set 'half way through the Stone Age before they took it from him'.

If vain delusions and hypocritical aberrations were the chief appeal in Leacock's Mariposa, his book would be a not unpleasing, ironic account of quaint manners and regional North American customs with provision of some vivid local colour. This local colour undoubtedly contributes to the artistic appeal of the book. But it is less important than the particular attitude which the author brings to his subject, one that allows Leacock to record Mariposan failings absolutely without contempt or distaste, and with a characteristic lack of harshness. This is the sustaining appeal of his writing: that vain, hypocritical, jealous and mean-spirited people, who could evoke a response as savage as Swift's to Lilliputians and Yahoos, form, in Leacock's vision, perhaps the most endearing community on earth. Instead of condemning the Mariposans for what he clearly perceives and describes as faults, Leacock regards them with warm affection. This apparently contradictory stance—of loving what he has described as limited or ridiculous—constitutes the uniqueness of Leacock's sensibility. That it also informs an outlook dominant among his Canadian contemporaries is the crux of the argument that follows.

According to R. E. Watters, the apparently contradictory stance in Leacock's fiction amounts to 'calculated diffidence',[6] a good-tempered restraint which avoids both the anarchic humour and 'amiable nonsense' of an English writer like P. G. Wodehouse, and the vindictive, 'iconoclastic satire' of an American like Sinclair Lewis. Interestingly, Watters attributes this neither-British, neither-American stance, in some degree at least, to the fact that Canadians 'have never known the easy national security and laurelled self-confidence' out of which Wodehouse's 'nonsense' issued. According to him Canadians also lacked the 'wealth and strength which can both provoke and withstand' Lewis's satire.[7]

The British novelist J. B. Priestley is more explicit than Watters in declaring that Leacock 'achieves an outlook, manner, style, that typically British or American humorists would find it impossible to achieve.' Priestley calls Leacock 'a unique national humorist' and relates his literary point of view to 'the humour of a nation that notoriously finds national self-expression not at all easy'. Priestley emphasizes this connection between Leacock's humour and the outlook of the typical Canadian, a 'baffled man'[8] who is partly British and partly American, and yet different from either. As Priestley implies, the typical Canadian tends to adopt an ambivalent stance partly because he is unable to express cultural difference from his British and American brethren.

Claude Bissell also links Leacock's ambivalent literary sensibility to Canada's mixed but flexible 'political and social conditions'; a situation that 'decreed reconciliation rather than polarization, diversity rather than integration.' Bissell observes that such conditions have 'political advantages'. But he claims they have 'literary advantages'[9] as well, and cites the work of Leacock (and of Thomas Chandler Haliburton) as 'proof'. For Leacock to take 'literary advantage' of such conditions was to give expression, as he did, to this uncertain sensibility, the logical inheritance of a people whose British ancestors settled in North America and became culturally Americanized while nevertheless *resisting* Americanization. This dynamically shifting, half-British, half-American historical inheritance had the practical effect of ensuring Canada's survival as a nation, through fending off both political absorption by the United States and complete colonial domination by Great Britain. It also engendered and strengthened that instinct for pragmatic compromise and for undeclared, wavering attitudes that registers as ambivalence in Canadian culture and in the writing of Stephen Leacock.

6. R. E. Watters, "A Special Tang," *Canadian Literature*, 5 (Summer, 1960), p. 25.
7. *Ibid.*
8. J. B. Priestley, "Introduction," *The Bodley Head Leacock* (London, 1957), p. 10.
9. Claude Bissell, *"Haliburton, Leacock and the American Humorous Tradition,"* *Canadian Literature*, 39 (Winter 1969), p. 19.

*   *   *

* * * [O]f course * * * [a]mbivalent attitudes are the stock-in-trade of writers the world over; they are abundant certainly in English literature, at least from Chaucer onward. Yet, as R. E. Watters and J. B. Priestley have argued, there is a difference between Leacock's writing and the literary humour produced in Britain and America. To identify this difference as the 'calculated diffidence' of a 'baffled man' who is typically Canadian seems largely justified by the historical factors in Canadian culture that have been already mentioned. The fundamental historical factor in this culture is one of transplantation from Britain; and it has parallels which can be seen in territories of European settlement overseas, for example, Australia, New Zealand, the Caribbean, and nineteenth century America.[1] Leacock's writing reveals closer similarities with these transplanted, British-colonial or neo-colonial literatures (including that of the U.S.A. during the first two or three generations after Independence) than with the literature of Great Britain or twentieth century U.S.A.

In Leacock's story "My Financial Career," the man who opens and closes his first bank account in one blind, desperate gesture is bewildered and rendered helpless by the incongruity between his unreal expectations of banking and the reality of actual, routine banking procedure. His exhibition of incongruity is similar to that of the character, Mallory Tompkins, or of V. S. Naipaul's Pundit Ganesh,[2] both of whom measure the scope of their learning by the number, or yardage, of books on their shelves. Because Leacock defined humour as "the kindly contemplation of the incongruities of life and the artistic expression thereof,"[3] one would imagine that the contemplation of incongruity in "My Financial Career" would have much in common not only with *The Mystic Masseur*, but also with the *Prologue* to the *Canterbury Tales, Joseph Andrews, The Pickwick Papers, The Diary of A Nobody*, and so on.

But although their behaviour is just as incongruous as that of Chaucer's Prioress or Parson Adams, or Mr. Pickwick or Pooter, Leacock's one-day financier and Naipaul's Ganesh differ from their British counterparts in that *their* uncertainty must be placed in a social milieu. They stand in their environment on fresh, untested ground in intimate contact with an unsettled mixture of transplanted cultural forms. Thus, while a good deal of British humour may also rely on incongruities of human behaviour as expressed through features of social class, the affectation, vanity and hypoc-

---

1. British culture is dominant in the English-speaking Caribbean although it is not an area of predominantly European settlement.
2. V. S. Naipaul, *The Mystic Masseur* (London, 1957).
3. Stephen Leacock, *Humour and Humanity* (London, 1937), p. 11.

risy of Chaucer's Prioress rely, for instance, more on her own individual waverings than on any confusion of social and cultural practices. It is this latter state of affairs which motivates and sustains the characters in Leacock's stories and in the early novels of V. S. Naipaul.

Similar comparisons may be drawn between Leacock's writing and the stories of Frank Sargeson of New Zealand, or between Leacock's humour and the fiction of several nineteenth century American humorists.[4] But at the same time, however closely the social milieu and moral situation of Leacock's stories may correspond with those of other neo-colonial writers, the correspondence is not to be taken as uniform or complete. As Beverly Rasporich has pointed out, the attitudes of Leacock's 'little man' do not correspond exactly with the attitudes of characters created by nineteenth century American humorists: 'the real voice of the humour (Leacock's) is distinctly that of Canadian gentility.'[5] The real voice of Naipaul's early writing is equally distinctive—more hypercritical and wounding than is compatible with Leacock's genial chuckles in *Sunshine Sketches*, while the moral earnestness of Frank Sargeson's stories appears more stern and severe, although as replete with examples of affectation and incongruity.

As Northrop Frye has hinted, perhaps there is no 'causal relation' between social conditions and art. Yet some writers—Leacock is a good example—show a definite relationship between their social environment and the art which they create, which is not to say of course that Leacock's art depends wholly on cultural factors. The aim here has been to identify a Canadian literary sensibility, and to sketch Leacock's role in its growth and development. For those still not convinced that Leacock's literary sensibility is intimately connected to the social environment in which he lived, it might be worth considering how difficult it is to define this environment. The difficulty arises precisely because of the ambivalence of Canada's cultural and historical traditions. This might help to explain why Leacock denied the existence of Canadian literature even though his own writing provides the best and most enduring expression of the Canadian literary sensibility existing in our imaginative literature.

In *Humour: Its Theory and Technique*, Leacock wrote:

> The idea of national characteristics has been greatly overdone
> . . . The world is being unified into one, and the human race
> being standardized into a type.[6]

4. See B. Rasporich, "The Leacock Persona."
5. *Ibid.*, p. 80.
6. Stephen Leacock, *Humour: Its Theory and Technique* (Toronto, 1935), p. 198.

Here is why Leacock denies the Canadian quality of so many things, creating instead a persona who is 'a Canadian and an internationally minded man.' It is possible that Leacock's idea for this persona stems from a 'national fantasy.' As Ms. Rasporich acknowledges[7] however, it is the same fantasy that informed Canada's role as a mediating power in the 1950s and 60s, the professional go-between, proponent of pragmatic compromise on the international scene, and the first to offer peace-keeping troops whenever needed by the United Nations. It is perhaps the same fantasy that contributed to Marshall McLuhan's vision of the global village, and Frye's conjectures on Canada's 'post national' society.

Expectations of a standardized, urban, industrial, affluent lifestyle which have been realized in much of the world, certainly in Canada, lend support to Leacock's view of an ever-increasing standardization in modern twentieth century civilization. The civilization that has realized these expectations, through machines and technology, has also nurtured writers whose main themes deal with self-diminution, loss, exile, cultural dislocation, placelessness, and a sense of global insecurity, foreshadowed by Leacock, and today most eloquently expressed by fellow Commonwealth writer, V. S. Naipaul. With the resilient example of Leacock's calculated ambivalence firmly established in the Canadian literary sensibility nearly a century ago, it is not surprising that contemporary Canadian writers should accept these modern literary themes as readily as they do, and that they should, for good historical and cultural reasons, feel qualified to consider them with special sympathy and insight.

GERALD LYNCH

From Stephen Leacock: Humour and Humanity†

* * *

"L'Envoi: The Train to Mariposa" takes the completed picture of Mariposa and throws a new light on *Sunshine Sketches* by applying its perceptions of the little town to life in the city. In a manner that parallels the movements between reality and illusion within each previous sketch, there is in "L'Envoi" a quite literal traffic between reality and illusion—"the train to Mariposa."

As this train crosses the bridge over the Ossawippi and moves

7. See B. Rasporich, p. 91, for two preceding excerpts as well.
† From *Stephen Leacock: Humour and Humanity* (Kingston and Montreal: McGill-Queen's UP, 1988), pp. 111–20. Reprinted by permission of the publisher.

ever closer to Mariposa, the Envoi narrator exclaims, "We must be
close now!" In a manner that resembles a technique of the dramatic monologue, the auditor interrupts his anticipation with an
unrecorded, though apparently apprehensive, remark. The narrator
considers the cause of his companion's anxiety: "What? It feels
nervous and strange to be coming here again after all these years?
It must indeed. No, don't bother to look at the reflection of your
face in the window-pane shadowed by the night outside. Nobody
could tell you now after all these years. Your face has changed in
these long years of money-getting in the city. Perhaps if you had
come back now and again, just at odd times, it wouldn't have been
so" (SS, 263). The mirror image here focuses the concerns of
"L'Envoi": self-identity in relation to Mariposa. The Envoi narrator
admonishes his auditor for the relentlessness of his "money-getting
in the city," a relentlessness that has told on his features, making
him unrecognizable to those who have remained in touch with
their Mariposan roots. However, the Envoi narrator is not suggesting that his auditor go home again, only that he should "perhaps"
have "come back now and again, just at odd times."[1] Note, also,
that the nostalgically maudlin and simplistic perception of Mariposa as "home" (SS, 256–57) is not the Envoi narrator's; it is,
rather, the homesick auditor's.

The reader of the *Sketches* may experience at "L'Envoi" a sense
of dislocation similar to its auditor's sense of displacement. Here,
for the first time since the preface, the reader is outside of Mariposa. He is situated now in the "dull" Mausoleum Club, and like
the auditor, he may yearn to return to colourful Mariposa. But before such an imaginative return can be attempted, the Envoi narrator, in a manner reminiscent of the practice of the prefacer and the
narrator of the sketches, must first correct his auditor's mispercep-
tions.

The Envoi narrator initially suggests his auditor's displacement
and ignorance of Mariposa by remarking continually on what he
"knows" and does not "know" (SS, 255–56). The auditor does not
know—or remember—that there is a train to Mariposa, though he
came "from the little town" and once spent many an evening yearning after the returning train. The auditor does not have a definite
reference for the repeatedly emphasized word, "home." Home once
referred to Mariposa, but now home "means that big red sandstone
house . . . in the costlier part of the city," or " 'Home' means, in a

---

1. See Gordon Roper, Rupert Schieder and S. Ross Beharriell, "The Kinds of Fiction,
1880–1920," in *Literary History of Canada*, 3 vols., 2nd ed., eds. Carl F. Klinck et al.
(Toronto: University of Toronto Press, 1976), 1, 352: "The feeling expressed with such
fine modulation in 'L'Envoi: The Train to Mariposa' . . . is much more prevalent than is
the feeling 'You can't go home again.' "

way, this Mausoleum Club" (SS, 255). And, finally, home can once again mean Mariposa when the auditor sits "reading in a quiet corner somewhere such a book as the present one" (SS, 255). Essentially, *Sunshine Sketches* is a reminder of what "home" is, and "L'Envoi" is a concluding lesson in how memories of Mariposa should be employed. But the reader would be as ignorant as the auditor to presume that Mariposa-as-home is an ideal to be set apart in some musty, nostalgically maudlin corner of a Mausoleum Club—an ideal that is occasionally dusted off and shined up. The reader, who is familiar with Mr Smith and with Drone's "beacon," should know better. The Envoi narrator is determined to correct just such a misperception of Mariposa. He does not want his auditor to misread *Sunshine Sketches* and misapply the lessons that it contains.

The Envoi narrator proceeds to recount his auditor's career. Upon first arriving in the city, the auditor, a homesick boy, had planned to "make money," to become "really rich," and then to return to Mariposa and build an ostentatious house—the best that money could buy" (SS, 256). The Envoi narrator remarks that such a house would be "much finer in true reality, than the vast palace of sandstone with the porte-cochère and the sweeping conservatories that you afterwards built in the costlier part of the city" (SS, 256). No doubt the narrator's perception is to some extent "true reality": such a house in Mariposa would be "much finer" than a "palace of sandstone" in the city. The ostentatious house that the auditor had dreamed of building in Mariposa dwindles, however, in comparison with the enchanted home of Peter and Zena Pupkin, which home is located in the "newer part of town" (SS, 211). "Cost" has little to do with the relative enchantments of a Mariposan home; in fact, it can effect enchantment inversely, for, as the reader knows, "some of the most completely enchanted [homes of Mariposa] are the cheapest" (SS, 169). Or to state the point directly, the auditor's early ambition betrays his dream as the gaudy dream of the *nouveau riche*: the small-town boy makes a pile and returns to impress the locals.

The salient characteristics of the auditor are his desire for wealth and his mistaken, nostalgic perception of Mariposa as "home." The auditor changed when he left Mariposa and lost a part of himself. A large part of the cause for his change and loss is that to which the narrator later refers in the central passage on self-identity—"these long years of money-getting in the city." The auditor's obsessive desire for material riches suggests further that he possesses something of a Smithian bent. His ambition also recalls Jeff Thorpe's mistaken desire for impressive wealth and Dean Drone's mistaken faith in his ostentatious beacon. And yet, though the auditor is uninformed in his nostalgic perception of Mariposa and mistaken in his desire for riches with which to build an impressive home in Mariposa, he is nonetheless still thinking of Mariposa. Mariposa remains his reference point. The more threatening trouble arises when he begins to forget Mariposa.

The Envoi narrator regrets that his auditor has "half forgotten Mariposa, and long since lost the way to it" (SS, 256–57). He notes that his auditor is in this respect "only like the greater part of the men in this Mausoleum Club in the city" (SS, 257). And it is here especially that "Mariposa" acquires a degree of abstraction, for it is difficult to conceive that "practically every one of [the Mausoleum Club members] came from Mariposa once upon a time" (SS, 257). Rather, "Mariposa" is intended to suggest collective origins and the past, an interpretation supported by the fairy-tale "once upon a time" which assists temporal suspension. (As the prefacer concluded, "the inspiration of the book . . . is large enough" [SS, xii].) Like the auditor who "half forgets" his origins, the members of the Mausoleum Club are "half ashamed to own" their beginnings in "Mariposa" (SS, 257). Just as the earlier comparison of houses recalled the enchanted houses of the three-sketch love interest, the most favourable treatment of Mariposa, so here the restrained criticism of forgetting and disowning remembers the three sketches on Mariposan religion, the most unfavourable treatment of Mariposa. The auditor and his fellow clubbers are forgetting "Mariposa" in a manner that parallels the way Mariposa discarded the quaint old church which, "like so much else in life, was forgotten" (SS, 105). In an attempt to induce his auditor to remember correctly his origins and the value of Mariposa, the Envoi narrator begins to recall for him some of Mariposa's allurements and to lead him to board, in his imagination, the train to Mariposa. Only such an imaginative re-affiliation with his origins can offset "the long dull evening" (SS, 257) of the Mausoleum Club—a place that, judging from his anxious reaction to his reflection in the window of the train to Mariposa, negates the auditor's fully integrated personality.

The Envoi narrator first entices his auditor with a sensuous appeal. The auditor is asked if his club meals can compare to the fish and fowl that he once caught near Mariposa (SS, 257). (Perhaps memory must begin so, with the body, in order to counter the maudlin musings of the mistaken mind. Certainly Proust thought so.) By a sudden leap of imagination, the narrator and his auditor are aboard the train to Mariposa. "The joke is" (SS, 258) that the city dwellers do not realize that the suburban train transforms into the Mariposa train. This may well be "the joke"—the humorous purpose—of Sunshine Sketches, for, like the train, the book itself provides access to Mariposa. Sunshine Sketches provides the opportunity for an imaginative return to "Mariposa"—to the past, to home, to origins. The community is transformed in Leacock's humorous vision so that it is perceived simultaneously as more real and more illusory, as ironically revealed and colorfully heightened. It may be, moreover, that the shift to the train is not so sudden a leap of imagination. The Envoi narrator began by recalling Mariposa and then unapologetically required his auditor (and the reader) to board the train. Without informed memories of Mariposa, an imaginative return is not possible.

By feigning ignorance of the appropriate, fashionable terminology, the narrator not only insinuates an opposition between himself and his travelling companion but also identifies himself with the temporarily displaced Mariposans aboard the train: "Those people with the clothes that are perfectly all right and yet look odd in some way, the women with the peculiar hats and the— what do you say?—last year's fashions? Ah yes, of course, that must be it" (SS, 258). While in the city, the Mariposans are not individualized. When the narrator points out "one of the greatest judges that ever adorned the bench of Missinaba County" and "that clerical gentleman . . . who is explaining to the man with him the marvellous mechanism of the new air brake (one of the most conspicuous illustrations of the divine structure of the physical universe)" (SS, 258–59), the references are, of course, to Judge Pepperleigh and Dean Drone, although neither is named. In a sense, Pepperleigh and Drone are here accorded a degree of abstraction similar to "Mariposa," in accordance, perhaps, with the prefacer's claim that his characters are types (SS, xi–xii). More important, the references to Pepperleigh and Drone pointedly recall the most favourable treatment of Mariposan life (the romance) and the most disillusioning aspect of life in the little town (the beacon). Only as a result of temporal and spatial distance—such as the auditor has interposed—is Mariposa remembered incorrectly as the ideal "home" or as an untroubled idyllic community. As the train moves towards Mariposa, the two characters of Pepperleigh and Drone emerge hazily to suggest the good and the bad of Mariposan life. "But of course you hardly recognize them while the train is passing through the suburbs and the golf district and the outlying parts of the city area" (SS, 259).

As the train departs from city environs, it undergoes a transformation reminiscent of the electricity which "turned into coal oil again" by the time it entered Mariposa (SS, 8). The electric locomotive "changes its character" and turns into an "old wood engine . . . with sparks enough to light up a suit for damages once in every mile" (SS, 259). Metaphorically, the city and the present, set afire by the retreating train, are left in the distance as the train to

Mariposa enters the country and the past and continues "thundering and pounding towards the north" (SS, 258), "up to the higher
ground of the country of the pines and the lakes" (SS, 260). It is at
this juncture that the Envoi narrator instructs his auditor to "look
from the window as you go" (SS, 260). And there are hints that the
auditor's fleeting journey towards Mariposa/home reflects his country's, Canada's, ongoing struggle for the preservation of a distinctive
identity vis-à-vis the United States of America.

In a passage that anticipates the ultimate indictment of the auditor for having half-forgotten Mariposa, the Envoi narrator regrets
that it is not a lack of opportunity that has kept the auditor away
from Mariposa:

> As you sit back half dreaming in the car, you keep wondering
> why it is that you never came up before in all these years. Ever
> so many times you planned that just as soon as the rush and
> strain of business eased up a little, you would take the train and
> go back to the little town to see what it was like now, and if
> things had changed much since your day. But each time when
> your holidays came, somehow you changed your mind and went
> down to Naragansett or Nagahuckett or Nagasomething, and
> left over the visit to Mariposa for another time. (SS, 260)

Rather than coming up to the country of his origins and affirming
his bond with its changing reality, the materialistic auditor has
spent what free time he could steal going down to vacation in the
United States. (Narragansett is a resort town and its adjoining bay
in Rhode Island; "Nagahuckett" appears to be a conflation of the
names of two other US resort areas, Naugatuck in Connecticut and
Nantucket Island off Massachussetts.) Compared to the melliflu-
ous "Mariposa"—the Spanish word for butterfly—the US names
onomatopoeically suggest the grinding gears of a machine. These
areas are the vacation spots that the auditor has chosen—"you
changed your mind and went down."

The Envoi narrator then contrasts this "Nagasomething" to the
Mariposan countryside that the auditor has been avoiding: "At
every crossway we can hear the long muffled roar of the whistle, dying to a melancholy wail that echoes into the woods; the woods, I
say, for the farms are thinning out and the track plunges here and
there into great stretches of bush,—tall tamarack and red scrub
willow and with a tangled undergrowth of brush that has defied for
two generations all attempts to clear it into the form of fields (SS,
260–61). This is suggestively a view of the country (to borrow from
the title of an Al Purdy poem) north of Toronto.[2] This view is of-

2. See Al Purdy, "The Country North of Belleville," in *Selected Poems* (Toronto: McClelland and Stewart, 1972), 118–19.

fered in opposition to "the city," but it is contrasted also to those vacation spots in the US that were referred to in the immediately preceding paragraph. A recalcitrant land that defies "all attempts to clear it into the form of fields" is a strikingly poetic image that echoes forward to several later Canadian works. Here is an approach to the Canadian landscapes of Lawren Harris, F. R. Scott and A. J. M. Smith, and Leacock has captured the spirit of the land in one seemingly endless sentence. (Of course, the implications arising from the image of a land resistant to "the form of fields" are ones to which later modernists such as Margaret Atwood have devoted much literary exploration.) For Leacock the Canadian hinterland—"the higher ground of the country of pines and the lakes" (SS, 260)—is the place "where the town of Mariposa has lain waiting for you . . . for thirty years" (SS, 261). Mariposa has lain waiting to reaffirm the auditor's sense of self and identity. Mariposa waits as the place to which city dwellers (Mausoleum Clubbers) may yet return, and should return, to revitalize their lives—both individual and collective. But the auditor has "half forgotten" Mariposa, having dismissed the train to Mariposa to ride instead the "Empire State Express" and the aptly named "New Limited" (SS, 261). The auditor is aboard the train to Mariposa only because the Envoi narrator has brought him there. By extension, the representative auditor is aboard only because "such a book" as *Sunshine Sketches* has provided memories and induced imaginings of Mariposa. Still, Leacock does not portray the auditor as a hopeless case. The auditor is on the train in a "half dreaming" state, which suggests an equal mixture of romance and reality and, consequently, the possibility of transcendent, yet accepting, insight into his condition. Furthermore, the positive side to "half forgotten" is that the auditor has "half remembered" Mariposa and so has read such a book as *Sunshine Sketches*.

Significantly, when nearing Mariposa, the Envoi narrator feels none of his auditor's anxiety. Having alternated his narrative mode from "you," to "they," to "you" (SS, 255, 257, 258), the narrator finally clarifies his own position in a passage that employs the first person, thereby stressing his identification with the Mariposans as the train approaches its destination. He refers to some other of the world's fast trains and proceeds in what has previously been termed a Maripocentric manner:

> But what are they to this, this mad career, this breakneck speed, this thundering roar of the Mariposa local driving hard to its home! Don't tell me that the speed is only twenty-five miles an hour. I don't care what it is. I tell you, and you can prove it for yourself if you will, that that train of mingled flat cars and coaches that goes tearing into the night, its engine

whistle shrieking out its warning into the silent woods and
echoing over the dull still lake, is the fastest train in the whole
world.

Yes, and the best too,—the most comfortable, the most reliable, the most luxurious and the speediest train that ever
turned a wheel. (SS, 262)

In a sense the "wheel" is coming full circle. The Envoi narrator's
childish petulance and pride in *his* "Mariposa local" as the best,
most comfortable and speediest "train in the whole world" is of
course quintessentially Mariporentric. Most important, he desires
to be so wholly Mariposan because the Mariposans aboard the train
are "the most genial, the most sociable" of people; having shed
"that dull reserve" of the city, they call to one another by name "as
if they were all one family" (SS, 262). There is no need at this point
to rehearse the numerous times within the *Sketches* when the
virtues of such a communal familiarity—in contrast to Mr Smith
and "the city"—proved overwhelmingly attractive to the narrator of
the sketches.

In the passage that describes the auditor's anxiety over his own
reflection, the narrator at once sympathizes with his apprehensive-
ness and forthrightly reveals its causes. The indictment is twofold:
the auditor is guilty of an over-emphasis on "money-getting" and of
going down to the US instead of occasionally returning to the typically Canadian and somewhat northern town of Mariposa. The two
offences—materialism and a US bias—are suggestively related.
Leacock may well be implying that the obsessive desire for material
gain nurtures an affinity for the "home" of liberal individualism.
Such a relationship is suggested in "L'Envoi," though it would be
mistaken to over-simplify. The auditor lives, after all, in a Canadian
city. Rather, *Sunshine Sketches* disparages unrestrained individualism and crass materialism in favour of the humane virtues of the
Mariposan community. And yet, individualism and materialism are
gaining ground in Mariposa; these are two of the changes the auditor would have noticed had he "come back now and again, just at
odd times." Had he met Smith or attended services in Drone's (or
Mr Uttermost's) new church, he would have seen that "things had
changed" (SS, 260). Perhaps the incongruity between his mistaken
nostalgic memories of "home" and the reality of change for the
worse would have prompted him to perceive and arrest such devel-
opments within himself.

In fulfilment of his credo that humour be "kindly," Leacock portrays the Envoi narrator's final position as one of sympathetic identification with his auditor's plight. "L'Envoi" could have ended with
the train's arrival in Mariposa, with "the cry of the brakemen and
the porters:

MARIPOSA! MARIPOSA!"[3]

The cry recalls the conclusion to "The Marine Excursion," that other, most Canadian of the sketches: "O-CAN-A-DA!" (SS, 93). The cry "Mariposa" would seem similarly to offer a fitting conclusion to *Sunshine Sketches*, but only if the reader is unrealistically predisposed to the escapist, idyllic literature that enjoyed such popularity at the turn of the century. A physical and permanent return to Mariposa was never the Envoi narrator's intention, either for himself or for his auditor. The auditor should have returned "now and again" (SS, 263). For the book to have terminated with the train *in* Mariposa would have been to leave the reader with a falsely comfortable impression, an impression that satisfies an emotional indulgence similar to the auditor's mistaken nostalgia. And, of course, a successful return to and entry into Mariposa would have devalued the criticism of materialism and uninformed memories that the Envoi narrator levels at his auditor.

The final paragraph (the postscript, as it were) of "L'Envoi" serves two critical purposes: first, it shows that the Envoi narrator sympathizes with the plight of his auditor. The narrator adopts the narrative mode "we," thus effectively unifying himself and his auditor back in the Mausoleum Club at precisely the point where an escape into an idealized "Mariposa" appeared imminently realizable: "And as we listen, the cry grows fainter and fainter in our ears and we are sitting here again in the leather chairs of the Mausoleum Club, talking of the little Town in the Sunshine that once we knew" (SS, 264). With Maripocentrism as its communally binding force, the little Town in the Sunshine gathers to its enchanted heart those residents who have visited the city. Leacock closes his "circle of affection," but he sympathetically leaves his philosopher-guide, the Envoi narrator, with the auditor.[4] The pair, now a community of two within the world of the Mausoleum Club, are returned to the real world. The conclusion of "L'Envoi" displays Leacock's humanism: an imaginative and visionary journey out of the self and the present to a northern, ideal community—"The country of the Ought to be"—is followed by a return to "a land of baser men."[5] A conclusion that left

3. When the train carrying a weary Tartarin home from his mock-heroic adventures arrives in Tarascon, two words are shouted, "Tarascon! Tarascon!" I should also note here that my term "Maripocentric" owes something to Daudet's frequently used word for a similar manner of thought and action in Tarascon, the *"Tarasconnade,"* as well as owing something to Dickens' "in a Pickwickian sense."

4. The phrase "circle of affection" is Duncan Campbell Scott's, *The Circle of Affection* (Toronto: McClelland and Stewart, 1947). To repeat, Leacock as prefacer claims that any "fault" of *Sunshine Sketches* "lies rather with an art that is deficient than in an affection that is wanting" (SS, xii).

5. "The Country of the Ought to be" was Archibald Lampman's intended subtitle to his poem, "The Land of Pallus"; see Richard Arnold, "The Clearer Self: Lampman's Transcendental-Visionary Development," *Canadian Poetry: Studies, Documents, Reviews*

the narrator and his auditor in "Mariposa" would have suggested a *contemptus mundi* that was foreign to Leacock's humanistic vision.

The second purpose of the "postcript" is to emphasize what has become increasingly clear throughout "L'Envoi": there is no literal "train to Mariposa." In the context of "L'Envoi," there is no real Mariposa. Mariposa is geographically real to the narrator of the sketches, but it is not to the Envoi narrator. For the Envoi narrator, "Mariposa" is an abstraction, the extrapolation finally from "seventy or eighty" Canadian towns, as the prefacer protested (*SS*, xi). "We are sitting here in the leather chairs of the Mausoleum Club," which, of course, "we" never left physically. The real and only "train to Mariposa" is *Sunshine Sketches*. Imaginative literature, "such a book as the present one," provides access to a correct perception of the past, of origins both individual and collective; and it helps make available in the present the *informed* memories from which imagination can fashion a vision of the future.

The Envoi narrator stresses the importance of periodic imaginative "returns" to Mariposa and demonstrates that, in imagination, by means of realistically and romantically informed memories, he is quite capable of reaffirming his bond to Mariposa. If Mariposa remains only "the little Town in the Sunshine that once we knew," if "we" forget and deny our origins, then "we" are condemned to remain entombed in a Mausoleum Club, waxing nostalgically and with mistaken eloquence on misconceptions of Mariposa as "home." It is just such an ignorance of Mariposa that allows the auditor to fancy that he possesses the proper feelings, thereby freeing himself to pursue competitively his materialistic, individualistic ends. However, the threatened fracturing of the representative auditor's identity, which he experiences when his face is reflected on the window of the imaginative train, is but one of the consequences of forgetting Mariposa. Without realistically informed memories of Mariposa, the auditor also lacks the material of imagination from which to fashion a future based on a correct understanding of the worthwhile from his and his country's past. The Envoi narrator has shown, as has *Sunshine Sketches*, how such an imaginative recreation operates—how, in Margaret Avison's expression, the "optic heart must venture."[6]

"*Quo vadimus?*" asked Leacock with regard to mankind's moral development (*ELS*, 52). In *Arcadian Adventures With the Idle Rich*, he offers a humorous vision of present tendencies in "the City," an American city.

---

no. 8 (Spring/Summer 1981): 50; the second phrase is from Lampman's "The Land of Pallus," in *The Poems of Archibald Lampman*, ed. Margaret Coulby Whitridge, Literature of Canada, Series 12 (Toronto: University of Toronto Press, 1974), 209.

6. Margaret Avison, "Snow," in *Winter Sun* (Toronto: University of Toronto Press, 1960), 17.

GLENN WILLMOTT

The Cost of a Drink in Mariposa†

* * *

As [Gerald Lynch, in *Stephen Leacock: Humour and Humanity* (1988)] shows, importantly, Leacock took a strong, explicit, and consistent stand against the generic realism that, like naturalism, attempts to document and to analyse in the laboratory of fiction the ideological forces and material facts of social history (48 ff.). His concern was to defend nonrealist literary values against a contemporary realist standard of mimetic truth. In a range of writings on literature from 1916 onward, Leacock defended romanticism and idealism in general and methods of selectiveness and exaggeration in practice. This writing has been significantly explored by Lynch, who argues that the romance element draws Leacock's style away from merely destructive satire in the "sentimental" direction of a more explicitly idealist mode of irony. Leacock saw the value of realism not as the basis of a mimetic truth in itself but as the necessary corrective to an ideal or abstract representation. I have introduced the term "abstraction" because it is important to think of this defence of idealism, not primarily in the sense of an assumed metaphysical order or optimistic sentiment thereof, but in the neutral sense proper to his defence of exaggeration and selectiveness from the actual world. What he defends is literary abstraction, the creation of ideal figures whose truth, like mathematics, is conceptual rather than mimetic.

It is the truth of abstraction that Leacock wishes to justify when he puts the characters of Dickens on trial in "Fiction and Reality: A Study of the Art of Charles Dickens." Various characters are called to stand before an imaginary court and prove that they are "real," and their defence always involves asking whether there are not hundreds of persons subject to the same typical quality. For example, Mr. Pecksniff is proud to be judged every bit as real as any other self-serving hypocrite who claims the work of others for his own pecuniary advancement. Indeed, the narrator tells us, as the expression "of the whole spirit and essence of modern business and modern politics, it appeared not merely as if Mr. Pecksniff were extremely real and actually existed, but as if there were more of him than any other human being" (225). Mr. Pecksniff is declared "real" not because his name, appearance, mind, or manner corresponds to that of an actual modern businessman or politician but because

† From *Essays on Canadian Writing* 68 (Summer 1999): 46–76. Reprinted by permission.

what he represents through such details, as a conceptual abstraction, is true to a significant number of them (unless evidence drawn from actually could correct or refute such an abstraction). For Leacock, concepts are more important than mimetic representations.

Idealism, in the form of abstraction, is morally neutral and, like secular or existential humanism, subtle in its metaphysical assumptions. Mr. Pecksniff is the type of certain ideal concepts, but not good ones, and, unlike those that Plato or Augustine imagined fixed beyond the stars, they are historical concepts whose significance is contextual, depending upon the modernizing worlds in which Dickens and Leacock saw them. Whether the concept abstracted is the gregarious self-interest of Smith, the hidden love of Judge Pepperleigh, or the innocent altruism of Edward Drone, what is meaningful is the significance that each has in relation to the other in the larger conceptual field of Mariposa—where, for example, the first might have the stabilizing role discussed above, the second might act as a consolation for the weakness of law before the world's inevitable violence and violent instincts (whether in drunkenness or war), and the third might demonstrate the dead end of a radical politics. It should also be apparent that the world of Mariposa, the entire world of fictional description in *Sunshine Sketches*, need not be organized according to the mimetic coherence of Mariposa to a real landscape or of its characters to real persons. We can assume, rather, that it is organized conceptually, as a field of concepts each selected and drawn from reality but organized as a whole according to a nonmimetic aesthetic structure of imagery and ideas. In this way, it is easier to appreciate how Leacock's characters can seem to oscillate so suddenly between diversely realist qualities—such as the description of Judge Pepperleigh, which combines the most caricatural details (howling at the sprinkler on the lawn, throwing a songful canary's cage into the hushes, uniformed in a tennis blazer [*Sunshine Sketches* 114, 110]) with what [R. D. MacDonald] has called the "profound" evocation of his and his wife's love (101). Characters are called upon to mediate very different kinds of emotional and ideological effects, not to approximate better a real psychology but to place certain concepts side by side in an abstract and wholly aesthetic unity. Whether Smith is a good or evil businessman in Leacock's political-economic vision is a false question if we think of the characters as abstract systems in which elements of this system are not mirrored such as they are but selected and shuffled into new forms. The same aesthetic transformation may produce Mariposa itself, not as a realist model of a good, bad, or transitional society, but as a nonrealist social landscape governed by aesthetic principles.

We do not have to search far for a generic category for such a
nonrealist form, for Leacock himself provides one: humour. Lynch
has already pointed the way in illustrating Leacock's idea of humour in the context of his engagement in the modern Canadian debate between romance and realism, while linking it to the social
vision of his "tory-humanism." It will be similarly useful for us to
think of this idea of humour, which Leacock calls the humour of
sublimity, as both a unique aesthetic form—a solution to problems
of literary genre—and a unique ideological belief—a solution to
modern losses of faith. Both aspects of form and content in Lea-
cockian sublime humour bear further discussion. As Lynch has in-
sightfully shown, this kind of humour was not merely a literary
practice or occasional attitude but also an encompassing perspective and abiding resource in modern life. As the explicit ideological
substitute for obsolescent religious institutions, it may even be considered as a kind of "religion" (24).[1] However usefully this comparison illuminates the nature of sublime humour as an ideology, I
prefer the term "ideology" itself because it better conveys the secular stance contrary to religious tradition that Leacock explicitly
took.[2] As he argued in 1935 in *Humor: Its Theory and Technique*
(HITT), the progress of humour depends on the Enlightenment de-
mystification of magical thinking and authority:

> Only with the modern world, and only in proportion as it loses
> its primitive credulity and the intense earnestness of its beliefs
> and superstitions, does humor enter largely into literature. Hu-
> mor in a world of waning beliefs remains like Hope still left at
> the bottom of Pandora's box when all the evils of the gods flew
> out from it upon the world. (13)

Leacock is not talking about Greek civilization as opposed to bar-
barism or about later Christian civilizations from the Middle Ages
through the Renaissance. For him, the "world of waning beliefs"
emerges in the eighteenth century and fulfils itself only in the nineteenth century. Not only humour but also culture as a whole became enlightened in the Victorian age, which "represents an epoch
in the history of letters greater than any that preceded it" (14). Far

---

1. Lynch's interest in this humour as the expression of an ideology is devoted to his identification of that ideology with "tory-humanism," a set of beliefs in individual freedom in
   the context of responsibility, in rational reform in the context of tolerance for human
   limitations, in a practical "middle way" between liberalism and socialism, and in the
   ideal of a conservative "organic society" recalling to itself forms of order and the good to
   be carried forward from its past (3–5).
2. Commenting on *Sunshine Sketches*, Robertson Davies observes: "The Dean exemplifies
   a feeling of Leacock's that seems to have had the strength of conviction, that the clergy,
   and organized religion itself, were not forces in any community, great or small, and that
   the advances of mankind were brought about by economic and political, rather than by
   spiritual agencies. For him the clergy, and one supposes Christianity as well, had not
   much to do with life" (16).

from decrying the "waning" of beliefs based on traditional authority, he is promoting it as a necessary step in the progress from
"primitive" to the "highest" understanding of life itself, which sublime humour represents. It expresses the "wistfulness" of a "new
ignorance—contrasted with the brazen certainty of bygone dogma"
of its modern society (15). In harmony with the new existential-
ism of the day, it finds meaning in the total uncertainty and corrigi-
bility of meaning and values themselves by regarding "compassion"
as the only ethical response to the "fever and fret of our earthly lot"
when "contrasted with its shortcomings, its lost illusions and its inevitable end" (261). Like Schopenhauer, the humourist attempts to
rescue from a world of lost illusions a merely human, rationally justified, transcending pity. The humourist is resigned to a world of
incongruity—between what should be and what is, between illusions of value and meaning by which we must live and the truth of
their defeat. To recognize the incongruity of life is to understand
and accept a fundamentally chaotic existence as opposed to any
knowable metaphysical order. In "American Humour" (1916), Leacock expresses this just as he would in his later books on the
subject:

> The final stage of development of humour is reached when
> amusement no longer arises from a single "funny" idea, mean-
> ingless contrast, or odd play upon words, but rests upon a pro-
> longed and sustained conception of the incongruities of
> human life itself. The shortcomings of our existence, the sad
> contrast of our aims and our achievements, the little fretting
> aspiration of the day that fades into the nothingness of tomor-
> row, kindle in the mellowed mind a sense of gentle amusement
> from which all selfish exultation has been chastened by the re-
> alisation of our common lot of sorrow. (92–93)

There is an authentic existentialist perception here, of the inessen-
tial nature of human values and concepts, in the romantic irony
that focuses on lost illusions, on the undoing of ideals by the real,
on the corrosion of what essentially we think we are and want to be
by the temporal and mortal inevitabilities of existence. This perception takes on a specific ideological colouring, however, where the
repeated emphasis is on suffering, sorrow, and futility. Despite the
contradiction of doing so, Leacock repeatedly claims that the emotions proper to sublime humour are unlikely to cause laughter and
more likely to cause tears (see, e.g., *Humor and Humanity* [HH] 21;
and HITT 7, 261). Repeatedly, he suggests that the fundamental experience of existence is suffering and pain (see, e.g., HH 211–12,
215; and HITT 261). This experience is not the result of meaningful
action, as in romance; rather, as in absurdist narrative, it is the cor-

relative of futility. We are to learn this in the contrast between the "fret of our life and its final nothingness," which renders our life not only "incongruous" but also "vain" (HH 219–20, 21). A kind of pessimistic faith in the futility and pain of existence is suggested above all by Leacock's image of a "sublime" perspective beyond existence in death or in nothingness, where in either case the simple point is that nothing matters anymore—except the joke of nothing mattering and the ambiguous hope that on Earth, "where the dead are better companions than the living," the joke may be shared and enjoyed (HITT 262, 266–67). Leacock is even tempted to see such annihilated futility and sorrow, as the essence of humour, in the very nature of things, human or inhuman:

> Thus does life, if we look at it from sufficient distance, dissolve itself into "humor." Seen through an indefinite vista it ends with a smile. In this, if what the scientists tell us is true, it only offers a parallel to what must ultimately happen to the physical universe in which it exists. Matter, we are told, is not matter in the real or solid sense. It is only a manifestation of force or energy, seeking to come to rest. An atom is not an atom in the sense of being a particle or thing. It is just an area inside whose vast empty dimensions unmatched forces, stresses and strains are trying to come together and neutralize one another. When they do this—at some inconceivable distance of time—then the universe ends, finishes; there is nothing left of it but nothingness. With it goes out in extinction all that was thought of as matter, and with that all the framework of time and space that held it, and the conscious life that matched it. All ends with a cancellation of forces and comes to nothing; and our universe ends thus with one vast, silent, unappreciated joke. (HITT 268)

This expression of an ideology regarding the nature of life, in which resignation before nothingness and meaninglessness is the inevitable horizon of present-day struggles between "unmatched forces, stresses and strains," echoes too uncannily for comfort a resignation before the apotheosis of the society that Leacock saw before him—that is, a plutocratic marketplace in which all values have dissolved into exchange values and a perpetual struggle of forces has cancelled out the meaning of production itself in a final, absolute idleness. It is a truly "religious," if nihilistic, vision.[3]

This ideology of humour is so inclusive, then, that it demands to be squared with Leacock's political-economic writing. But since

---

3. One is reminded of Marshall Berman's description of the experience of modernity, according to Marx, as a world in which "all that is solid melts into air." Marx meant that capitalist modernity degrades all values into exchange values but liberates humanity for a new kind of power over history. Berman extends the insight in order to gesture toward a new freedom as well as a new frailty in modernity, in the sceptical undoing of stable, authoritative values in general.

this writing emphasizes the possibility of progressive social change
and the meaningfulness of individual work, it is hardly of a piece
with the tendentially nihilistic, if sympathetic, mood of the "sublime" humourist. A similar contradiction is found in the politics of
the literary work of Leacock's contemporary Sara Jeannette Duncan, in whose A Daughter of Today (1895), for example, an independent woman's attempts to establish a professional career, which
ends in partial success and death, are overseen by the transcendent, liberating, but ultimately nihilistic "smile" of a statue of
Buddha (59 and elsewhere), her private muse. Although the
conservative-liberal contradictions of Duncan, as of Leacock, have
been attributed to red toryism, doing so recognizes the generality of
the problem more than explains it. The problem with "sublime humour," if we wish to argue that Leacock is dedicated to a meaningful critique of modern society or a positive vision of social change,
is that in theorizing it he explicitly offers neither satirical nor romantic correctives for the miseries of a ductile society but consolatory or escapist distances from the miseries of a world that appears
inevitable.[4] The "Hope" in Pandora's box appropriately remains
contained in it, unable to reverse the "cancellation of forces." The
hope is that we may feel it doesn't matter.[5]

What I have just described sounds suspiciously resonant with the
self-cancelling plot forms of Sunshine Sketches, in which seemingly
conflicting actions and forces continually turn out not to matter
and to dissolve thus into humour. Perhaps the ideology of sublime
humour lies darkly behind whatever sunnier communal ideals appear to be represented by the Mariposa status quo. If this is so,
then [Francis Zichy] is right to argue that the book fulfils the subtle ideological function of providing a consolation for the failure of
consolation. The "cost" of its "plea for the preservation of the Mariposa status quo as the best thing we have" is that it simultaneously
"reveals that the Mariposa game, which may never have been worth
playing, has at any rate been lost long ago" ("Narrator" 65). All that
is left of it is the "appeal" of an illusion whose value is suspended
by a "ruling equivocation" (63). The point is not only whether there
remains a concept of the social good but also what function the
concept has in the book's imagination of the reader and his or her
modern world. This function seems to be consolatory rather than

---

4. Although it is tempting to cite Leacock's gloomy prison-of-life imagery (HITT 262–64),
   doing so would be a mistake. Leacock imagines us to be prisoners of the present, of a fi-
   nite history, wishing for escape into a more stable and absolute "eternity" and "infinity."
5. "Life is full of anxiety, of fret, of pain. At the end of it is death, and when we look upon
   a dead face somehow the pain is gone from it—there is 'all eternity to rest in.' So, when
   we see them in retrospect, what were the troubles of to-day become the trifles of yesterday; as things drift into the past, animosity and anger fade out of them; the hate is gone,
   the bitterness is washed out" (HH 215).

activist, caught as an unsolid thing in the ideological net of sublime, self-cancelling equivocations and in the futile sympathies of a
plutocrat neutralized for a moment by his armchair.[6] This is the
gloomy side—the ideological side that traps ideals in a specialized
box apart from life—of the humour that Reginald Watters finds in
Leacock and that Zichy dryly affirms: "the ideal is repeatedly
thwarted by the real but never quite annihilated" (qtd. 64). For
what does it matter if the "real" is always against it?

Sublime humour also has the formal dimension indicated above,
as a generic ideal conceived by its author to improve upon romance
and realism alike. Lynch developed this point in order to show, using Northrop Frye's definitions, that Leacock's ideal form is ironic
rather than satiric and is best realized in *Sunshine Sketches* (38,
122). But Leacock's engagement in a debate regarding two other
generic forms, then dividing literary opinion in Canada, is itself
suggestive for reasons now apparent. His practice of and—like
other modernist writers—theorization of a definitively "new," alternative aesthetic to both romance and realism is at one with his desire to express his own, definitively modern ideology. His "sublime"
perspective resigns itself to parting with past systems of metaphysical faith while rejecting newer systems of materialist faith (in liberal progress to be achieved in capitalist development, the invisible
hand of the marketplace, or in socialist progress to be achieved in
rationalist restraint in the rule of the people). It holds faith, instead, in a world in which all forces and values are tendentially
futile and meaningless, all inequalities tendentially cancelled out,
and all suffering tendentially painless. In this world, "incongruity"
is the purely negative, principal feature of life itself, against which
any bid for order or value must find itself unexpectedly measured.
Under this kind of "incongruity," the narrative structure of romance—the plotted conflict between worlds of heaven and hell, of
good and evil—will never have a reliable meaning. Nor, for example, will realist detail—the realist description of an object, action,
or desire—have any but an equivocal reality.

It may be useful, in short, to consider sublime humour as a modernist form. It similarly answers to the need, which the modernist
avant-garde expressed in experimental aesthetics, for a new way of
expressing a vision of "incongruity" that had broken the bounds of

6. This interpretation of Zichy's conclusions is consistent with his assertion, in a review of
Lynch's book, that the "continuity" between Leacock's "comic fiction and his non-fiction
. . . is not that of fiction which reflects or 'enacts' serious ideas" but more likely that of a
"kind of uncertainty in his thinking" ("Problem Tory" 170). That this "uncertainty" results in an ideological displacement of his political-economic discourse of social change
is suggested by Zichy's concluding his review with an approving citation of Watt (172),
who offers the most cynical reading of Leacock's work as complicit with rather than critical of the plutocracy that Leacock mocked.

romantic irony and infiltrated, like the transvaluation of values wrought by the pervasive irony of commodification, the very authenticity of story and language themselves. Sublime humour responds to this need by presenting elements of story and language in their own undoing—which Leacock felt was both funny and pathetic and would generate a chastened modesty and sympathy in his audience that might, ultimately, soften the aggressive and dissolve the materialist impulses in his modern world.

*   *   *

WORKS CITED

Berman, Marshall. *All That Is Solid Melts into Air: The Experience of Modernity*. New York: Simon, 1982.

Davies, Robertson. *Feast of Stephen*. Toronto: McClelland, 1970.

Duncan, Sara Jeannette. *A Daughter of Today*. 1895. Ottawa: Tecumseh, 1988.

Leacock, Stephen. "American Humour." *Essays and Literary Studies*. London: Lane, 1916. 79–112.

———. "Fiction and Reality: A Study of the Art of Charles Dickens." *Essays and Literary Studies*. New York: Lane, 1916. 193–230.

———. *Humor: Its Theory and Technique*. Toronto: Dodd, 1935.

———. *Humor and Humanity*. New York: Holt, 1938.

———. *Sunshine Sketches of a Little Town*. 1912. Toronto: McClelland, 1989.

Lynch, Gerald. *Stephen Leacock: Humour and Humanity*. Kingston: McGill-Queen's UP, 1988.

MacDonald, R. D. "Measuring Leacock's Mariposa against Lewis's Gopher Prairie: A Question of Monuments." *Dalhousie Review* 71 (1991): 84–103.

Watt, F. W. "Critic or Entertainer? Stephen Leacock and the Growth of Materialism." *Canadian Literature* 5 (1960): 33–42.

Zichy, Francis. "The Narrator, the Reader, and Mariposa: The Cost of Preserving the Status Quo in *Sunshine Sketches of a Little Town*." *Journal of Canadian Studies* 22.1 (1987): 51–65.

———. "Problem Tory." Rev. of *Stephen Leacock: Humour and Humanity*, by Gerald Lynch. *Canadian Literature* 127 (1990): 169–72.

Responses of Canadian Novelists

ROBERTSON DAVIES

From Stephen Leacock†

* * *

* * * His next production, in 1912, was *Sunshine Sketches of a Little Town*, and if it may not be called a novel, it has a strong appearance of being the work of a man who will write a novel very soon. The twelve chapters have a single setting and a group of characters who are developed by means of description from a variety of viewpoints. Although the term "sketches" suggests looseness of form, we find that the book must be read straight through, if we are to comprehend it fully; chapters may be extracted, as they have been by more than one anthologist, but no chapter is wholly self-contained. Read it as a novel, and all the characters fall into a coherent pattern, and the strongest sense of the Little Town itself becomes so palpable that we know the Little Town to be the hero, the theme to which all else is contributory.

Descriptions of small-town life have become commonplace, especially in the literature of this continent. In Leacock's day they tended, with a handful of notable exceptions, to look on the sunny side of village and rural life and to accept the widely-held view that small-town people were kindlier, less corrupt, and more chaste than dwellers in great cities. Since then, of course, a school has arisen which portrays small towns, very profitably, as microcosms of Sodom and Gomorrah in which everybody but a handful of just men and women are deep in corruption, especially of the sexual order. Leacock tried very hard to keep his Sunshine Sketches sunny.

He succeeds, but only because he takes a determinedly godlike view of his community. Josh Smith, the hotel-keeper, is plainly the ablest man in Mariposa. He cannot read, though he can write his name, and he seems to have started his career as a cook in a logging-camp. But he has the Napoleonic touch. He disregards the

† From *Stephen Leacock* (Toronto: McClelland and Stewart, 1970), pp. 23–30. Used by permission of McClelland & Stewart Ltd., *The Canadian Publishers*.

law by keeping his saloon open after hours, and when the licensing authorities become troublesome, he exerts himself and spends a great deal of money to make his hotel so attractive that his fellow-citizens cannot bear to be without it and petition the licensing authorities to overlook his fault. As soon as this can be achieved, Josh cuts his expenses; the "caff" and the Rats' Cooler lose their gloss. (Josh never establishes the "Girl Room" that he has seen in big-city hotels, and this is a fine touch; a "Girl Room" would never do in Mariposa.) When the big mining boom comes north of the village, everybody invests but only Josh knows what will make money. When the *Mariposa Belle* sinks in Lake Wissanotti, Josh is the man who knows how to get her off a sandbank. When the Anglican Church gets into deeper water than the *Mariposa Belle* ever sailed, it is Josh who resolves its problems by burning it down and, as self-elected head of the fire brigade, knows how to keep the fire from spreading to the rest of the wooden town. And at last Josh gets himself elected to Parliament because he is willing to put money rather than principle into the campaign. We are not told so, but we can imagine that Josh went to Ottaway with one determination—to protect the interests of his constituents in every respect in which they happened to coincide with his own. Josh is indeed a finely executed portrait of a type of local tycoon and politician very important in Canadian politics so long as Canada remained a predominantly rural country and by no means yet extinct. He is also a creature for whom Leacock never lost his admiration—the Man of Horse Sense, the leader who will always rise above the commonalty whatever his want of education or principle.

When reading this book we should not miss the slight but convincing portrait of Josh's clerk, Billy, who does all the leg-work and spreads the word of the leader among the ranks. Billy is shadowy, because Billies always are so, but anybody with any experience of politics knows that every Josh has his Billy and could not work without him.

After Josh, the most carefully realized character is that of the Reverend Rupert Drone, the rural dean who has been rector of the Anglican Church for forty years. He is as innocent and ineffectual as Josh Smith is worldly-wise and energetic. Yet there burns in him, as it does in the bosom of so many priests, the ambition to build, to set up a bigger church, and with the aid of his congregation, he does it. The Dean is wholly unable to keep his accounts straight, probably because his education concentrated chiefly on Classics; indeed, though he cannot positively be said to read Greek, he is frequently to be seen sleeping with a volume of Theocritus on his knee. His real enthusiasm is for the minor achievements of engineering; he makes toys for children and makes them with skill. His world seems peaceful—though he thinks he is run off his feet with church concerns—until he hears a parishioner say that the church would be better off if that old mugwump were out of the pulpit. This remark preys on him until he determines to resign his charge. His decision coincides with Josh Smith's recognition of the fact that the only way to save the church from the Dean's mismanagement is to burn it down and get its unrealistically large insurance value. And so Josh saves the Dean, too, for although his wits are a little astray, Dean Drone is able to remain in his charge, assisted by a curate.

Exaggerated? Only enough to be in key with the prevailing harmony of the book; not so much as to be absurd, for who does not know of good, ineffectual men who have lingered in a backwater until, to their dismay, the backwater becomes troubled water. The Dean exemplifies a feeling of Leacock that seems to have had the strength of a conviction, a feeling that the clergy, and organized religion itself, were not forces in any community, great or small, and that the advances of mankind were brought about by economic and political, rather than by spiritual agencies. For him the clergy, and one supposes Christianity as well, had not much to do with life.

Jefferson Thorpe, the barber of Mariposa, is given an extended but sufficient examination. Like all the Mariposa people, Jeff is at once a type and an individual. When a mining boom north of the little town awakens its cupidity, he becomes an investor and, because of his stubbornness rather than through any acuteness, he is a lucky one. He gets forty thousand dollars — a fortune to a man who charges five cents for a shave. But Jeff also acquires a conviction that he is a shrewd fellow, although he knows nothing of investment except what he reads in the city papers. He is deferred to by his customers as a man of uncommon insight. But he puts his fortune in Cuban land speculation and loses it, and thus goes right on shaving for five cents a shave, and his wife continues to supply eggs to Josh Smith's "caff." This too is a familiar story. Indeed, the writer of this study can recall himself as a little boy sitting on the board across the arms of a barber's chair, getting a haircut while the barber (a man who had probably never possessed $250 all at one time in his life) blew the scent of Wrigley's Spearmint Gum into his ear as he whispered: "If I had a cool fifty thou right this minute, I'd crack 'er all into Hollinger."

The fourth theme given extended treatment in the book is the romance of Peter Pupkin, the bank clerk, and Zena Pepperleigh, daughter of the district judge of Missinaba County. Here Leacock is less sure of his ground, and his tone moves farther from comedy into the realm of farce. He never had a completely assured hand when he wrote of love, which he seems to have linked with religion as one of those amiable delusions to which clouded or inferior intellects are subject. But who knows? In Mariposa it may have been so; rural Ontario has never been renowned as one of Aphrodite's favourite domains. Marriage—yes, Leacock can speak well of marriage. The link between the Judge and Martha Pepperleigh easily stands the strain of the Judge's fiery temper. Dean Drone's tender memories of his wife are first among the elements in his character that raise him above the level of the comic person of platitudinous farce. But love—? We are never persuaded that Peter and Zena find anything of more than superficial value in one another. Zena is pretty: Peter proves to be the son of a rich man. The Judge and Peter's father have known each other in earlier days. And this is deemed enough. If there is to be anything of greater worth, it will presumably come after marriage and the baby. Leacock, like so many writers who aspire to popularity, declares himself to be fond of youth, but he writes most warmly when youth is disposed in well-ordered ranks in the university.

This is not to say that Leacock knew nothing of tenderness. Jeff Thorpe, who refers to his wife simply as "the woman," is delighted with his gains because they will further the histrionic ambitions of his daughter Myra. Judge Pepperleigh is presented to us as something more than a legal bully because of his unwillingness to see that his son Neil is worthless, and the few sentences in which his grief at Neil's death in the South African war is described are among the most powerful in the book. Certainly Leacock knew tenderness; perhaps he knew too much of it and feared to allow himself to write of it. But a man who seeks to be a novelist must conquer such fears and discipline his emotions to serve his artistic needs. The fact that Leacock never wrote of love except in a jocular and scoffing spirit tells us much about him. That he could love we know; that he could not write about love, except as a joke, suggests that he never completely trusted his talent to express his deepest feelings.

Certainly *Sunshine Sketches* looks like a move toward writing novels, as Leacock's heroes and exemplars, Dickens and Mark Twain, had done. The godlike view, the assumption by the writer of a power to judge his characters, certainly leads toward the composition of novels of a particular kind. If he had persisted, Leacock might have written another kind of novel—the kind in which characters are described from the inside, instead of being examined from the outside; *David Copperfield* and *Huckleberry Finn* are such novels known by him and admired by him. But something happened that seems to have warned Leacock away from this sort of work. The Little Town sharply resented the way in which it had been examined; the author's idea of sunshine seemed to it much more like an inquisitor's spotlight. Only a man of Leacock's remarkable self-confidence and lack of sensitivity toward other people could have thought that it would be otherwise. Sap the book of its humour, and what have you? A community in which the acknowledged leaders are windbags and self-serving clowns, and where the real leader is an illiterate saloon-keeper, a community that sees financial acuity in a lucky little barber who makes a one-in-a-thousand killing in the stock-market, a community that will not support a church, but will swindle an insurance company with a fraudulent fire; a community in which an election is shamelessly rigged; to say nothing of a community where a school-teacher who takes an occasional glass of beer is "the one who drinks" (and thus an unfit person to receive a raise in pay), where the captain of the lake-boat cannot keep it off a shoal, and where a chance encounter between a nightwatchman and a bank clerk becomes a tale of heroism. We may all know of towns where some of these things or others of the same kind are true, but which of us would boast of being the original of Dean Drone, Judge Pepperleigh, or John Henry Bagshaw? The Little Town was very angry, and some of its citizens were still angry after Leacock died. It was later that he became a tourist attraction and the occasion of an annual award and banquet to which his own pen could do proper satiric justice.

During the greater part of his career Leacock reiterated, at intervals, his conviction that true humour springs from kindness and gives no pain. He must have known, in his heart of hearts, that humour is a razor, and even in the most skilled hand it sometimes cuts. The humorist, if we take the work seriously, is akin to the writer of tragedy in his ability to see beneath the surface of life and to see what other men do not see. Of both the comic and the tragic writer, people of commonplace outlook say the same thing—that he has exaggerated. Many artists, both in comedy and tragedy, are so naïve as to expect that humanity will be grateful to them for showing how absurd or how desperate human life can be. Leacock showed such naïveté toward Orillia and seems to have been both astonished and warned by the fury and hurt feelings he provoked. He never struck so truly again. He wanted to be liked, and that is a serious weakness in an artist of any kind. He gained his desire, for he was greatly liked—even loved, as time wore on. But his artistry was nipped by an early frost that succeeded the sunshine of the Little Town.

Throughout his life Leacock showed a strange innocence, a lack of self-knowledge, and a corresponding insensitivity toward others. He had no desire to hurt anybody's feelings, but he lacked insight into other people's feelings. The originals of some of the characters in *Sunshine Sketches* were indignant, others were wounded. In an article he wrote for the *Orillia Packet and Times* (March 12, 1957), Dr. C. H. Hale identifies several of those who were originals of characters in the book, and says that

> It was in deference to his mother that in the book version of *Sunshine Sketches*, Stephen disclaimed "any intention of doing anything so ridiculous as writing about a real place and real people" and in particular declared that "the Rev. Mr. Drone is not one person but about eight or ten." Mrs. Leacock had reproached her gifted son for lampooning her rector, Canon Greene, easily the most beloved man who ever lived in Orillia, whose tolerant kindliness was demonstrated by the fact that he never resented the rather cruel exploitation of his idiosyncracies.

Dr. Hale says that in its original version, which appeared serially in the Montreal *Star*, the names were even less disguised than in the book: Rapley and McCosh, who first appeared as Popley and McGraw, became Mullins and Pepperleigh. But Jeff Shortt, the Orillia barber, was still clearly Jefferson Thorpe, just as Bingham the undertaker was Golgotha Gingham. Josh Smith was—quite simply— still Josh Smith. It was for his caricature of Canon R. W. E. Greene that Leacock's mother, as Dr. Hale says, "gave Stephen Hail Columbia!"

It cannot have been the hurt feelings caused by *Sunshine Sketches* that brought about the scrappy form and shallow tone of *Behind the Beyond*, which succeeded it in 1913 Leacock wrote and published so much that one book was in the process of writing while its predecessor was still at the publisher's. There is nothing in this new volume that suggests the earlier and richer vein. The title-piece is a satire on the "problem plays" of the period; Leacock attacks them with his broad-axe but he has not been as concise here as he was in *Nonsense Novels*. He could touch off "Gertrude the Governess" in twenty pages; "Behind the Beyond" trudges on for forty, and it is too much for anything he has to say. He is happier in the group of five "Familiar Incidents" that follow it. But "Parisian Pastimes" is in his Mark Twain manner, here we have the Innocent Abroad comparing Paris with things back home. What Mark Twain did well in 1869 Leacock does poorly in 1913. We simply do not believe in him. Mark Twain was a genuine Innocent—ill-educated, and confined by a frontier outlook; Leacock is highly educated and has seen much of the world. Spurious naïveté is even more depressing than spurious sophistication. In the last piece in this book. "Homer and Humbug", he makes one of his many assaults on the

Classics, and the theme brings out much of what is best in his wit. It also reveals one of his convictions that time has not treated kindly—his faith in progress as a simple effect of the passing of time. "The classics are only primitive literature. They belong in the same class as primitive machinery and primitive music and primitive medicine," he says. We now see virtues in what is primitive, and we do not think of the passing of time as inevitably bringing improvement. In his faith in progress Leacock was very much a Victorian—a surprisingly simple Victorian.

*   *   *

GUY VANDERHAEGHE

Leacock and Understanding Canada†

*   *   *

* * * [S]omething about Leacock * * * has always puzzled me. I had wondered why it was that a man who had lived as many years as Leacock had in Montreal never, to my knowledge, introduced a French-Canadian into his fiction. And why were there plenty of Anglican rectors and English peers but no Catholics or Jews? Montreal could certainly boast significant numbers of these last two communities.

In raising these points I do not wish to make a criticism of Leacock but to raise a point. I am not saving that we *ought* to find in Leacock's books French-Canadians, Catholics, or Jews, only that we do not. After all, a writer defines his fictional universe as much by what he excludes as by what he includes. It is not an original remark to say that writers who are contemporaries and who share a common citizenship produce very different work. Henry James is one kind of American writer and Mark Twain another. Writing at roughly the same time, these writers produced their finest work when their talents and imagination discovered what, for want of a better word, I will call their subjects. Their masterpieces proclaim to the world a part of what it meant to be American then and, by extension, a part of what it means to be American now.

The same, I think, can be said of Leacock.

What was his subject? Mariposa. And what is Mariposa? I do not think it is what the back cover of the New Canadian Library edition of *Sunshine Sketches of a Little Town* proclaims it to be in

† From *Stephen Leacock: A Reappraisal*, ed. David Staines (Ottawa: University of Ottawa Press, 1986), pp. 17–22. Reprinted by permission of the publisher.

announcing that "although Mariposa can be identified as Orillia, Ontario, it is also true that it represents any small town anywhere in Canada." An orthodox opinion, I suspect.

But I don't believe it for a minute. To claim that Leacock's Mariposa *is* the Canadian small town, a generic village that can be plopped down anywhere in the country to do duty like a Hollywood set, is to misrepresent what the rest of English-speaking Canada is and to diminish what Leacock achieved in his portrait. What Leacock drew with such love and conviction is not necessarily common to us all. Leacock's small town is not Alice Munro's small town, nor Margaret Laurence's small town, nor Sinclair Ross's small town. Nor should we expect it to be. To ignore differences is to diminish Mariposa in all its glorious particularity. As Czeslaw Milosz has written in *The Witness of Poetry*, "we apprehend the human condition with pity and terror not in the abstract but always in relation to a given place and time, in one particular province, one particular country."

Mariposa is a small town of a particular time, place, and people. It is important not to forget that this is a picture of a lost world, an Edwardian town basking in a bright sunshine of confidence, peace, and stability; a town that has no inkling that it will soon send its sons to perish in the bloody mud of Flanders. We also ought not to forget that it is an Ontario town and a British town.

In some sense Mariposa is also the closest thing to a utopia that the small "c" conservative who denies the notion of human perfectibility will permit himself to dream. Here is the organic society so much applauded, a society whose members are bound to one another by common values, traditions, a longing for stability, and a belief in a deity. For a writer of Leacock's convictions and temperament this was a subject he both loved and understood. In no other of his works does his gentle humour illuminate human idiosyncrasy with a steadier light, or does the pathos he evokes seem so much a natural outcome of our common human journey.

Of course, perhaps this Mariposa he created was never more than a dream. But Leacock's dream tells me something about my country as Twain's and James's dreams tell me something about America. In *Sunshine Sketches* I am allowed to glimpse what people of a certain time and place wanted life to be. And such dreams, projected by the force of desire, have consequences far into the future.

Yet how can I, an admitted foreigner to Mariposa, offer these speculations, separated from it as I am by time, region, and perhaps even sympathy? I could offer the suggestion that the love and skill with which Leacock writes lead me to perceive these things. * * *

One test of the dream is to imagine [my British, Tory grandfather from Ontario] in Mariposa. I have no difficulty in doing so.

I have no doubt that my grandfather would have been completely at home in Jeff Thorpe's barber shop, as he would have been at his ease promenading the deck of the Mariposa Belle. And how gladly he would have raised his voice in a Mariposa church or a glass in Smith's hostelry. Best of all. I see him as a Knight of Pythias. His Eastern European neighbours were not given to joining fraternal organizations. And what pleasure he would have taken in fighting a *real* election, the kind they fought in Missinaba County.

It is in this fictional landscape that my grandfather appears at home to me, rather than the one he inhabited for most of his life. Perhaps this is some kind of testament to the strange reciprocity which exists between Life and Art. If it is, it suggests another way of looking at *Sunshine Sketches*, not as the embodiment of some kind of vague "Canadianism," but as a distinct and local expression. Perhaps even, to press a point, as a regional and ethnic work. Looked at in this way *Sunshine Sketches* can lay claim to being not only a fine, funny, sad book, but also a book which possesses the power to reveal one Canadian to another, even across the daunting gulfs of space and time.

MORDECAI RICHLER

Spend a Few Hours in Mariposa†

Going through my library recently, I plucked Stephen Leacock's *Sunshine Sketches of a Little Town* off the shelves, and reread it with considerable pleasure.

In his biography of Mark Twain, Leacock wrote that at the time Twain established himself as the first true master of the American idiom, "of American literature there was much doubt in Europe; of American honesty, much more, of American manners more still." With considerably more licence, the same could have been said of Canadian letters and manners when Leacock published his first collection of humorous pieces, *Literary Lapses*, in 1910. That initial effort, as rich as anything he would write later, included the anthology gem "My Financial Career," which my generation was grateful to discover in our otherwise disconcertingly worthy high-school reader. *Nonsense Novels*, published a year later, gave us that immortal phrase about the horseman "who rode off in all directions" and it was understandably an early influence on S. J. Perlman. But it is his 1912 novel, *Sunshine Sketches of a Little Town*, that is easily the most cherished of his books, as much good honest fun to read today as it was when first published. * * *

"Dying is easy," said the actor Edmund Gwenn on his deathbed. "Comedy is difficult." Obviously Leacock agreed. "There is no difficulty in writing a scientific treatise on the folk-lore of Central China," he wrote. "But to write something out of one's own mind, worth reading for its own sake, is an arduous contrivance only to be achieved in fortunate moments, few and far between."

An aggrieved author, Leacock felt insufficiently rewarded for his first two books, both of which, he complained, could be had in any bookshop for a total of 7 shillings. A biographer of Dickens himself, I suspect he warmed to the ostensibly innocent, but clearly precocious Oliver Twist, who at the age of 10 had a sure grasp of where the real money was in the book trade.

"How would you like to grow up a clever man, and write books, eh?" asked the kindly Mr. Brownlow. "I think I would rather read them, sir," replied Oliver. "What! Wouldn't you like to be a bookwriter?" said the old gentleman.

Oliver considered a little while; and at last said he should think it a much better thing to be a book-seller.

The main street of the fictional town of Mariposa (pop. 6,000, 7,500 or 10,000 depending on which town booster you credited), on the shores of Lake Wissanotti, boasted, as you might expect, lodges for the Knights of Pythias and the Sons of Temperance, as well as an Oddfellow's Hall and a YMCA. Today, no doubt, these institutions have been displaced by a McDonald's, a video-game centre and possibly even a massage parlour. But in Leacock's day there was, above all, Smith's Hotel, JOS SMITH, PROP. The illiterate Smith, who goes on to become the MP for Missinaba County, in one of the book's many risible set pieces, weighed 280 pounds, favoured a loud check suit and diamonds, and must be accounted Sunshine's finest comic creation. However, in this affectionate but knowing celebration of small-town Ontario verities, Judge Pepperleigh, the Reverend Mr. Drone and Mr. Pupkin, who "is found whenever a Canadian bank opens a branch in a county town and needs a teller," do not lag far behind. For my money, the far-from-tragic July sinking of the Mariposa Belle in less than six feet of lake water on the Knights of Pythias Excursion Day (wherein the rescuers have to be rescued, as it were, by the victims) is the most memorable episode in a novel that is far from deficient in comic inventions.

"When you do comedy," Woody Allen once said, "you are not sitting at the grown-ups table." A complaint, I think, that Leacock would have taken as a compliment. In any event, his line in comedy is not the coruscating stuff readers will find in Evelyn Waugh, Nathaniel West or Terry Southern. Leacock sprung from a gentler age, an age more given to forgiving parody rather than full-blown satire. There is no anger in Sunshine Sketches, as there is in Garrison Keillor's later sketches of small-town life in Minnesota.

Avarice, nefarious rather than endearing hypocrisy, social pretensions that infuriate more than they amuse, and lust, are strangers to Mariposa. Leacock's take on life in Mariposa is filtered through rose-tinted glasses. It's benign. Sunshine sketches is what we are promised and sunshine sketches is what we get, albeit delivered with assurance and enviable skill.

Leacock's fetching account of small-town life makes no allowances for repression. There is no sex whatsoever to be found there, but even on the shores of Lake Wissanotti, circa 1910, I suspect that it did exist. Leacock's wholesome vision can be appreciated as an antidote to more rigorous American renditions of similar cultural backwaters: say, Sherwood Anderson's Winesburg, Ohio, Sinclair Lewis' Main Street, or Hemingway's famously cruel but accurate short story Up in Michigan.

The tunes Leacock plays with such panache will not evoke Mozart or Wagner. But there is also Gilbert and Sullivan. And those who adore that make-believe world as much as I do will find many delights in this mischievous book, which was also the first work to establish a Canadian voice and deservedly gain international recognition.

Stephen Leacock: A Chronology

1869   Stephen Butler Leacock, the third of eleven children, born to Peter and Agnes Leacock on December 30 at Swanmore, Hampshire, England.

1876   Leacock family joins Peter on farm near Lake Simcoe, Ontario.

1882   Leacock enrolls in Upper Canada College (UCC), Toronto.

1887   Publishes first article, "The Vision of Mirza (New Edition)," in UCC *College Times*, graduates as head boy and enrolls in University of Toronto (U of T). His father abandons family and farm.

1888   Withdraws from U of T for financial reasons and enrolls in Strathroy Collegiate Institute in Strathroy, Ontario, to obtain teacher's certificate.

1889   Becomes junior master at UCC.

1890   Returns to U of T and publishes humourous articles in *Varsity*.

1891   Graduates from U of T with honours BA.

1894   Publishes humorous articles in the satirical magazine *Grip* and in the general-circulation magazine *Saturday Night* (both Toronto).

1895   Publishes "My Financial Career" in *Life*.

1899   Resigns from UCC and begins graduate work in political economy at University of Chicago (U of C) with view to studying under Thorstein Veblen, whose *The Theory of the Leisure Class* was published in 1899.

1900   Offered a sessional lectureship by the political science department at McGill University, Montreal. He marries Beatrix Hamilton.

1903   Doctoral thesis, "The Doctrine of Laissez Faire," accepted and Leacock graduates from U of C *magna summa cum laude*.

1906   *Elements of Political Science* published.

1907   Tours the British Empire for eleven months beginning in April, lecturing on "Imperial Organization." *Baldwin, Lafontaine, Hinks: Responsible Government* published.

1908   Purchases property on Lake Simcoe near Orillia, Ontario, and appointed to professorship in political economy at McGill.

1910 *Literary Lapses* published.

1911 *Nonsense Novels* published. Campaigns against free trade with the United States in Canadian federal election.

1912 *Sunshine Sketches of a Little Town* published in instalments in the *Montreal Daily Star* and then in book form.

1913 *Behind the Beyond and Other Contributions to Human Knowledge* published.

1914 *Arcadian Adventures with the Idle Rich* and three books on Canadian history published.

1915 Only child, Stephen, born and *Moonbeams from the Larger Lunacy* published.

1916 *Further Foolishness* published.

1917 *Frenzied Fiction* published.

1919 *The Hohenzollerns in America with the Bolsheviks in Berlin and Other Impossibilities* published.

1920 *The Unsolved Riddle of Social Justice* and *Winsome Winnie and Other New Nonsense Novels* published.

1921 Lectures in England and Scotland.

1922 *My Discovery of England* published.

1923 *Over the Footlights and Other Fancies* and *College Days* published.

1924 *The Garden of Folly* published.

1925 Wife, Beatrix, dies.

1926 *Winnowed Wisdom* published.

1928 *Short Circuits* published.

1929 *The Iron Man and the Tin Woman and Other Futurities* published.

1930 *Economic Prosperity in the British Empire, The Leacock Book*, and *Laugh with Leacock* published.

1931 *Wet and Dry Humour* published.

1932 *Back to Prosperity, The Dry Pickwick and Other Incongruities, Afternoons in Utopia*, and *Mark Twain* published.

1933 *Charles Dickens: His Life and Work* published.

1934 *Lincoln Frees the Slaves, The Greatest Pages of Charles Dickens*, and *The Pursuit of Knowledge* published.

1935 Awarded Mark Twain Medal. *Humor, Its Theory and Technique* published.

1936 *The Greatest Pages of American Humor, Hellements of Hickonomics*, and *Funny Pieces: A Book of Random Sketches* published. Retires from McGill and tours western Canada lecturing and reciting.

1937 *My Discovery of the West, Here Are My Lectures and Stories, Humour and Humanity* published. Awarded Lorne Pierce

Medal by the Royal Society of Canada for his contributions to Canadian letters.

1938   Governor General's Prize for nonfiction awarded for *My Discoveries of the West*. *Model Memoirs and Other Sketches from Simple to Serious* published.

1939   *Too Much College* published.

1940   *The British Empire* and *Stephen Leacock's Laugh Parade* published.

1941   *Canada: The Foundations of Empire* published.

1942   *My Remarkable Uncle* and *Other Sketches*, *Our Heritage of Liberty*, and *Montreal, Seaport and City* published.

1943   *How to Write* and *Happy Stories Just to Laugh* published.

1944   Dies on March 28 in Toronto after operation for throat cancer.

Selected Bibliography

• indicates a work included or excerpted in this Norton Critical Edition.

• "Amusing Sketches." Review of *Sunshine Sketches of a Little Town*. *New York Times*, 29 September 1912, 540.

Anderson, Allan. *Remembering Leacock: An Oral History*. Ottawa: Deneau, 1983.

Bentley, D. M. R. "Rummagings 2: Stephen Leacock." *Canadian Poetry: Studies, Documents, Reviews* 53 (Fall/Winter 2003): 5–8.

———. "Rummagings 4: John Maynard in Leacock's *Sunshine Sketches of a Little Town*." *Canadian Poetry: Studies, Documents, Reviews* 54 (Spring/Summer 2004): 5–11.

Berger, Carl. "The Other Mr. Leacock." *Canadian Literature* 55 (Winter 1973): 23–40.

———. *The Sense of Power: Studies in the Ideas of Canadian Imperialism, 1867–1914*. Toronto: U of Toronto P, 1970.

• Birbalsingh, Frank. "Stephen Leacock and the Canadian Literary Sensibility." *Canadian Literary Review* 1 (Fall/Winter 1982): 73–84.

Bissell, C. T. "Haliburton, Leacock and the American Humorous Tradition." *Canadian Literature* 39 (Winter 1969): 5–19.

Bush, Douglas. "Stephen Leacock." *The Canadian Imagination: Dimensions of a Literary Culture*. Ed. David Staines. Cambridge: Harvard UP, 1977. 123–51.

• Cameron, Donald. "The Enchanted Houses: Leacock's Irony." *Canadian Literature* 23 (Winter 1965): 31–44.

———. *Faces of Leacock*. Toronto: Ryerson, 1967.

Clever, Glenn. "Leacock's Dunciad." *Studies in Canadian Literature* 1 (Summer 1976): 238–41.

Cook, Ramsay. "Stephen Leacock and the Age of Plutocracy, 1903–1921." *Character and Circumstance: Essays in Honour of Donald Grant Creighton*. Ed. John S. Moir. Toronto: Macmillan, 1970. 163–81.

Curry, Ralph L. *Stephen Leacock: Humorist and Humanist*. Garden City, NY: Doubleday, 1959.

Davies, Robertson. "Stephen Leacock." *Our Living Tradition: Seven Canadians*. Ed. Claude T. Bissell. Toronto: Published in association with Carleton University by U of Toronto P, 1957. 128–49.

———. *Stephen Leacock*. Canadian Writers 7. Toronto: McClelland and Stewart, 1970.

Doyle, James. *Stephen Leacock: The Sage of Orillia*. Toronto: ECW P, 1992.

El-Hassan, Karla. "Reflections on the Special Unity of Stephen Leacock's *Sunshine Sketches of a Little Town*." *Gaining Ground: European Critics on Canadian Literature*. Ed. Robert Kroetsch and Reingard M. Nischik. Edmonton: NeWest Press, 1985. 171–85.

Edgar, Pelham. "Stephen Leacock." *Queen's Quarterly* 53.2 (1946): 173–84. Reprinted in *Across My Path*. Toronto: Ryerson P, 1952. 90–98.

• Ferris, Ina. "The Face in the Window: *Sunshine Sketches* Reconsidered." *Studies in Canadian Literature* 3.2 (Summer 1978): 178–85.

Finlayson, Carolyn. "A Literary and Introductory Preamble: Dean Drone and Dr. Gallagher." *Mnemographia Canadensis: Essays on Memory, Community, and Environment in Canada*. Vol 2: Remember and See. Ed. D. M. R. Bentley. London: Canadian Poetry P, 1999. 195–97.

Hodgins, Jack. "Afterword." *Sunshine Sketches of a Little Town*. By Stephen Leacock. New Canadian Library. Toronto: McClelland and Stewart, 1987.

Keith, W. J. *Canadian Literature in English*. Longman Literature in English. London and New York: Longman, 1985. 23–25.

Kushner, J., and R. D. MacDonald. "Leacock: Economist/Satirist in *Arcadian Adventures* and *Sunshine Sketches*." *Dalhousie Review* 56.3 (Autumn 1976): 493–509.

Legate, David. *Stephen Leacock: A Biography*. Toronto: Macmillan of Canada, 1978.

Lomer, Gerhard R. *Stephen Leacock: A Check-List and Index of His Writings*. Ottawa: National Library, 1954.

Lower, Arthur. "The Mariposa Belle." *Queen's Quarterly* 58.2 (Summer 1951): 220–26.

Lynch, Gerald. "Leacock's Debt to Daudet." *Canadian Literature* 107 (Winter 1985): 186–89.

• ———. *Stephen Leacock: Humor and Humanity*. Montreal and Kingston: McGill-Queen's UP, 1988.

———. *The One and the Many: English-Canadian Short Story Cycles*. Toronto: U of Toronto P, 2001.

McArthur, Peter. *Stephen Leacock*. Toronto: Ryerson P, 1923.

MacDonald, R. D. "Measuring Leacock's Mariposa Against Lewis's Gopher Prairie: A Question of Monuments." *Dalhousie Review* 71.1 (Spring 1991): 84–103.

———. "Small Town Ontario in Robertson Davies' *Fifth Business*: Mariposa Revised?" *Studies in Canadian Literature* 9.1 (1984): 61–77.

MacLulich, T. D. "Mariposa Revisited." *Studies in Canadian Literature* 4 (Winter 1979): 167–76.

Magee, William H. "Genial Humour in Stephen Leacock." *Dalhousie Review* 56 (Summer 1976): 268–82.

———. "Parody and Perspective: Form in Leacock's Sketches." *Thalia* 3 (Fall/Winter 1980–81): 31–37.

• ———. "Stephen Leacock: Local Colourist." *Canadian Literature* 39 (Winter 1969): 34–42.

Mantz, Douglas. "The Preposterous and the Profound: A New Look at the Envoi of *Sunshine Sketches*." *Journal of Canadian Fiction* 19 (1977): 95–105.

Marshall, Tom. "False Pastoral: Stephen Leacock's Conflicting Worlds." *Journal of Canadian Fiction* 19 (1977): 86–94.

Meyers, Leonard E. "Stephen Leacock, Canada's Mark Twain." *Antigonish Review* 98 (Summer 1994): 35–39.

• Moritz, Albert, and Theresa Moritz. *Leacock: A Biography*. Toronto: Stoddart, 1985.

Norris, Darrel A. "Preserving Main Street: Some Lessons of Leacock's Mariposa." *Journal of Canadian Studies* 17.2 (Summer 1982): 128–36.

Pacey, Desmond. *Creative Writing in Canada: A Short History of English-Canadian Literature*. 1952. Rev. ed. Toronto: McGraw-Hill Ryerson, 1961. 108–18.

• ———. "Leacock as a Satirist." *Queen's Quarterly* 58 (Summer 1951): 208–9.

• Rasporich, Beverly J. "Charles Dickens and Stephen Leacock: A Legacy of Sentimental Humour." *Thalia* 3 (Fall/Winter 1980–81): 17–24.

———. "Leacock Persona and the Canadian Character." *Mosaic* 14 (Spring 1981): 76–92.

———. "The New Eden: The Source of Canadian Humour: McCulloch, Haliburton, and Leacock." *Studies in Canadian Literature* 7.2 (1982): 227–40.

• Richler, Mordecai. "Spend a Few Hours in the Town of Mariposa." *National Post* (Toronto), 25 March 2000: B8.

Roper, Gordon, S. Ross Beharriell and Rupert Schieder. "Writers of Fiction, 1880–1920. *Literary History of Canada: Canadian Literature in English*. Ed. Carl F. Klinck. Toronto: U of Toronto P, 1973. 334–39.

Ross, Malcolm. "1965 Editor's Preface." *Sunshine Sketches of a Little Town*. By Stephen Leacock. New Canadian Library 15. Toronto: McClelland and Stewart, 1960. ix–xi.

Sandwell, B. K. "Leacock Recalled: How the 'Sketches' Started." *Saturday Night* 67.46 (23 August 1952): 7.

Sedgewick, G. G. "Stephen Leacock as Man of Letters." *University of Toronto Quarterly* 15 (Oct 1945): 17–26.

Sharman, Vincent. "Satire of Stephen Leacock's Sunshine Sketches'." *Queen's Quarterly* 78.2 (Summer 1971): 261–67.

Spadoni, Carl. *A Bibliography of Stephen Leacock*. Toronto: ECW P, 1998.

———. "Introduction." *Sunshine Sketches of a Little Town*. By Stephen Leacock. Broadview Literary Texts. Peterborough, ON: Broadview P, 2002. vii–lxxxi.

Spettigue, Douglas. "A Partisan Reading of Leacock." *Literary Half-Yearly* 13 (July 1972): 171–80.

Staines, David, ed. *Stephen Leacock: A Reappraisal*. Ottawa: U of Ottawa P, 1986.

• "Sunshine Sketches." Review. *Times Literary Supplement* (London) 15 August 1912: 320.

• "Sunshine Sketches of a Little Town." Review. *Canadian Magazine* (Toronto) 40.1 (November 1912): 89–90.

• "Sunshine Sketches of a Little Town." Review. *Spectator* (London) 24 August 1912: 277–78.

Watt, F. W. "Critic or Entertainer? Stephen Leacock and the Growth of Materialism." *Canadian Literature* 5 (Summer 1960): 33–42.

Watters, R. E. "Special Tang: Leacock's Canadian Humour." *Canadian Literature* 5 (Summer 1960): 21–32.

- Willmott, Glenn. "The Cost of a Drink in Mariposa." *Essays on Canadian Writing* 68 (Summer 1999): 46–76.
Zezulka, J. M. "Passionate Provincials: Imperialism, Regionalism, and Point of View." *Journal of Canadian Fiction* 22 (1978): 80–92.
Zichy, Francis. "The Narrator, the Reader, and Mariposa: The Cost of Preserving the Status Quo in *Sunshine Sketches of a Little Town*." *Journal of Canadian Studies* 22 (Spring 1987): 51–65.